The Great
Disappointment

ADVANCE PRAISE FOR THE BOOK

'For anyone interested in the economic history of India from after Independence to now, this is the book to read—an objective analysis of our economic journey through the decades of Independence. The last half decade has been especially disappointing. A huge opportunity provided by both domestic and global factors has been wasted by a government busy with only event and headline management.'—Yashwant Sinha, former minister of finance and external affairs

'As the Modi-led NDA reaches the end of an underwhelming term, Salman Soz eviscerates its economics in prose that is refreshingly accessible, engaging and lucid. *The Great Disappointment* offers a straightforward and timely appraisal of five years of confused economic policymaking and catalogues the great opportunities squandered by the ruling dispensation. In this masterful, far-reaching volume, Salman Soz seals his credentials as one of contemporary India's most authoritative voices on the state of our political economy.'—Shashi Tharoor, member of Parliament and author

'In *The Great Disappointment*, Salman Soz has placed his finger unerringly on the single-most intriguing political economy question of our times: How did Narendra Modi, elected with such fanfare to transform the Indian economy, end up wasting the opportunity of a lifetime? This book is a must-read for anyone with a serious interest in the Indian economy.'— Sadanand Dhume, columnist, *Wall Street Journal*

'Salman Soz has produced a very timely must-read on the Modi government's economic record, carefully separating fact from fiction. Despite good luck in the form of low oil prices and a benign global environment, the outcomes— especially on job creation and farm distress—are as the carefully researched book aptly shows, hugely disappointing. For *"achhe din"*, India needs a carefully thought through vision for the future—not a compendium of political slogans and flashy schemes.'—Ajay Chhibber, former assistant secretary general, United Nations and senior World Bank official

'In *The Great Disappointment*, Salman Soz prosecutes a sustained, empirical critique of the Modi government's stewardship of the economy. With lucid prose and rich detail, Soz provokes a timely debate that every Indian has a stake in.'—Milan Vaishnav, senior fellow and director of the South Asia Program, Carnegie Endowment for International Peace

The Great
Disappointment

HOW
NARENDRA
MODI
SQUANDERED
A UNIQUE
OPPORTUNITY
TO TRANSFORM
THE INDIAN
ECONOMY

SALMAN ANEES SOZ

EBURY
PRESS
An imprint of Penguin Random House

EBURY PRESS

USA | Canada | UK | Ireland | Australia
New Zealand | India | South Africa | China

Ebury Press is part of the Penguin Random House group of companies
whose addresses can be found at global.penguinrandomhouse.com

Published by Penguin Random House India Pvt. Ltd
7th Floor, Infinity Tower C, DLF Cyber City,
Gurgaon 122 002, Haryana, India

Penguin
Random House
India

First published in Ebury Press by Penguin Random House India 2019

10 9 8 7 6 5 4 3 2 1

This book is a work of non-fiction and is based on the author's involvement in the
political arena, evidence and materials collected by him from various sources and
through interviews conducted by the author. The instances in the book are based
on a variety of sources, including, but not limited to, the personal interactions of
the author with various persons mentioned in the book. The views and opinions
expressed in the chapters of this book are those of the author only and do not
reflect or represent the views and opinions held by any other person or the
publishers; the publishers are not in any way liable for the same.

This book is based on actual events and is based on the materials collected by the
author with respect to the events enumerated. It reflects the author's representation
of the events enumerated as truthfully as possible and, as far as recollection
permits. All persons within the book are actual individuals.

The objective of this book is not to hurt any sentiments or be biased in favour of or
against any particular person, political party, society, gender, creed, nation or religion.

ISBN 9780670091799

Typeset in Bembo Std by Manipal Digital Systems, Manipal
Printed at Replika Press Pvt. Ltd, India

www.penguin.co.in

MIX
Paper from
responsible sources
FSC® C016779

To my father, Saifuddin Soz, and my life partner, Asia Mubashir,
for pushing me to write this book

To my mother, Mumtaz Soz, for her endless supply of love
and encouragement

To my amazing little children, Asmara and Zaydan, for patiently
waiting for Daddy to finish writing and being more excited about it
than even I was

To Soola, my adorable dog, for always sitting by my side and
keeping me company while I wrote this book

Contents

Introduction

The first single-party majority government in three decades raised hopes for change and a significant step-up for India, a country that remains poor despite progress in recent decades. In 2014, Narendra Modi and the Bharatiya Janata Party (BJP) campaigned on promises of limited government, good governance and economic transformation. Modi presented himself as a masterful leader, ready to launch India into a new era of prosperity. Hopes ran high. The atmosphere was heady and feverish. There was a general perception in the country that Narendra Modi's performance as chief minister of Gujarat was demonstrative of his credentials as a pro-business leader with a can-do attitude. During his highly successful 2014 election campaign, candidate Modi railed against big government, declaring, 'I believe government has no business to do business. The focus should be on Minimum Government but Maximum Governance.'[1] It appeared as if a conservative, right-of-centre political party had finally taken root in India.[2] As the National Democratic Alliance (NDA) completes its term in 2019, the government's economic policies and programmes are due for a proper and full assessment.

With the biggest political mandate in almost three decades and under a leader widely perceived to be one of the most powerful prime ministers India has ever had, did India's economic trajectory make a decisive break from its past? This is the central question of this book project. The fundamental question raised and investigated in this book is not simply about the usual political question: 'Are you better off today than you were five years ago?' It is deeper. In Modi's case, it was never about a new government performing better than the one it was replacing. It was about making the case that given a chance, the Modi government would not just outperform all predecessor governments but would match their cumulative performance within its first term. Hence Modi's famous line from the election, 'You gave Congress 60 years, give BJP just 60 months,' is a running theme in this book.

Of course, some of this is political positioning and campaign management but the expectations were so high that the former ruling party, Indian National Congress, ended up with just forty-four seats in the Lok Sabha (lower house of Parliament), by far its worst performance ever. It is therefore important to cast this promise of transformation as the central question of this book. This broader question includes several components:

- Has the Modi government been able to deliver on its campaign's economic narrative, one that promised a conservative, minimum-government stance?
- Has the Modi government promoted the next generation of reforms that the previous government was unable to pursue?
- Have macroeconomic policies led to the promised spurt in growth and job creation?
- Has the investment scenario significantly improved compared to that under the previous economic regime?
- Have agricultural development and the rural–urban transition happened in a fundamentally different way than past experience?

- Has the Modi government focused adequately on human-development policies that can help young people become productive members of society?

The question of transformation is not just about Modi's success or failure. It is much bigger than that. We in India must think critically about policies for the future. We are at a critical moment in our history and the next government's policies could have lasting effects as the world's pace of change accelerates, driven in part by disruption and technology, and a new populist, anti-globalist political environment. Countries around the world confront the question of how best to effectively manage these changes, driven in large measure by technological innovation, climate change and demographic shifts. Prosaic needs anchor these big themes—the well-being of the human race, most commonly projected through a desire to ensure a good future for the next generation. Worries about the future, especially the future of work, are dominating the discourse in international economic development. There are also worries about how unequal progress will be and if some people will inevitably be left behind.

Along with these global trends, each country faces bread-and-butter development challenges. In India, we confront endemic problems in the agricultural and industrial sectors. Infrastructure needs are vast, even as investments have slowed. The rural economy is unable to slow the migration of workers to urban areas, which remain unprepared for a large influx of people. Environmental degradation and pollution are exacting a heavy toll at a time when India's growth is enabled by fossil fuels. The biggest challenge is that of jobs. As life expectancy has increased in India, people are ageing at much lower income levels compared to the experience of advanced economies. At the other end of the spectrum, India has a youth bulge that would be the envy of any country were it not for the fact that creation of decent jobs is lagging. A demographic dividend threatens to become a demographic curse.

Connecting global trends to India's circumstances is a vast topic, beyond the scope of this book. However, it would be a missed opportunity to not present some broad ideas that should become part of India's development discourse. It is also important to present some principles that should serve as the basis of policy formulation in India. We can come up with sectoral visions or strategic plans, but we also need some cross-cutting principles that are good to keep in mind as we navigate increasingly complex global, national and local development contexts. The few principles presented here are not exhaustive. However, their inclusion is meant to catalyse a debate on the need for such principles. To address the gamut of India's development challenges, this book issues a call to action in a number of important areas. In doing so, we also reflect on India's public discourse and contrast it with what is happening globally.

In five parts, this book attempts to answer the overarching question of whether or not the Modi government transformed India's economy and what the next government's agenda should look like. The **first** chapter sets the stage by describing the economic landscape inherited by Modi and the NDA in 2014. The **second** chapter focuses on the 2014 Lok Sabha election, revisiting the narrative around economic issues and promises crafted by the PM and the BJP. **Chapter 3** considers the key economic policies and programmes enacted by the Modi government while also analysing other economic initiatives that were, perhaps, ignored. **Chapter 4** presents the current state of the economy as a way of assessing the effectiveness of Prime Minister Modi's economic policies. **Chapter 5** highlights India's central economic challenges and recommends a policy framework and an actionable agenda for the next government.

1

The Inheritance

'I have done as best as I could under the circumstances.'[1]—Manmohan Singh (2014)

On 25 October 2013, at a public rally in Jhansi, the then prime-ministerial candidate of the Bharatiya Janata Party (BJP), Narendra Modi, addressed the people thus: 'You gave Congress 60 years, give BJP just 60 months.'[2] He went on to boldly promise, 'We will change India's future and bring about development in 60 months.' Essentially, Modi argued that those who came before him didn't do much and asked the electorate for a chance to show them what he could do. This simple argument resonated greatly with the population, propelling Modi and the BJP to a resounding electoral victory. However, it also created very high expectations of fast growth and economic development.

The Modi narrative minimized the efforts of past governments, particularly those led by the Indian National Congress (INC or Congress). While some of this rhetoric was part of the rough-and-tumble world of Indian politics, there is an ideological context to it. The Rashtriya Swayamsevak

Sangh (RSS), BJP's parent organization, has built an ideological narrative based on Hindu nationalism that has been unable to digest India's secular, democratic traditions. In that context, casting the legacy of the founders of modern India in a negative light is part of the RSS's long-term strategy. The RSS and BJP have been successful in crafting this narrative and in sowing doubts in the minds of Indians about the effectiveness of past efforts directed at economic development.

It is therefore important to review key policies introduced and results achieved by previous governments. This background will help establish a counterfactual to the efforts of the Modi government, which we will come to later. The other introductory point to note is that in this book, and in most discussions of India's political economy, the Central government's economic stewardship is the object of the analysis. However, India's states and their governments have a major role in the country's economic progress. No discussion of India's economy is complete without an assessment of what is happening in the states. Details of state-level efforts are beyond the scope of this book, however. For the purpose of this book, we assume that under the Modi government the states performed as well or as badly as they have done in the past.

To assess the success of economic policymaking under PM Modi, and to get to the heart of the sixty-months-versus-sixty-years debate, it is necessary to take a short historical tour. The challenges that confronted various governments and the policy frameworks and solutions put forward are a fascinating study. Reviewing the results of those efforts will be useful for most readers. Without a glimpse into our past, today's progress or lack thereof would be difficult to measure. Having said that, it would be unwieldy to offer a detailed account of each government's economic stewardship. To deal with that, I will do what some others have done in the past. I will look at distinct phases of India's economic history that characterize 'clear breaks in economic policies'.[3] These phases include the period from Independence to the end of the third five-year plan in 1965, 1966–80, 1981–91 and the post-1991 reform period. However, given the context of this book, the period during which the United Progressive Alliance (UPA) government held office will receive special attention since it provides the most immediate comparator against which to assess the performance of the Modi government.

1947–65—The birth of a democratic nation, a postcolonial fledgling economy

'At the stroke of the midnight hour, when the world sleeps, India will awake to life and freedom. A moment comes, which comes but rarely in history, when we step out from the old to the new, when an age ends, and when the soul of a nation, long suppressed, finds utterance.'[4]— Jawaharlal Nehru

Managing Partition and the postcolonial period

The Partition and the bloodletting that accompanied our Independence took up much of our founders' energy. An opinion piece by an unnamed Indian official in the July 1949 issue of *Foreign Affairs* magazine describes the challenge: 'In its [Partition's] wake came the immense task of organizing, within a few weeks, the movement of no less than 6,000,000 refugees, of improvising arrangements for their immediate relief, and devising plans for their permanent resettlement and rehabilitation. When was a "refugee problem" of this magnitude set before an untried government in the very first days of its existence and solved with equal expedition and success?'[5] There was no significant foreign assistance to deal with a refugee crisis that was second in scale only to that of World War II. While presenting the first budget of independent India on 26 November 1947, finance minister R.K. Shanmukham Chetty noted that the immediate impact of the Partition's 'tragic developments has been to divert the attention of the Government almost completely from normal activities'.[6]

The Partition was an unwanted addition to an already full plate of immense problems. Most of India's 35 crore people then lived in staggering poverty. One of the biggest problems facing the young nation was shortage of food. The Bengal famine of 1943, which claimed 30 lakh lives, was still a fresh memory. India was predominantly rural, and agricultural life dominated not just politics but also India's economy. Harvard economist John Kenneth Galbraith, writing in *Foreign Affairs* magazine[7] almost a decade after Independence, summed up the situation: 'The isolation of the Indian village is something that can be both seen and felt. The thin, searching people, the mud and thatch, the patrol of silent cows, the meagre surrounding fields, all convey a sense of solitude. Village government is primitive but slightly tied to central authority. There is no priest who is in communication with his hierarchy and no telephone or telegraph lines to the city. Often the village can be approached only on foot.' Pointing to an inherent mistrust of authority, Galbraith notes that, 'Those who have approached it [village] over the mud dikes or along the dusty paths in centuries past have been the agents of old oppressions or the harbingers of new misfortunes. At best they have been bearers of promises that were never kept or prophets of reforms that were never made. Out of the depths of this experience the village has a deeply ingrained mistrust of the world outside, and this mistrust is directed first of all at those who presume to govern.'

Early challenges of a fledgling economy

When we think about development challenges today, considerable as they are, the challenges India's founders confronted seem a world away. In his maiden budget speech, former finance minister Sir Ramasamy Chetty noted that India's 'food position has continued to cause grave anxiety both to the Provincial Governments and the Central Government'. Galbraith was of the view that India's villages, where 83 per cent of Indians lived, were 'preoccupied, with the production of food'. He noted that 'Indian economic life as a whole' was mostly about food production. Poverty was endemic, with about 70 per cent of Indians living in poverty in 1947.[8] According to the 1951 census, adult literacy rate was a mere 18 per cent. In 1950, life expectancy was thirty-two years and the infant mortality rate (IMR) was 145 per 1000 live births.[9] In the 1940s, maternal mortality ratio (MMR) was 2000 (per 1,00,000) live births.[10] The country had built only 750 primary health centres and had only about 50,000 doctors.[11]

Agriculture accounted for 50 per cent of national output and only 0.2 per cent of India's villages (there are over six lakh forty thousand of them) had electric connections. While today we keenly observe the ups and downs of the index of industrial production (IIP), India imported 90 per cent of industrial goods at the time of Independence. What India's founders confronted in 1947 had accumulated over time. From 1900 to 1947, India's gross domestic product (GDP) grew at an average rate of a meagre 0.9 per cent per annum. In this period, per capita GDP grew at only 0.1 per cent per annum.

Despite the focus on refugee and food-production challenges, India's first government, led by Jawaharlal Nehru, understood the critical need for balanced development and for reviving the economy. There was also a degree of consensus among the founders on the centrality of industrialization to poverty reduction. Nehru, Sardar Patel and others were among the main players behind the Industrial Policy Resolution of 1948, which set the stage for 'planned' development and a major role for the state. In fact, the public sector gained a monopoly in some industries while recognizing the private sector's role in the economy.

The Industrial Policy Resolution also set the basis of the Planning Commission, which was formed in 1950. The government also initiated the planning process by producing the first five-year plan. The Planning Commission and the five-year plans remained, except for some interruptions, a mainstay of India's economic landscape for over sixty years until their discontinuation by the Modi government. The twelfth five-year plan was the last one of its kind and it ended in March 2017.[12]

The dawn of India's five-year plans

A 1956 resolution followed the 1948 resolution, and gave the public sector a more dominant role in economic affairs. The architect of the second five-year plan was P.C. Mahalanobis, a statistician and scientist of great repute. From his perspective, economic growth was dependent on increased investment, which in turn required capital goods. However, as pointed out earlier, India imported such goods, and it was a widely held view at that time that the country did not have sufficient resources for those imports. It is for this reason that the architects of the five-year plans emphasized a greater role for the public sector to produce these goods. In the words of Mahalanobis, 'The only way of eliminating unemployment in India is to build up a sufficiently large stock of capital which will enable all unemployed persons being absorbed into productive capacity. Increasing the rate of investment is, therefore, the only fundamental remedy for unemployment in India.'[13]

India needed a diversified production base even as it tried to stabilize agriculture. Many accounts of that time indicate that the consumer-goods sector did not receive adequate attention, but even here the policies seemed to focus on self-reliance.

One must view this focus on what was part of the Swadeshi movement, in the context of a history of foreign rule and what that had wrought on India.[14] For India's founders, political freedom was not sufficient. They also needed economic freedom because the colonial economic policies of the past had created near universal poverty in India. There wasn't the kind of focus on exports that we see today and it is likely that this was due to the circumstances of that period where the needs of a large swathe of Indians were unmet.

In their desire for rapid development, the founders displayed breathtaking ambition. Since food production was of critical importance initially, the first government under Pandit Nehru focused on expanding India's irrigation capacity. Chester Bowles, an American diplomat, noted in an opinion piece that India embarked on creating three large dam systems (Damodar, Hirakud and Bhakra-Nangal) that had an irrigation capacity 70 per cent more than that of the Grand Coulee (in the US state of Washington) which was at that time the 'largest irrigation system in the world'.[15] For a country that had just become free from an exploitative occupation, the scale of these projects spoke of the frantic pace that was being set on the development front.

The five-year plans that some criticize today for their 'one-size fits all', top-down approach in a diverse country such as India, did help the industrial sector grow by an average of 7 per cent over the 1950–65 period. The government helped reverse the decline under the British and put in place the basic building blocks of a new socio-economic order. In the fifty years before Independence, India's GDP growth averaged about 0.9 per cent per annum. During the first three five-year plans, India's GDP growth averaged 4 per cent. Today, we can say that 4 per cent was low and that our founders were ineffective, but who in the year 1900 could imagine that India would grow at 4 per cent a year over a fifteen-year stretch? In those fifteen years (1950–65),

India's average GDP per capita growth rate was almost nineteen times that achieved during the 1900–47 time period.[16]

No doubt the strategy of industrialization through a focus on capital goods has come in for criticism, particularly from right-leaning economists. Even so, the state-led interventions in the 1950–65 period have not received the kind of criticism that the policies of the 1960s and 1970s did. The former vice chairman of the NITI Aayog, Arvind Panagariya, makes this distinction clear: 'Most analysts, including those critical of India's controlled regime, broadly approve of the economic policies and performance in the 1950s. Difference between the advocates of pro-market and state-driven development strategy relate principally to the period beginning in the 1960s when the Republic of Korea successfully switched from import substitution policies to outward oriented policies and India did not.' Panagariya notes that Jagdish Bhagwati and Padma Desai, two economists who are known for being among the harshest critics of the policy regime of the 1960s, wrote 'approvingly of India's performance during the first three five-year plans'.[17]

India's first post-Independence economic growth spurt

One of the most nuanced essays on post-Independence economic performance is by Deepak Nayyar, a professor at Delhi's Jawaharlal Nehru University (JNU).[18] According to Nayyar, 'It is clear that the pace of economic growth during the period from 1950 to 1980 constituted a radical departure from the colonial past.' Nayyar reviewed two sets of national income data for the period 1900 to 1947. He estimated that growth rates based on national income calculated by S. Sivasubramonian estimates indicate that India's 'national income would have doubled in 70 years whereas per capita income would have doubled in 350 years'. However, if India's economy had grown at the lower rate estimated by Angus Maddison, 'national income would have doubled in 87.5 years whereas per capita income would have doubled in 1,750 years'. However, Nayyar points out, 'The reality in independent India turned out to be different. The growth rates achieved during the period from 1950 to 1980 meant that GDP doubled in 20 years while GDP per capita would have doubled in 50 years.'

A cottage industry has opened up to bemoan the legacy of 'Nehruvian socialism', as opponents of Pandit Nehru like to term the mixed-economy model adopted by our founders. In the 21st century, it appears that we have become more impatient about development. It may even seem to us that earlier generations of Indians were less impatient and, as a result, did not focus sufficiently or with a sense of urgency in dealing with India's challenges and putting the country on the fast track to economic development. Some politicians have sought to stoke this sense of dissatisfaction. However, there is absolutely no question that India's founders were exceedingly concerned with the pace of its development. They had little choice in the matter because they were dealing with survival issues such as sufficient food for the impoverished citizens of the country. Nehru and his team were constantly grappling with issues such as land reform, food production, use of technology and anything that would help alleviate the suffering of India's poor. It may be fashionable for today's pundits to call this 'povertarianism', but in those days it was about saving lives and giving hope that things would be better now that India's destiny was in its own hands.

However, not only does data indicate that India's economic performance was reasonably good but even the most authoritative critics of India's 'licence raj' or 'permit raj' have shown appreciation for the work done in the early years after Independence. In the process, when the first prime minister passed away in 1964, the economy was bigger, health and education indicators had improved, the number of villages connected to electricity had grown and the production of industrial goods was up. And, yes, food production had gone up significantly too. This brief discussion of a few pages cannot do justice to the enormous work accomplished in those years when independent India was still young. But it is my hope that I leave the reader with the thought that those years were not a waste, and, in fact, they achieved a lot. If we are where we are today, for better or for worse, it is because our founders were ambitious and wedded to the idea that India deserved not just political freedom but economic freedom as well.

State of India's economy

To illustrate economic progress since Independence, the reader can review data on a few basic indicators for each period under discussion. These range from broad macroeconomic indicators such as GDP to human development indicators related to health and education. An indicator on power generation will act as a proxy for infrastructure development. The information presented in the table may be obvious to many readers but is a necessary reminder that Narendra Modi did craft a narrative that sought to minimize India's achievements under past governments. Replications of this table will later on show India's progress at different points since Independence.

Progress on key indicators (1947–65)

	1947–50 (earliest available)	1965
GDP (constant 2010 US$) (in billions)	N.A.	162
GDP per capita (constant 2010 US$)	N.A.	325

	1947–50 (earliest available)	1965
Foreign exchange reserves (US$ million)	2	524
Infant mortality rate	155	152
Life expectancy at birth[19]	32	44
Literacy rate	18%	28%
Power generation (installed capacity, megawatts)	1362	9027

Source: Compiled from World Development Indicators (World Bank), Economic Surveys, Reserve Bank of India Statistical Database, Ministry of Finance, Ministry of Power.

By the time Nehru passed away, he had led the country in taking the first steps as a new democracy. His government faced many severe challenges but he secured for his successors a foundation to build upon.

1966–80—Political tumult, nationalization, the Green Revolution and slower growth

'Jai Jawan, Jai Kisan' ('Long live the soldier, long live the farmer')—Lal Bahadur Shastri
'Garibi Hatao' ('End poverty')—Indira Gandhi

A hint of liberalization

With Nehru's passing and in the aftermath of the wars with China (1962) and Pakistan (1965), the state was set for a renewed economic development push. The victory over Pakistan had enhanced the popularity of Lal Bahadur Shastri, India's second prime minister. Niranjan Rajadhyaksha, formerly the executive editor of Mint newspaper, has written extensively about economic developments since Independence. According to him, Shastri assumed the figure of a quiet but determined reformer who recognized the limitations of state-led planning and paved the way for greater participation of the private sector in economic activity. Rajadhyaksha quotes P.N. Dhar, an adviser to Indira Gandhi, India's third prime minister, to buttress his point.

In his memoir, *Indira Gandhi, the 'Emergency' and Indian Democracy*,[20] Dhar notes:

> He [Shastri] wore no ideological blinkers; he saw facts as they were in all their starkness. Chronic food shortages made him shift investment from basic industries to agriculture. Roaring black markets persuaded him to make a relative shift from controls to incentives, and the glaring inefficiency of the public sector made him accept a larger role for the private sector and foreign investment. He also took measures to shift the locus of economic decision-making from the Planning Commission to the ministries and from the Centre to the states.[21]

Shastri died while in office without a full opportunity to pursue his vision. We shall never know what the full impact of his economic stewardship may have been.

The take-off of India's neighbours

India's growth rate in the 1965–80 period stagnated partly on account of even greater control of the economy by the state, especially after the Indira Gandhi government took charge. Before examining the impact of Indira Gandhi's first tenure from an economic perspective, I will address the following argument that right-of-centre economists make regularly: In the mid

1960s, India and South Korea had a similar average income, and now the gap between the two countries is large. For reference, GDP per capita (current US$) in India was 118 and only 108 in Korea. In 2017, per capita GDP for the two countries was 1940 and 29,743 respectively.

Panagariya makes the case thus: 'Through macroeconomic stability, policy credibility and legal institutions capable of enforcing contracts, India was successful in pushing its GDP growth rate from less than 1 percent during the first half of the 20th century to the 3–4 percent range during 1950–80. But it came nowhere near the ultra-high growth rates experienced by Korea during the sixties and seventies principally because it opted for an increasingly protectionist trade policy regime with nearly all imports coming under strict licensing by early 1970s.'

Panagariya adds that, 'By the mid-1970s, India's trade regime was so constrained that imports (other than oil and cereals) had fallen from the already low level of 7 percent of GDP in 1957–58 to 3 percent in 1975–76. Whereas Korea recognized the importance of competing against the world's most efficient producers and the need for importing the state-of-the-art machinery from abroad, India chose to hide behind a steel wall of protection, manufacturing its own machinery (and steel!). The result was an annual per-capita GDP growth of 6.3 percent in Korea and 1.1 per cent in India during 1961–80.'[22]

Countries like Korea succeeded in securing higher growth due to a strategy that was different from what India pursued. However, simplistic explanations distort our understanding of what policymakers confront when they make decisions based on the information and choices at their disposal. Were the conditions in Korea and India really similar in the mid 1960s?

While incomes were broadly similar, there were other, arguably more important determinants of future progress.

Korea had a big lead as far as key human development indicators were concerned. According to data from the Organisation for Economic Cooperation and Development (OECD), Korea's literacy rate in 1970 was 87.6 per cent. In 1971, India was still struggling at 34.5 per cent, with female literacy at only 21.9 per cent.[23] In 1965, Korea's infant mortality rate (IMR) was 64.9 versus 152.3 in India.[24] In 1965, life expectancy at birth was fifty-seven years in Korea versus only forty-four years in India. These human development indicators have a major impact on economic development. This does not absolve Indian policymakers but it contextualizes India's relative underperformance.

One could argue as to why India did not improve its human development indicators after 1947. The answer is simple: India improved its position significantly compared to 1947 when adult literacy was only 18 per cent (Korea: 22 per cent in 1945), IMR was 186 (Korea: 138 in 1953), and life expectancy at birth was just thirty-two years (Korea: forty-eight years in 1953).

Roots of an economic slowdown

It is important to understand the policy framework under Indira Gandhi as well as the short-lived Janata Party government that succeeded her in 1977. Many experts point out that this period is notable for the entrenchment of the state in economic activity, a 'permit raj' that inhibited the private sector and stagnated economic growth. This gave birth to what came to be called the 'Hindu rate of growth'. While we mostly hear about Indira Gandhi's decision to nationalize banks in 1969, we should begin with looking at the time around which she took over as prime minister for the first time. In 1965 and 1966, India suffered two successive droughts on account of monsoon failure. Given the post-Independence strategy of prioritizing industrialization, especially of heavy industry, the agricultural sector was lagging behind during the first two five-year plans.

Experts believe that policy changes in favour of the agricultural sector in the third five-year plan 'did not go far enough'.[25] With an increasing population and limits to how much institutional changes such as a focus on cooperative farming could improve production, 'agriculture remained highly dependent on the weather'.[26] The failure of monsoons in 1965–66 contributed to a decline in 'agricultural production by 17 percent and food grain output by 20 percent'. In the next year, food grain production fell further to a level below that of 1960–61. The rate of inflation crossed 10 per cent in 1966–67 and 1967–68, with food price inflation at around 20 per cent.[27]

Another cause of this severe inflation was a mounting fiscal deficit caused in part by the wars against China (1962) and Pakistan (1965). Defence expenditures as a share of GDP doubled between 1960–61 and 1965–66 from 1.6 per cent to 3.2 per cent. To make matters worse, the balance-of-payments position, which had been relatively weak since Independence, worsened with falling exports and the need to import food. With limited degrees of freedom, the Indira Gandhi government took three steps, primarily as a way of securing external assistance. The government devalued the rupee by 36.5 per cent in 1966, rationalized export subsidies and import duties, and adopted a new agricultural strategy aimed at promoting fertilizers and high-yield seeds.

Politics overshadows economics

While there appeared to be support for a change in the agricultural strategy, many saw the devaluation as a 'sell-out' to institutions such as the World Bank. In the 1967 election, Mrs Gandhi had to pay a political price in terms of a reduced margin of victory for the Congress party. Despite political losses, the economy showed some improvement. The Green Revolution commenced and agricultural production rose rapidly, exports recovered and inflation slowed. GDP grew by 6 per cent in those years. The industrial sector took a hit, however, and the 'oil shock' that saw crude oil prices jump over 300 per cent between September 1973 and September 1974 marked an especially challenging time for the Indian economy.

The experience of economic crises and failed monsoons caused a degree of disenchantment with five-year plans. This led to a 'plan holiday' from 1966 to 1969. It is during this time that Indira Gandhi's relationship with a powerful faction in the Congress party, which included the then finance minister Morarji Desai, worsened. She relieved Desai of the finance portfolio and embarked on a path of building support for her own vision. During this time, a key decision, and one that has received criticism since then, led to the nationalization (government control) of fourteen of India's largest banks. In addition, the government brought in the stringent Monopolies and Restrictive Trade Practices (MRTP) Act to closely regulate the activities of private businesses.

Indira Gandhi's bank nationalization had some context to it. In an interesting paper on banking-sector reforms, three professors at the Massachusetts Institute of Technology (MIT)[28] observe that 'the Indian government felt that banks in private hands did not lend enough to those who needed it most'. They cite the following quote by Prakash Tandon, former chairman of the Punjab National Bank:

> 'Many bank failures and crises over two centuries, and the damage they did under "laissez faire" conditions; the needs of planned growth and equitable distribution of credit, which in privately owned banks was concentrated mainly on the controlling industrial houses and influential borrowers; the needs of growing small scale industry and farming regarding finance, equipment and inputs; from all these there emerged an

inexorable demand for banking legislation, some government control and a central banking authority, adding up, in the final analysis, to social control and nationalization.'

The Indian banking sector changed dramatically after nationalization. Agricultural credit, which was about 2 per cent of the total prior to nationalization, rose to 9 per cent within a decade, and the number of bank branches in rural areas went up from about 18 per cent before nationalization to almost 58 per cent in 1985, a year after Indira Gandhi's death. The policy framework 'required banks to open four branches in unbanked locations for every branch opened in banked locations'.

As a financial inclusion policy, bank nationalization and bringing banking to unbanked communities is comparable with financial inclusion under the current government as well as the previous UPA government. Both governments used the platform of public-sector banks (PSBs), developed as a result of Indira Gandhi's nationalization policy, to take financial inclusion to the next level.

However, private-sector activity also continued. According to the MIT professors mentioned above 'Between 1969 and 1980, the number of private branches grew more quickly than public banks, and on April 1, 1980, they accounted for approximately 17.5 percent of bank branches in India.' This does not prove Indira Gandhi's detractors wrong when they complain about the heavy hand of the state in economic activity. However, it does show that things are not always as they are made out to be.

The state exerts control

Buoyed by her stupendous victory in the general election of 1971 (on the Garibi Hatao slogan) and India's victory over Pakistan in the 1971 war, Indira Gandhi consolidated her power and initiated further populist measures that effectively increased government control over the economy. The takeover of hundreds of sick units, including textile mills, followed the nationalization of insurance and coal sectors.[29] The government enacted the Industrial Licensing Acts of 1970 and 1973 followed by the Foreign Exchange Regulation Act (FERA) in 1973 to regulate foreign investment in India, thereby adding to an already burdensome regulatory framework.[30]

The state's dominance over economic affairs grew considerably under Indira Gandhi. Critics such as Bhagwati and Panagariya have pointed out that such over-regulation had a lasting impact on India's economic development trajectory. They point out that between 1965 and 1975, before Indira Gandhi implemented the Emergency, India's per capita income grew by a measly 0.3 per cent per annum.[31] GDP growth during that period averaged only 2.6 per cent. It is true that growth picked up after the imposition of the Emergency, but the entire period under Indira Gandhi saw an average annual growth of about 3.2 per cent. This was lower than that achieved under the first three five-year plans.

The Janata Party government that took charge after defeating the Congress in 1977 benefited from two good monsoons, and agricultural production rose to a record level of 21 million tons in 1979. In their book on India's political economy, Vijay Joshi and I.M.D. Little note that while exports grew, imports rose due to import liberalization. However, 'remittances remained so buoyant that foreign exchange reserves rose to more than $7 billion in 1978, providing 9 months of import cover'.[32] In essence, India's food and foreign exchange positions were strong. However, the government appeared to be unable to benefit from these benign conditions as investments (both public and private) fell. By 1979, the Janata Party was plagued by internal squabbles. This political turbulence could not have come at a worse time.

A severe drought in 1979 and an oil-price shock led to high inflation and fiscal deficit. Food prices, particularly onion prices, became an emotive issue. After Morarji Desai's ouster as prime minister, Chaudhary Charan Singh led a Congress-supported government for a mere twenty-eight days. Overall, as one can expect, the short-lived Janata Party government did not leave a lasting impact on India's economic trajectory. In some ways, it extended the path that Indira Gandhi's policies had created for the Indian economy.

Progress on key indicators (1966–80)

	1966	1980
GDP (constant 2010 US$) (in billions)	162	272
GDP per capita (constant 2010 US$)	318	390
Foreign exchange reserves (US$ million)	626	7361
Infant mortality rate	150	114
Life expectancy at birth[33]	45	54
Literacy rate	28%	44%
Power generation (installed capacity, megawatts)	9027	26,680

Source: Compiled from World Development Indicators (World Bank), Economic Surveys, Reserve Bank of India Statistical Database, Ministry of Finance, Ministry of Power.

During 1966–80, India experienced the hugely important Green Revolution and witnessed major progress in financial inclusion. It also witnessed the advent of an overly regulated economy impacted by fractious politics which resulted in the slowest economic growth in the postcolonial period. It was a period of policy experiments with mixed efficacy. Despite the challenges of the period, it also contributed to economic gains of the following decade. By the end of this period, India was ready for change and a new direction.

1981–90—The economy regains speed; pro-business reforms initiated

> Our economy owes much to the enterprise of our industrialists. But there are some reputed business and industrial establishments which shelter battalions of law-breakers and tax evaders. We have industrialists untouched by the thrusting spirit of the great risk-takers and innovators. The trader's instinct for quick profits prevails. They flourish on sick industries. Many have not cared to learn the fundamental lesson that industrialisation springs from the development of indigenous technology, not from dependence on others. Industrial empire built on the shaky foundations of excessive protection, social irresponsibility, import orientation and corruption may not last long.[34]—Rajiv Gandhi (1985)

The year 1981 marked the beginning of a new economic period that is more significant than it gets credit for. The narrative that the years preceding the reforms of 1991 were a period marked by 'stagnant' or 'low' growth dominates general public perception. The only economic reforms ordinary citizens are aware of are the ones undertaken under the leadership of former prime minister P.V. Narasimha Rao and his finance minister, Manmohan Singh. However, the 1981–91 period has an interesting story that we must remember, both for its positive aspects and also the difficulties that ultimately led to a crisis that paved the way for the 1991 reforms.

India's second growth spurt

As Deepak Nayyar noted in his seminal essay ('Lumbering Elephant, Running Tiger'),[35] in the post-Independence era, there were two structural breaks in economic growth. The first, as we noted earlier, came in the period 1950–65. The second, argues Nayyar, was in 1980 and not in 1991, as is widely perceived. Nayyar notes that ideological narratives drive some of the hypotheses around relatively rapid growth between 1980 and 2004. However, one widely accepted cause of higher growth starting in 1980 has to do with increased public investment and consumption.

Nayyar's view of 1980 representing a structural break receives support from the work of well-known economists Dani Rodrik and Arvind Subramanian.[36] In a 2004 paper, Rodrik and Subramanian argued,

> It is indeed the case that, until recently, India had one of the most over regulated and closed economies in the world. It is also true that the economic liberalization of 1991 constitutes a watershed event for the Indian economy. But the main difficulty with the standard account, as summarized here, is that the pickup in India's economic growth precedes the 1991 liberalization by a full decade. Even a cursory glance at the growth record reveals that the more-than-doubling of India's growth rate takes place sometime around 1980, with very little discernible change in trend after 1991.

Pro-business reforms

According to Rodrik and Subramanian, 'The trigger for India's economic growth was an attitudinal shift on the part of the national government in 1980 in favor of private business.' From their perspective, the government's attitude toward business 'went from being outright hostile to supportive'. Their research led them to believe that this switch in attitude 'was further reinforced, in a more explicit manner, by Rajiv Gandhi following his rise to power in 1984. This, in our view, was the key change that unleashed the animal spirits of the Indian private sector in the early 1980s.'

However, the two economists made a distinction between 'pro-business' and 'pro-market' reforms. Clearly, the strategy of the 1980s appeared to be to improve the environment for established businesses and avoid creating losers, which market reforms can create along with winners. The policy changes that marked this shift in attitude included cuts in corporate taxes, removal of price controls and easing of restrictions on the output of businesses. Rodrik and Subramanian point out that trade liberalization, which would have been an example of market reforms, was not part of the 1980s attitudinal shift. Trade liberalization followed in the 1990s.[37]

Rodrik and Subramanian are matter-of-fact in characterizing the 1980s as a period that marked a shift towards higher growth rates. They conclude, 'India's growth transition began in the early 1980s rather than after the crisis of 1991.' If you just read this sentence, it has a certain unrealness about it. The 1991 reforms have left such a deep impression on our collective memory that it is difficult for us to think of the 1980s as anything but a period of disappointing growth. In reality, the growth was high. The other interesting aspect of their conclusion is how they link the changes of the 1980s to both the past as well as the future. As a nod to the past policy frameworks, they note that 'the learning generated under the earlier policy regime and the modern manufacturing base created thereby provided a permissive environment for eventual takeoff once the policy stance softened vis-à-vis the private sector'.

Rodrik and Subramanian also argue that 'unlike what one may have otherwise expected (from accounts of how costly import substituting industrialization [ISI] was), growth occurred where the earlier investments had been made.

They also suggest a link to the reforms of the 1990s. 'The reforms of the 1990s were, of course, triggered by the crisis of 1991. The quick rebound from the crisis has been almost entirely attributed to the decisive break from the dirigiste past. But if the 1980s experience was as successful as we think it might have been in creating a strong base of manufacturing and productivity growth, it is hard not to draw the conclusion that the quick rebound was also rendered possible by the strength of the 1980s performance.[38]

India hits double-digit growth

That manufacturing received a boost in the 1980s, especially in the latter half of the decade, is shown vividly in an essay by Pulapre Balakrishnan in a 1990 volume of the *Economic and Political Weekly* (EPW).[39] In his view, the high growth in the production of consumer durables (electrical machinery and appliances as a proxy) and the relatively slow growth in the textiles sector could be explained by the changing consumption patterns in India in the 1980s. Broader macroeconomic aggregates reflect some of these changes.

As documented in a paper by Arvind Panagariya, GDP growth was above 6 per cent in five of the ten years from 1980–81 to 1989–90. In the other five years, it was below 5 per cent but never below 3 per cent. In 1988–89, the Indian economy hit double-digit growth for the first time since Independence. On a per capita basis, the economy grew 3.3 per cent and investment went from about 19 per cent of the GDP in the early 1970s to nearly 25 per cent in the early 1980s. Exports, which had grown annually at a paltry 1.2 per cent rate during 1980–85, registered a hefty annual growth of 14.4 per cent during 1985–90.[40]

The thinking towards more impactful and broader economic reforms started towards the end of Rajiv Gandhi's tenure. A two-member committee comprising then finance secretary (and later RBI governor) S. Venkitaramanan and economist Vijay Kelkar, who headed the Bureau of Industrial Costs and Prices (BICP), prepared an interim report on an agenda for reforms commissioned by Rajiv Gandhi but submitted after his assassination to the V.P. Singh government. Due to a variety of factors, not least of which had to do with the social churning around the Mandal Commission report, the Venkitaramanan-Kelkar report saw little action.

This was also the time that an economic crisis was building up, which many economists, especially on the right, have blamed on the high fiscal and current account deficits that built up over the 1980s.[41] Many believe that expansionary macroeconomic policies culminated in the crisis of 1990–91. For example, Joshi and Little argue that, 'The expansionary policies in the first half of the 1980s (combined with modest liberalization) did lead to faster growth. But problems were stored up for the future by the fiscal deterioration and the lack of current account adjustment.' Nayyar does not agree with such narratives. He believes that the pick-up in aggregate demand led to relatively high growth rates in the 1980s, and laying the blame on the unsustainability of fiscal deficits does not present the full picture.

In any event, there is much more to say on the 1991 crisis and the reforms initiated as a result. Here's a look at India's basic development indicators at the end of 1990.

Progress on key indicators (1981–90)

	1981	1990
GDP (constant 2010 US$) (in billions)	288	471
GDP per capita (constant 2010 US$)	404	530
Foreign exchange reserves (US$ million)	6823	3962
Infant mortality rate	111	86
Life expectancy at birth[42]	54	58
Literacy rate	44%	48%
Power generation (installed capacity, megawatts)	26,680	63,636

Source: Compiled from World Development Indicators (World Bank), Economic Surveys, Reserve Bank of India Statistical Database, Ministry of Finance, Ministry of Power.

1991–2004—Structural reforms and stable, moderate growth

In 1991, a balance-of-payments crisis led to the adoption of an International Monetary Fund (IMF) programme, which included a substantive reform package. Economists such as Panagariya point out that high fiscal deficits and heavy external borrowing may have kept economic growth high but it came at a cost. After the V.P. Singh and Chandrasekhar governments bowed out, fresh elections brought in the P.V. Narasimha Rao government in June 1991. It was a leadership change that coincided with a fresh economic crisis that eventually led to some of the most consequential economic reforms enacted in India. While many experts have opined on the nature of the crisis, the budget speech delivered by Manmohan Singh, then finance minister, provides a clear sense of the challenge India faced and how the government of the day chose to address it.

A crisis and an opportunity

In his budget speech, Singh was remarkably candid and got to the heart of the matter, 'The new Government, which assumed office barely a month ago, inherited an economy in deep crisis. The balance of payments situation is precarious.'[43] He noted that while international confidence in the Indian economy was strong until late 1989, political instability in the country along with high fiscal deficits and the Iraq War resulted in the erosion of confidence in the economy. Capital inflows, including remittances by non-resident Indians (NRIs), had declined and despite IMF support, foreign exchange reserves were insufficient to cover more than two weeks of imports.

Prices were growing by double digits, making life extremely tough for poor and low-income families. The Central government's fiscal deficit had reached 8 per cent of the GDP in 1990–91 and its internal public debt had reached 55 per cent of the GDP. In short, Singh noted, 'We have not experienced anything similar in the history of independent India . . . There is no time to lose. Neither the Government nor the economy can live beyond its means year after year. The room for maneuver, to live on borrowed money or time, does not exist any more.' The government's acknowledgement of such dire economic straits midwifed the famous 1991 reforms.

Trade liberalization and domestic reforms

The 1991 crisis provided an opportunity to shift decisively away from India's import-substitution model, which supported the growth of Indian industry by restricting imports. The public sector's role diminished and the private sector's role expanded. Prior to the reforms, import licencing was an integral part of the foreign-trade regime. Trade tariffs were high too. The maximum tariffs were set at about 400 per cent while only 4 per cent of tariff rates were below 60 per cent. Restrictions on foreign investment meant that India received only US$100–200 million in foreign direct investment (FDI) annually.[44] After the 1991 reforms, the government abolished import licencing and the average tariffs declined to about 25 per cent. It announced liberalization of the foreign investment regime, opening up of the telecom and insurance sectors as well as minor adjustments to fuel and fertilizer subsidies.

The first two years after the reforms proved to be challenging but growth eventually picked up between 1994 and 1997 during which the economy grew by over 7 per cent in three successive years.[45] Exports grew as well and, in 1992, exceeded 10 per cent of the GDP for the first time. Short-term debt as a ratio of foreign exchange reserves stood at a very high 129 per cent in 1990. By 1994, this ratio had come down to just 14 per cent and

by 2002, it stood at a mere 10 per cent. The debt-service ratio
dropped from 35 per cent in 1990 to 26 per cent in 1994 and
only 14 per cent by 2002.[46]

Why structural reforms differed from past efforts

Deepak Nayyar, the chief economic adviser to three
governments between 1989 and 1991, penned one of the most
interesting perspectives on the 1991 reforms. He distinguished
between the objectives of the 1991 reforms and those of
earlier reforms. While Nayyar acknowledges reform efforts
in the late 1970s and the mid 1980s, he notes that these did
not 'contemplate any fundamental changes in the objectives
or strategy of development'. He goes on to argue that, 'The
changes in 1991 were significant enough to be characterised
as a shift of paradigm.'[47]

Nayyar highlights three dimensions of the 1991 reforms as
markers of change from past efforts. First, economic growth
and efficiency received greater recognition as policy objectives
as opposed to reduction of income inequality. Simply put, the
reforms envisioned growth as a means to reducing poverty
and inequality. Second, the role of the state in economic
development diminished. Third, the government sought
to quickly dismantle trade barriers while encouraging new
investments and technologies.[48] One thing to keep in mind is
that Nayyar was clear, as were some economists such as Rodrik,
Subramanian, J. Bradford DeLong, Kaushik Basu and others,
that India experienced a structural break in long-term trend
growth in 1980–81 and not as a result of the 1991 reforms.
However, the 1991 reforms constituted a fundamental break in
terms of the kinds of reforms enacted in India. This is a subtle
point but it is important to keep in mind as we course through
this book and look to assess other episodes of major reforms.

Furthermore, Nayyar points out that the 1991 reforms had two components: 'macroeconomic stabilization and structural reform'.[49] The first component aimed at stabilizing the economy, reducing the fiscal deficit, easing the balance-of-payments situation and curbing inflationary expectations. According to Nayyar, macroeconomic stabilization was a short-term objective. The structural reforms component sought medium-term changes aimed at raising the rate of growth using two specific levers: increasing exports and encouraging the private sector to play a bigger role in the economy. Such a shift in thinking and policies constitutes a 'structural' change, a helpful distinction in assessing reforms undertaken by other governments.

Role of institutions in the success of structural reforms

While many experts attribute the successes of the 1991 reforms solely to the policies themselves, Nayyar also credits India's 'institutional capacities', such as a higher-education system, social institutions and legal frameworks, for its pivot to market economy.[50] Directly linking historic socio-economic developments to the sustainability of the 1991 reforms, Nayyar writes, 'Given the importance of initial conditions, it must also be recognized that economic reforms in India yielded benefits in significant part because of the essential foundations that were laid in the preceding four decades. The politics of democracy was the other critical factor that sustained the process in India.'

The 1991 reforms put India on a path that yielded solid economic development and historically high poverty reduction. The Economic Survey of 1995–96 notes the marked improvements since the crisis year of 1990–91. Growth of GDP at Factor Cost was 6.3 per cent in 1994–95 and projected at 6.2 per cent in 1995–96. This was a far cry from the 0.8 per cent growth recorded in the crisis year. This growth was also more sustainable with fiscal and current account deficits declining, inflation coming down below the historic 8 per cent figure, and savings rates reaching historic highs.

Real agricultural wage growth recovered sharply, mortality rates fell and employment growth was substantial. From 1992–93 to 1994–95, employment growth was an estimated 63 lakh jobs per year. Gross fixed capital formation as a share of real GDP reached a record of 22.2 per cent in 1994–95. Export growth averaged over 19 per cent during 1993–94 to 1995–96. Foreign exchange reserves, which stood at US$1 billion in 1990–91 rose to US$16.3 billion by January 1996, equivalent to five months of import cover. External debt as a share of GDP fell from a peak of 41 per cent in 1991–92 to 29 per cent in September 1995.

Sustaining progress after 1991

While acknowledging the powerful impact of the structural changes unleashed by the 1991 reforms, the contributions of other governments in the post-1991 period merit attention as well. The United Democratic Front (UDF) governments led by H.D. Deve Gowda and I.K. Gujral also contributed to India's growth story. However, these short-lived governments suffered from greater political instability, hampering their ability to institute major changes. Still, it was under the UDF government that the Infrastructural Development Finance Company (IDFC) was set up in 1997 to provide long-term infrastructure finance. At the time, the IDFC had an authorized share capital of Rs 5000 crore.[51] Over time, IDFC has branched out into different segments including banking. IDFC Bank had assets of US$16 billion as of 2017. It was also during the UDF government that the Telecom Regulatory Authority of India (TRAI) was set up in 1997.[52] On 25 April 1998, the government promulgated an ordinance for setting up the Central Electricity Regulatory Commission (CERC) at the Centre and State Electricity Regulatory Commissions (SERCs) in the states.[53]

These types of institutions have played a critical role in strengthening infrastructure services in India. We sometimes think of GDP growth or other socio-economic development improvements as abstract or automatic. However, institutional development goes hand in hand with socio-economic development, and all the governments that have contributed to institution-building deserve recognition. We will keep coming back to this point because it is one of the core objectives of this book to remind the reader of all that goes into improving living standards and sustaining progress.

The significance of the Vajpayee years

In the post-1991 reform period, the Vajpayee government deserves special mention for a policy framework that has had a significant impact on the Indian economy. There are four major areas in which policy changes led to notable improvements down the road. On the fiscal side, the government introduced the Fiscal Responsibility and Budgetary Management (FRBM) Act, aimed at curbing high fiscal deficits while inculcating a culture of fiscal prudence in India. On the infrastructure front, the Vajpayee government conceived the Golden Quadrilateral road network that connected four major metropolitan cities (Delhi, Mumbai, Chennai and Kolkata). The Vajpayee government also launched the highly successful Pradhan Mantri Gram Sadak Yojana (PMGSY), the prime minister's rural roads scheme. For anyone who has lived in rural areas, the changes due to PMGSY are remarkable and a testament to Vajpayee's long-term vision. While the Congress could point out that much of the rural-roads construction boom happened under the UPA government, the Vajpayee government deserves credit as well.

In two other areas, the Vajpayee government established a path that would guide the work of his successors. The government established the first disinvestment ministry and the idea of privatizing some public-sector entities took hold. The Bharat Aluminium Company (BALCO) and Hindustan Zinc, Indian Petrochemicals Corporation Limited and VSNL represent some of the notable disinvestments from that era.[54] Finally, the Vajpayee government brought in the New Telecom Policy in 2002, which helped unleash the telecom market 'by replacing fixed license fees for telecom firms with a revenue-sharing arrangement'.[55] A Telecom Dispute Settlement Appellate Tribunal was set up and the government's regulatory and dispute-settlement roles were separated.[56]

A work in progress and persistent challenges

While there are many positives to report during the post-1991 reforms period up to the time of the first NDA government, a number of problems remained. As Panagariya noted in 2001, the 1991 reforms had been unable to pull workers from agriculture into non-agricultural sectors. Labour-intensive manufacturing was the preserve of small-scale businesses. This hampered industrial development. Rigid labour laws prevented firms with more than a hundred employees from laying off workers. From Panagariya's perspective, privatization was not proceeding fast enough, and he pitched for further trade liberalization and a focus on reallocating resources to labour-intensive products. Panagariya viewed the agricultural sector as largely untouched by reforms and worried that the pace of infrastructure development, especially in the power sector, was very sluggish. He also emphasized reform of the education sector and seemed disappointed with progress in financial-sector reform and civil-sector reforms. In 2001, he noted, 'The accomplishments of the past decade are dwarfed only by what remains to be done.'[57]

A different perspective on the remaining challenges after the 1991 reforms comes from Deepak Nayyar. Writing in 2017, Nayyar notes that, 'The biggest failure of the past 25 years is that, despite such rapid economic growth, employment creation has simply not been commensurate.' In fact, employment elasticity of output (jobs created as a result of economic growth) declined consistently from 1972–73 to 2011–12.[58] It is no surprise, therefore, to find employment creation as a recurrent topic of concern and debate, given the waves of young people who are coming out of schools and colleges, unable to find gainful employment.

The other problem that persists is that of poverty. While growth has helped lift hundreds of millions out of poverty, millions remain poor. According to Nayyar, 'If we were to use a higher poverty line that allows for other basic needs [beyond food and clothing] such as appropriate shelter, adequate healthcare and education, it is estimated that about 75% of the population lives in absolute poverty. These are the vulnerable poor.' The third persistent problem is that of growing inequality in India. A variety of estimates indicate that income and wealth inequality has risen sharply in the post-1991 era.

The Indian economy's structure leads to some of these persistent challenges, which will be dealt with later in the book. For now, it is sufficient to acknowledge that even as India faced a variety of socio-economic challenges at the end of the Vajpayee era, it is indisputable that his government helped sustain progress in the post-1991 era. As is our practice, we will take a look at the same basic indicators that we have been following since 1947. However, as India's economy developed, some more data became available that sheds light on results achieved under different governments and the kind of economy one government left to another. In this context, I will add an indicator for access to an improved water source and an indicator for trade to see how India has been changing.

Progress on key indicators (1991–2004)

	1991	2004
GDP (constant 2010 US$) (in billions)	471	1000
GDP per capita (constant 2010 US$)	530	903
Foreign exchange reserves (US$ million)	5834	112,959
Infant mortality rate	86	58
Life expectancy at birth[59]	58	64
Literacy rate	48%	61%
Power generation (installed capacity, megawatts)	63,636	105,046
People with access to at least basic drinking water services (% of population)	80.5%	81.9%
Exports of goods and services (% of GDP)	8.58%	18.05%

Source: Compiled from World Development Indicators (World Bank), Economic Surveys, Reserve Bank of India Statistical Database, Ministry of Finance, Ministry of Power.

2005–2014—The UPA years

Benchmarking the Modi government's performance vis-à-vis the UPA government is fairly common. Modi and the BJP were seeking to replace Manmohan Singh and the Congress. Naturally, the proximate comparator is the UPA government.

Modi argued that Congress had failed to deliver and that he would bring good governance and *achhe din* (good days). His promise of transformation won out and the Congress suffered a massive defeat. As we have done with other periods of India's economic history, we will now assess the economy's performance under the UPA to get a sense of the kind of economy Modi inherited.

A narrative of crisis

When the UPA suffered its 2014 electoral meltdown, there was a widespread impression that the country's economy was doing poorly. Economic growth, while recovering, was still weak compared to the high rates seen during the UPA's first term (UPA1) and the early years of its second term (UPA2). Allegations of widespread corruption, bolstered by reports of the Comptroller and Auditor General of India, strengthened the Opposition's case.[60] 'Policy paralysis', a euphemism for slowdown in investments and economic decision-making, became a defining feature of the latter part of UPA2. The banking sector was in distress, with non-performing assets (NPAs) rising to uncomfortable levels.

Another common refrain was that the UPA had focused far too much on 'doles' as opposed to economic empowerment, creating an unsustainable burden on the exchequer. Legislation such as the Mahatma Gandhi National Rural Employment Guarantee Act (MGNREGA) and the National Food Security Act (NFSA) came in for scathing criticism. Inflation levels were high, as were the fiscal deficit and the current account deficit. On 28 August 2013, the rupee reached a historic low leading to a nationwide uproar. Senior BJP leader Ravi Shankar Prasad said that the Indian economy is on a 'ventilator in the intensive care unit'. Former finance minister Yashwant Sinha argued that 'the only thing that will stabilize rupee and market

at this point of time is for the government to resign and go for
fresh elections'. Sushma Swaraj tweeted, 'On prime minister's
statement in parliament: The rupee has lost its value. The prime
minister has lost his grace.'[61, 62]

An era of historic progress

While the economy was indeed facing great challenges, the
picture was not as black and white as it was portrayed by the
Opposition. Historically high growth rates achieved under the
UPA quadrupled the economic output in nominal terms. For
much of the UPA's tenure, India grew faster than all major
economies, with the exception of China. Between 1994 and
2012, poverty was down by half. Research indicates that 'the
pace of poverty reduction accelerated over time and was three
times faster between 2005 and 2012'.[63] Investment and savings
ratios stood well above 30 per cent, the Sensex notched up
compound annual growth rates of 16 per cent, exports grew
at an average rate of 18 per cent per year and infrastructure
investment was 7–8 per cent of the GDP, much higher than that
achieved under previous governments.

It is helpful to unpack this data. Averaging out data for
several years can smoothen the kinks in a narrative. For
example, it is absolutely true that in an average year the
economy grew faster under the UPA than it did under NDA1
or even NDA2. Of course, those average years also included
some below-average years such as 2008–09, 2011–12, 2012–
13. But, in five out of ten years, India's economy grew by
8 per cent or more. It is also true that the economy was
recovering in 2013–14, when the Modi government took
over. The point is that we need to go beyond averages to get
a sense of when things were really good for the economy and
when they were not so rosy.

Populism or social protection?

That the UPA neglected economic growth and focused on populist schemes is a view widely ingrained in India's economic narrative. From the opposition BJP to influential opinion makers, the UPA's 'povertarianism' in the form of schemes such as MGNREGA was held responsible for a slowing economy and elevated inflation, and fiscal and current account deficits. However, this view did not go unchallenged. A trio of economists, Ashok Kotwal, Maitreesh Ghatak and Parikshit Ghosh, wrote a comprehensive paper in which they argued that 'the UPA period has been characterized by faster growth, higher savings and investment, growing foreign trade and capital inflows, and increased infrastructure spending in partnership with private capital'.[64] From the perspective of these and many other like-minded economists, 'The UPA's political troubles arise not from policies that hurt growth but from an inability to tackle the consequences of accelerated economic growth—increased conflict over land, rent seeking and corruption in the booming infrastructure and natural resource sectors, inability of public education to keep up with increased demand and rising aspirations, and poor delivery of welfare schemes made possible by growing revenues.'

When I look back at the time when I was defending the record of the UPA (I was then, and remain now, a Congress spokesperson), I couldn't fully understand why the government was under attack from both the left and the right. As Kotwal, Ghatak and Ghosh pointed out in 2014, 'It is a unique misfortune for any party to be charged with both crony capitalism and unbridled welfarism.'[65] One of the biggest critiques of the UPA government was that it reaped the benefits of policies pursued by the NDA government under Vajpayee and then squandered those gains by doling out welfare schemes.

A sober review of the Vajpayee years is sufficient to demonstrate that economic growth under NDA1 was modest, with average rates below even the growth rates witnessed under the UDF regime. It was only in the final year of the Vajpayee government that growth breached the 8 per cent mark. However, a 'base effect' partly explains this growth. That means growth in the previous year was about 4 per cent and that helped the economy show a bounce. An additional explanation is that the global economic environment was benign and there was a lot of liquidity sloshing around globally.[66]

Social infrastructure takes centre stage

For a variety of reasons, the Vajpayee years included some tough economic times, which ultimately contributed to the BJP's defeat in 2004. As is the case with any new government, the UPA inherited some positives and some negatives from the Vajpayee era and added its own policy initiatives to the mix. The UPA's legislative agenda was transformational in many respects. As Kotwal, Ghatak and Ghosh noted, 'The Right to Information, Forest Rights, Land Acquisition, Lokpal, Right to Education and National Rural Employment Guarantee Acts add up to a legislative record that is impressive in scope and aim. The UID scheme tried to clean up and modernise the entire infrastructure of providing entitlements and enabling experiments like cash transfers.'[67]

Beyond changes in the institutional framework, the UPA implemented a host of programmes in health, education and infrastructure to help maintain the momentum of socio-economic development. For instance, the UPA revamped the Rashtriya Swasthya Bima Yojana (RSBY), a health-insurance scheme for patients below the poverty line. Almost four crore smart cards for RSBY beneficiaries were issued. The UPA

converted the National Rural Health Mission (NRHM) into
the National Health Mission to bring urban-poor and middle-
class families within the ambit of increased health investments.
Health outcomes continued improving and life expectancy at
birth increased by five years during the UPA's tenure.[68]

Infrastructure, which many consider the UPA's weak point
especially in the road and power sectors, saw strong growth.
Infrastructure spending as a percentage of GDP increased from
5 to 7 per cent.[69] Rural roads grew by 2 lakh km; investments
under the PMGSY went up tenfold. India added more power
capacity during the UPA's tenure than in the preceding period
since Independence. Per capita consumption of electricity went
up from 559 kWh to 813 kWh.

Glass half-full or half-empty?

The point here is not to suggest that the UPA did a stellar job
and that there were no mistakes. There were plenty of mistakes,
as there are in the tenure of any government. The UPA also
missed opportunities for further economic reforms that could
have sustained growth at a higher level. Despite many years
of discussions on the goods and services tax (GST) and efforts
to reform the direct tax code (DTC), these reforms did not
happen. Reforms to the bankruptcy code also stalled, and the
land-acquisition bill ended up as an improvement over the
exploitative land-acquisition regime of the past but perhaps not
good enough for India's future needs. However, this is a far cry
from arguing that the UPA (or its predecessors) did not advance
India's socio-economic development.

In recent times, India's economic output has overtaken
the levels of output in advanced economies such as Italy and
France. India's economy is now the fifth biggest in the world.
In terms of purchasing power parity (PPP), it is the third biggest.

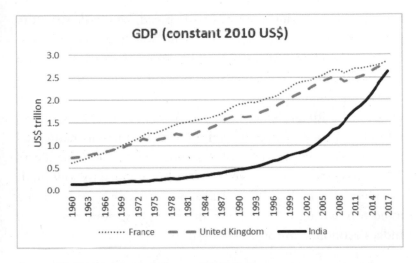

Source: World Development Indicators, World Bank

That did not happen overnight. World Bank data going back to 1960 shows how India narrowed the gap with countries such as France, and finally caught up with them in GDP terms (see chart). The contribution of the UPA government, or any other government for that matter is a part of this progress.

Undoubtedly, the Manmohan Singh–led UPA contributed significantly to this progress because of the high growth rates achieved in that time. However, one cannot argue that the UPA would have taken India so far without the work of its predecessors. Of course, India needs to do a lot more. In per capita terms, India badly trails behind not just advanced economies but also scores of middle-income countries. It is for this reason that governments must pursue sustainable growth and enact policies that give India the best chance of catching up with other countries in per capita income terms.

There were many positives associated with the UPA's tenure and that view finds greater acceptance in hindsight. The Indian economy had matured, poverty reduced drastically, access to basic health and education was widespread, basic infrastructure such as roads, power, water and sanitation had touched most Indians. Development frameworks embodied social protection and institutions were in place to support further progress. Of course, challenges remained as well. Limited job creation, quality of public health and education, problems in the banking sector, infrastructure weaknesses and agricultural productivity hampered progress. All this was part of Narendra Modi's inheritance in 2014. In the next section we see what he intended to do with it.

Here is a look at how India progressed on some of the indicators we have kept track of through various periods of India's economic history.

Progress on key indicators (2005–14)

	2005	2014
GDP (constant 2010 US$) (in billions)	1100	2129
GDP per capita (constant 2010 US$)	971	1645
Foreign exchange reserves (US$ million)	141,514	304,224
Infant mortality rate	56	38
Life expectancy at birth[70]	65	68
Literacy rate	64%	74%
Power generation (installed capacity, megawatts)	105,046	199,877
People using at least basic drinking water services (% of population)	81.9%	86.6%
Exports of goods and services (% of GDP)	19.8%	25.4%

Source: Compiled from World Development Indicators (World Bank), Economic Surveys, Reserve Bank of India Statistical Database, Ministry of Finance, Ministry of Power.

2

The Promise

'You gave Congress 60 years, give BJP just 60 months'
—Narendra Modi (2013)

In the run-up to the 2014 election, then candidate Narendra Modi promised 'a new India, with an efficient government free of corruption'.[1] PM Modi and his supporters ran a high-voltage campaign on a platform of remaking India with 'minimum government, maximum governance' that would usher in 'achhe din' or good days. A slowing economy, high inflation, allegations of corruption and a perception of 'policy paralysis' had hobbled the Manmohan Singh government.[2] Candidate Modi very astutely tapped into widespread public discontent and a palpable longing for change and speedier progress. He promised to build bullet trains, hydroelectric power plants, manufacturing hubs, roads, airports, ports and 100 'smart cities'. His party also wanted greater foreign direct investment (FDI), except in multi-brand retail, much higher growth and a massive employment generation effort.[3]

This part of the book highlights the BJP's promises to the electorate and gauges why those promises caught the imagination of the Indian voter. As a participant in that election, especially as a spokesperson on economic affairs for the Congress party, I had a bird's-eye view of what the BJP was promising and why it was so effective. The BJP's election manifesto is an obvious source for this part of the book, but it won't do to simply present a summary of the economic sections of that document. To better appreciate what was going on in the run-up to the 2014 election, it is important to trace the evolution of Modi as a change agent and his achhe din narrative.

According to many observers, PM Modi's victory in 2014 ushered in the dawn of right-of-centre economics in India. A *Los Angeles Times* headline summed it up as, 'India's Narendra Modi leads conservatives to election day victory.'[4] How were journalists persuaded to write such headlines? Modi's journey from chief minister of Gujarat to the point of an implied transformation to a Thatcherite is an interesting one. It is about how the 'Gujarat model' of economic development enabled Modi's rise and fed into the campaign promises that form the basis of assessing the government's performance.

The Amartya Sen–Jagdish Bhagwati debate and its relevance to Modi's rise

Modi's rise was in no small way aided by right-leaning economists and policy experts. The Gujarat model gained credibility because leading economists such as Jagdish Bhagwati gave it their blessings, so to speak. In fact, the highly publicized debates between 'rivals' Bhagwati and Amartya Sen included in-depth treatment of the Gujarat model and its comparison with economic models of other states such as Kerala. Views expressed by Bhagwati (and Panagariya) and Sen (and Jean Drèze) present a fascinating contrast between the paths that countries such as India could take for achieving economic development goals.

While the Sen–Bhagwati debate is a long-standing one, it gained greater prominence just as Modi's election campaign was heating up. In their book, *An Uncertain Glory: India and Its Contradictions*[5], Sen and Drèze attributed the deficiencies in India's development to its lack of 'proper' accountability to the 'needy majority'.[6] The implication is that stronger citizen rights (and entitlements) will help broad-based growth. Bhagwati and Panagariya have countered that stronger growth and liberalization were the answers to India's development challenges.[7]

The Sen/Drèze–Bhagwati/Panagariya debate became heated when the *Economist* published a book review of *An Uncertain Glory*. In response to the review, Bhagwati and Panagariya shot off a letter to the magazine disagreeing with the review's contention that Sen and Drèze wanted to go beyond economic growth. They wrote, 'The truth of the matter is that Mr. Sen has belatedly learned to give lip service to growth, which he has long excoriated as a fetish.'[8] Sen responded: 'Jagdish Bhagwati and Arvind Panagariya have misdescribed my past work as well as the book itself.' He argued that while economic growth is important for improving people's lives, 'to go much further, faster', growth needs 'to be combined with devoting resources to remove illiteracy, ill health, undernutrition and other deprivations'.

In this context, Sen rejected as confused the Bhagwati-Panagariya charge of his advocacy as 'redistribution' of incomes.[9] It is no secret that Sen has spoken approvingly of Kerala's development experience. Bhagwati, on the other hand, has supported the 'Gujarat template'. Of course, we are more interested in the Gujarat model because of its importance to Modi's rise and his successful prime-ministerial election campaign.

Writing in the *Mint*, Bhagwati argues, 'The Gujarat template is ideal: its people believe in accumulating wealth but they believe also in using it, not for self-indulgence but for social good.'[10] Bhagwati and Panagariya had also claimed that 'Gujarat has produced growth and also that the change in its social indicators is remarkable, whereas Kerala is by no means the great model of development that Sen has long extolled for its "redistribution" under the communist regimes . . .'[11]

The table below presents an interesting comparison of socio-economic indicators for both Gujarat and Kerala, including the time when Narendra Modi was chief minister of Gujarat. Readers should be mindful of averages as sometimes averages can hide more than they reveal. For example, given an average annual income of Rs 50 of a country with two individuals, the income distribution between these two individuals may be Rs 10/Rs 90 or Rs 40/Rs 60. To my mind, the latter distribution is healthier even though the average income is identical in both scenarios.

Indicator	Year	Gujarat	Kerala
Net State Domestic Product (NSDP) per capita at current prices (in Rs)	2010–11/ 2013–14	77,485/ 1,06,831	69,943/ 1,03,820
Adult literacy	2011–12	79.31	93.91
Life expectancy	2013	68.2	74.8
Infant mortality/1000 live births	2013	40	12
Maternal mortality/lakh live births	2013	212	81
Poverty rate	2011–12	16.63	7.05
Physical quality of life Index	2013	77.1 (7th rank)	92.64 (1st rank)

Source: Muhammed Salim. A.P., 'Kerala-Gujarat Models: A Comparative Study with Respect to Socio-Economic Environment.' Imperial Journal of Interdisciplinary Research 2, no. 7 (2016): 396–407. Accessed on 6 January 2019. http://www. imperialjournals.com/index.php/IJIR/article/download/1136/1090

Mainstreaming of the Gujarat model

Although the narrative of the Gujarat model was years in the making, it gathered momentum as Modi's ascent in the BJP became apparent. The Gujarat model first came into the limelight at the BJP's 2008 national meet. Modi had won a big victory in the 2007 elections to the Gujarat legislature. He had not only beaten anti-incumbency but had done it without being indebted to any other party leader. Modi had gained an iconic status by then. People seemed fully on board with 'Moditva', a smart combination of Modi's apparent focus on development as well as his readiness to take on any 'threat to Gujarat'.[12] The legend of the 'strong' and 'decisive' leader who would deliver 'good governance' was born.

Veteran journalist Harish Khare points out that the BJP, led by L.K. Advani and Rajnath Singh, was somewhat listless in its opposition to the first UPA government. Modi's victory appeared to give the BJP a template for other states. Khare notes, 'It was no coincidence that the day the 2008 BJP national council began its deliberations, the Gujarat government chose to put in full-page paid advertisements in newspapers, extolling the "Gujarat model", based on three claims: a strong, honest and efficient leadership; transparent governance that nurtures innovations; and a vision to make development a people's movement.' However, the senior leadership of the BJP did not go overboard in promoting the Gujarat model because that would have compromised the prime-ministerial ambitions of some top leaders, including L.K. Advani.[13]

Maximum governance, minimum government

An essay by Mukul G. Asher, professor at the Lee Kuan Yew School of Public Policy at the National University of Singapore, connected the 'maximum governance, minimum government' slogan to the Gujarat model. Writing in the March 2008 volume of *Pragati* magazine, Asher notes that 'The essence of the Gujarat model of governance comprises of three Cs— Competence, Corruption aversion, and Consistency, and two Ps—Performance-orientation and Public-private partnership management skills.'[14] Asher, who also served on the advisory panel of the *Indian National Interest Review*[15], the publisher of *Pragati*, argued, 'There is widespread consensus that India is experiencing a governance crisis—reflected in the poor quality, low accessibility and economic inefficiencies associated with goods and services provided by the public sector. It is also reflected in the inattention to the internal security.' Citing data on a variety of indicators including economic growth, availability of electricity, crime statistics and female-child sex ratios, Asher makes the case for a socio-economic development model that is 'more relevant for the twenty-first century India'.

Asher also refers to two themes that would later become an integral part of Modi's messaging. First, he discusses 'corruption aversion' that Modi had summed up as '*khato nathi, khava deto nathi*'. This phrase, later translated in Hindi, became a ubiquitous election campaign slogan: '*na khaunga na khane dunga*'. Loosely translated, this meant Modi would neither eat (steal), nor let others eat (steal). The second theme was the Beti Bachao Andolan (save the girl child campaign). Asher notes that this campaign 'helped increase the female child to male child sex ratio from 802 in 2001 to 870 in 2007'.

Asher's essay also hints at Modi's pro-business credentials by highlighting Gujarat's record on promoting public–private partnerships (PPPs) and the development of the Gujarat International Finance Tec-City (GIFT), a 500-acre special economic zone (SEZ) near Ahmedabad.[16] As an aside, it is pertinent to mention that many experts have raised serious questions about the Gujarat model. Some have accused its proponents of having vastly exaggerated its successes. We will discuss some of those critiques later, but Asher's views present a proximate example of such exaggeration. According to 2001 census data, Gujarat's child sex ratio was 883 (ranked thirty-first out of thirty-five states and union territories). The 2011 census showed that this ratio had improved to 890 (ranked twenty-ninth). It is not clear where Asher's data came from but it does not appear to have come from census data. Meanwhile, Kerala's child sex ratios were far better—960 in 2001 (ranked thirteenth) and 964 in 2011 (ranked seventh).[17]

Following Modi's 2007 election victory, the *Economist* noted, 'Always prosperous and enterprising, Gujarat is now booming. Its voters clearly credit some of this prosperity to Mr. Modi's administration, which is notably less venal and ineffectual than those Indians in most other states have to endure.' In a moment of prescience, the magazine noted that 'The BJP is short of "tall" leaders. L.K. Advani, its candidate for prime minister, is 80. The party's president, Rajnath Singh, has made little impression: no one is wearing masks made in his likeness. Mr. Modi, on the other hand, has attracted intelligent and ambitious strategists, such as Arun Jaitley, who would not waste their talents on him if they thought him no more than a provincial demagogue.'[18] Of course, the BJP lost in the 2009 Lok Sabha election and the ambitions of Advani and others suffered a serious blow. The path for Modi was becoming clearer even though mainstream India had not fully noticed it yet.

The 'economic right' joins the bandwagon

Others outside Gujarat had begun to take notice. Sadanand Dhume, a columnist and a Resident Fellow at the American Enterprise Institute (AEI), a conservative think tank in

Washington DC, wrote approvingly of Modi in a 2010 op-ed noting,

> It is as an administrator that Mr. Modi has earned his reputation. Over the past eight years, Gujarat's GDP has grown at a tigerish double digit rate. The state is bursting with malls and multiplexes, freshly surfaced roads and private ports. Outside Ahmedabad a new city, Gujarat International Finance Tec-City (GIFT), is rising as a thinly veiled threat to India's hopelessly misgoverned financial capital, Mumbai, in neighboring Maharashtra. Even in the hinterland of Gujarat, power cuts come only rarely.[19]

At this point, Dhume wasn't all in for Modi, observing, 'Mr. Modi is the wrong choice both for the BJP and for India. At some level his association with the Gujarat riots—regardless of the conclusion of the federal team investigating his role—tars him for life.'[20] However, those were still early days and Modi's legend would only grow.

In the aftermath of the global financial crisis (GFC), the Indian economy struggled to maintain its previous high growth trajectory. By 2012, the political situation had shifted and dissatisfaction had crept in. High-profile corruption scandals began to garner attention even as high inflation and fiscal deficits chipped away at Manmohan Singh's economic credentials. It was during this time that Modi became an increasingly acceptable idea 'whose time had come'. Dhume's writing is indicative of the shifts at that time. In an article in *Foreign Policy* magazine, he wonders about Modi: 'Could he be the next leader of India?' He answers in the negative: 'Narendra Modi may well be India's best chief minister.[21] But he'd still make a terrible choice for prime minister.' However, through much of the article, you can tell that Dhume can see that Modi as PM is a possibility even though at that time, he did not feel he would be the right choice. By June 2013, Dhume almost declares Modi a Thatcherite, even if he still doesn't believe Modi can make it to the top job, given that Indian politics rewarded 'consensus figures' up until that time. He writes in the *Wall Street Journal*: 'Pro-market liberals have lately begun to flirt with Mr Modi's Thatcherite message of "minimum government, maximum governance", and his willingness to broach such subjects as the privatization of state-owned railway lines. His record of building roads, ports, power plants and a generally business-friendly environment in Gujarat appeals to a new middle class that wants its politicians to offer people a hand up, not a handout.'

Vivek Dehejia, an economist and professor at Carleton University in Canada, is one such pro-market reformer although he is conservative in the American sense of the word. In a 2013 article, he too wonders if Modi could be PM but had this to say about his stint in Gujarat: 'It's evident that the "Gujarat model", or, rather, the "Modi model", perfectly suits the interests of corporate India and of foreign investors. They are looking for a place where it's easy to do business, there's a sure return on investment, and there isn't the scourge of bureaucratic delay and corruption which bedevil investment projects most elsewhere in India.'[22] Dehejia too pointed to the expectations of free-market enthusiasts when it came to Modi. Writing two days before election results, he asks 'Should free marketeers be popping champagne? Can we expect Modi to turn into an ardent economic liberalizer?' Dehejia notes that Modi's 'minimum government, maximum governance' slogan would make Ronald Reagan or Margaret Thatcher proud but, at the time, he wasn't sure if Modi was pro-business or pro free markets. However, by this time, even Dehejia appears a bit smitten when he ends optimistically: 'The good news is that a pro-business, results-oriented Modi cannot possibly be worse for the economy than the outgoing government.'[23]

In India, too, several experts had begun writing about the development experience in Gujarat. Prominent among them were economists Bibek Debroy and Surjit Bhalla. Bibek Debroy wrote a series of columns in the *Times of India* defending Gujarat's record on everything, from growth to poverty reduction to a variety of social indicators. When observers criticized the decline in Gujarat's inter-state human development index (HDI) from a ranking of sixth in 1991 to eleventh in 2007–08, Debroy stepped in with an explanation. He argued that since the rankings covered more states, the decline was because, presumably, the new states had better human development indices. He noted that the HDI for Gujarat was 0.431 in 1991, while in 2007–08 it stood at 0.527. The all-India scores were 0.381 (1991) and 0.467 (2007–08).[24] He neglected to mention that Gujarat's improvements mirrored the national average. There wasn't anything exceptional about them.

Surjit Bhalla also penned numerous articles to promote Modi's vision of development and believed that the hallmark of Modinomics would be 'a greater focus on outcomes rather than outlays, a vision of anti-dolenomics and fiscal responsibility'.[25] After Modi was formally nominated as BJP's prime-ministerial candidate, Bhalla wrote in his regular column in the *Indian Express* about 'Lessons from the Gujarat Model'. His conclusion is direct: 'If one looks jointly at poverty reduction and poverty levels, the preliminary conclusion has to be that the "Gujarat model" of development seems to have performed much better than most models on offer.'[26]

A wave washes over evidence

The preceding discussion should not give the reader the impression that the Gujarat model went unchallenged. In fact, there were many voices apart from Sen and Drèze who wrote extensively about the limitations of the Gujarat model. Some pointed to the fact that growth rates in Gujarat were high even before Modi came to power. Others pointed out correctly that Gujarat's social indicators lagged behind those of many other states. In human development rankings, states like Kerala did far better, while states such as Maharashtra and Tamil Nadu had their own growth stories to tell. I myself wrote about the inadequacies of the Gujarat model. From one of my articles in 2014, I will take the liberty of quoting a section that seemed to capture what many were saying at the time (see box). While I and many others felt the Gujarat model represented a discredited 'trickle-down' model of economics, Jagdish Bhagwati was arguing that its growth had a 'pull-up' effect.[27] That was in essence how the Gujarat model was positioned. As we learnt in 2014, this latter argument won spectacularly.

'The most serious indictment of Mr. Modi is not that he fails to provide a full picture of Gujarat's development path or that he is a quintessential braggart. It is simply that with high per capita income and growth, Gujarat could have done a lot better by focusing on the "software" of its society—poverty reduction, education, health, and other social development aspects. Poverty reduction and social development commensurate with Gujarat's growth and per capita income have, quite simply, not occurred.

'In this era of glibness, facts have little chance. But, to the extent that facts matter, here are a few key social indicators and Gujarat's rank in each (1 is best): Human Development Index (11th), Infant Mortality Rate (12th); Poverty (15th); Households with no assets (14th); Hunger Index: (13th); Under-5 Mortality Rate (12th); underweight children (19th) and literacy (13th). With two-thirds of rural people defecating in the open, where does Mr. Modi hide but behind a PR machine. Let's face it; Gujarat is by no means a stellar or even a good example of socio-economic development in India. Other states, led by quieter, more humble or perhaps less marketing-savvy leaders, may fit the bill.'

Source: '149 Months of "Gujarat Shining" . . . Really?' Economic Times, 25 March 2014. https://blogs.economictimes.indiatimes.com/Politiconomy/149-months-of-gujarat-shining-really/

The preceding discussion provides some context for the transformation of Narendra Modi, the man tainted forever by the 2002 Gujarat riots, into a Thatcherite reformer and decisive leader who would pursue good governance, fight corruption and bring achhe din. It is now time to recall what Modi actually promised in specific terms to the people of India. What was the vision and the policies and programmes that gave concrete shape to the exhortation: 'You gave Congress 60 years, give BJP just 60 months'?

Modi fought two successful campaigns. While we all focus on his spectacular victory in the 2014 election, he also fought an intra-BJP battle against other contenders who attempted to thwart his rise. He won his party's internal battle using a potent narrative with just the right amount of Hindu nationalism mixed with a heavy dose of development through 'good governance'. He had already built up a formidable reputation as a business-friendly chief minister who constantly marketed the Gujarat model of development. And he was already seen as an unabashed standard-bearer of Hindutva since the 2002 Gujarat riots. The BJP establishment had no answer to Modi's nationalist narrative that powered his inexorable rise to the top. In June 2013, he became chairman of the BJP's Central Election Committee over the resistance of some of its most senior leaders such as L.K. Advani.[28] Modi was well on his way.

The 'achhe din' campaign

Modi and BJP ran a terrific campaign promising to remake India with 'minimum government, maximum governance' and a pledge to usher in achhe din. In speeches at the Federation of Indian Chambers of Commerce and Industry (FICCI) and the BJP's national council meeting, Modi rolled out his vision for India's economy. He attacked the UPA for the 'despair' prevailing in India and how the country had become a country of 'underachievers'.[29] Modi presented an all-encompassing vision from the social sectors to infrastructure development to job creation and high economic growth. On education, he said the BJP's dream was 'to have an IIM [Indian Institute of Management], an IIT [Indian Institute of Technology] and an AIIMS [All India Institute of Medical Sciences] in all states'.[30] With an eye on middle-class voters, Modi talked up infrastructure and the rural to urban transition. He spoke of building 100 smart cities and bullet trains. He also promised to build hydroelectric power plants, manufacturing hubs, roads, airports and ports. The PM's party also wanted greater FDI for job and asset creation in all sectors except multi-brand retail. The BJP spoke of generating 10 per cent growth, creating millions of jobs and focusing on much-needed skill development.[31]

It was soon clear to everyone that Modi's impressive rhetorical style was endearing him to the public. While the speeches were not purely about economic development, it is fair to say that the development plank was central to the campaign. Yes, there were references to BJP's religious and social causes. However, for the most part, the 'achhe din' campaign was about good governance, improving economic performance, creating jobs and transforming India into an economic powerhouse that would lift poor people out of poverty and usher in high standards of living for the middle class.

The 'Modifesto' as BJP's manifesto

With opinion polls consistently showing that Modi would lead the next government, the BJP's manifesto, dubbed 'Modifesto', was to be the icing on the cake. However, the manifesto was inexplicably delayed.[32] In fact, the BJP released its manifesto on the first day of polling.[33] While not many people may read election manifestos, they are important for holding political parties to account.

As widely reported at that time, key members of the committee in charge of drafting the manifesto were not too fond of Modi. Murli Manohar Joshi, the head of the manifesto committee, had to give up his Lok Sabha constituency, Varanasi, so that Modi could contest from there. Former finance minister Yashwant Sinha was back-benched and another senior leader, Jaswant Singh, was expelled.

The delay in the release of the manifesto appeared to be strategic in nature, allowing Modi to grow stronger without revealing too many specifics about the delivery of promises.[34] The manifesto generously spouted feel-good statements but remained very stingy about specifics. However, at that point, voters seemed to have made up their minds and any critique of the manifesto for its lack of detail, especially by the Congress, had very few takers.

As a *Frontline* magazine article pointed out, Modi's imprint on the manifesto was clear. While the images of most senior BJP leaders were on its cover, Modi's popularity required help from neither the manifesto nor the party leaders gracing its cover.[35] The manifesto boldly declared BJP to be a modern and inclusive party, relegating its pet projects such as the Ram Temple, uniform civil code and cow protection to the peripheries of the document. *Frontline* noted wryly, 'So, for the BJP government, apparently both rural and urban areas are to be high priority. And all sections of people are to be empowered: the poor, the elderly, the new middle classes and entrepreneurs, rural dwellers, urban residents, Scheduled Castes, Scheduled Tribes, Other Backward Classes, minorities, other weaker sections, women, children, senior citizens, the "specially-abled", the youth, sportspersons, farmers and small-scale business owners.'[36] *Frontline* went on to ask: 'Did anyone get left out in this breathless attempt at inclusion?'

It is helpful to see the manifesto's broader context without drowning in its details. At the time of the election, I was doing all I could to run down this manifesto. Of course, as with any manifesto, there was a lot to genuinely criticize. However, I could also see the elegance of the presentation. The BJP contended that the next government had to deal with immediate concerns before building a framework supportive of systemic reforms. These reforms required a broader platform, hinting at the need for inclusion. To my mind, that was logical and smart. With immediate problems out of the way and a stronger and inclusive framework, India could leap forward. This presentation clearly captured the hearts and minds of many opinion makers; hence, the victory of hope over genuine fears was complete.

In the manifesto, the BJP painted the ten years under the UPA government as a 'Decade of Decay'. The document charged that India had a 'free fall' on all fronts, including the economy. According to the manifesto, the UPA had presided over 'gross misuse and total denigration of government and institutions'. In a pointed attack on the leadership of the Congress, the BJP highlights the 'erosion of the office of the Prime Minister'. In a tribute to the first NDA government, the document contrasts the UPA's 'casting gloom and doom on the country' with India's rise as an 'Emerging Superpower' in 2004. In discussing the legacy of the Vajpayee government, the manifesto talked about the 'near double digit growth' that UPA inherited (in Vajpayee's last year, growth was about 8 per cent).

The manifesto accused the UPA of not maintaining that growth and leaving the next government with sub–5 per cent growth.[37] The BJP charged that the UPA pushed the country backwards by twenty years and that millions of men and women were jobless. Arguing that the country had lost hope, the BJP cast itself as the party that would act decisively to address the country's challenges on a priority basis. The manifesto then set out to first summarize what it would do in key areas before expanding on a broader range of topics. What follows is basically an overview of key issues and the way the BJP manifesto addressed them.

POVERTY REDUCTION: This was a big theme of the campaign. In 2011, the Planning Commission in an affidavit before the Supreme Court indicated that the official poverty line was set at Rs 26 per day (53 cents at the time) for rural areas and Rs 32 per day for urban areas.[38] This created a national uproar, given that the figure was set so low. The BJP brought up the issue of poverty repeatedly during the campaign. In an election meeting in Uttar Pradesh, candidate Modi accused the Congress of 'chanting the poverty mantra when the elections approach'. He asked his audience, 'Who was in power at the Centre for 60 years?' He went on to assert, 'A government may be any party's but a government is meant only for the poor, for their welfare and not to fatten the pockets of the rich.' Asking why the Congress had not done anything to reduce poverty and bring prosperity, he complained that hard-working people suffered indignity. He then went back to his usual refrain: 'You give me 60 months to their 60 years and I will realize this dream. You have elected rulers for 60 years, try electing a servant for 60 months and watch what I do.'[39]

In its manifesto, the BJP committed to form a government that would be 'a government of the poor, marginalized and left behind'. Supporting the poorest Indians would be 'a national priority'. To fight poverty, the manifesto called for 'convergence, transparency and efficiency', identification of the 100 most backward districts of the country for prioritized integrated development, gainful employment for the rural poor in agriculture and allied activities and enabling the urban poor to 'develop skills so that they take advantage of the emerging opportunities'. On food security, the BJP noted it 'has always held that "universal food security" is integral to national security'. The BJP promised to ensure that the benefits of the scheme would reach the beneficiaries and that the right to food 'does not remain an act on paper or a political rhetoric'. The manifesto also underlined the BJP's commitment to provide equal opportunity and social justice to all sections of society, including the scheduled tribes, scheduled castes and minorities.

EMPLOYMENT AND ENTREPRENEURSHIP: Modi had correctly assessed India's shifting demographic profile. With 65 per cent of Indians below the age of thirty-five, job creation was clearly a priority, especially because job creation trailed economic growth under the UPA. Modi's pitch to India's youth was clear—if they voted for him, he would get them a job. Speaking at a public rally in Bhagalpur in Bihar, Modi addressed the younger generation when he said, 'This is the most important election for youth in the age group of 18–28 years. This election is about their future. If they miss this opportunity, they will miss crucial five years of their life.'[40]

Before that, in a speech in Agra in November 2013, Modi stated that 'If BJP comes to power, it will provide 1 crore jobs which the UPA Government could not do despite announcing it before the last Lok Sabha polls.' He made the case that the youth, who were struggling for jobs, could become a 'force for the development of the country'.[41] As discussed earlier, Modi's credentials received a boost by numerous reports from independent experts. For example, Goldman Sachs estimated that if other states emulated Gujarat's manufacturing employment levels, India could generate 4 crore industrial jobs in a decade.[42]

The manifesto acknowledged the importance of labour-intensive manufacturing, and the BJP talked about strategically developing sectors such as textiles, footwear, electronics assembly, etc., as well as tourism. The BJP also promised to 'strengthen employment bases of agriculture and allied industries, and retail—through modernization as well as stronger credit and market linkages'. A plan to leverage infrastructure and housing for job creation found its way into the manifesto as well. The BJP also promised to focus on youth self-employment (incubating entrepreneurship and credit facilitation) and addressing the skills gap through a 'multi-skills development program'. It further pledged to transform employment exchanges into career centres, connecting youth to jobs through technology and counselling.

ECONOMIC REVIVAL: Modi blamed the UPA for 'policy paralysis' and for closing down avenues for collaboration between the Centre and the states. He spoke about the need to simplify laws and use technology to facilitate decision-making. He was a proponent of greater autonomy for the states. In an interview to ETV, a news channel, Modi said, 'We need to simplify laws and shortcut the process. We should use technology to reduce files and connecting different departments. Centre's policy should be such that each state is allowed to function according to its own needs. Today there is no environment for the state and Centre to work together.'[43] However, despite campaign rhetoric, Modi did not appear to favour a reduced role for the states per se. He seemed to disagree with the strategy of privatizing loss-making public-sector undertakings (PSUs). Modi seemed to believe, based on his own experience in Gujarat, that he could revive such units if policymakers reposed faith in them. He argued that, 'The view that PSUs are *nikamma* (inefficient) has caused much damage.'[44, 45]

The BJP expressed concern about the banking sector and emphasized the need for its revival as well as for a variety of other initiatives aimed at reviving the broader economy.[46] In the manifesto, it argued that India suffered from 'a decade of maladministration and scams' as well as 'decision and policy paralysis'. The BJP promised to 'ignite again' the economy with a commitment to public interest and encourage the bureaucracy to take the right decisions. The BJP promised to remove bottlenecks and missing links in all sectors, activities and services; focus more on proper planning and execution for good outcomes; and strive for scale and speed with a futuristic vision.

The BJP also promised to 'strictly implement Fiscal discipline' and undertake 'banking reforms to enhance ease, access and accountability'. The manifesto did not include a detailed discussion on banking-sector NPAs but did state that the BJP would set up a strong regulatory framework for the non-banking financial companies to protect the investors.

BLACK MONEY AND CORRUPTION: This was a signature issue for the BJP. One of the defining moments of the campaign came during a speech wherein Modi appeared to promise that his government would bring back black (unaccounted) money from foreign banks and that the funds recovered would be so great that 15 lakh rupees could be deposited into each citizen's bank account.[47] Rajnath Singh, who led the BJP during the 2014 campaign, discussed bringing back black money within 150 days.[48] Amit Shah, the BJP's current president, later claimed that Modi's Rs 15 lakh comment was more like a political *jumla* (idiom). However, this statement has stuck in the country's collective consciousness.[49]

The BJP's manifesto, citing high-profile corruption scandals that marred UPA's second term, called corruption 'a manifestation of poor governance'. To deal with what they called a 'National Crisis', the BJP promised to 'establish a system, which eliminates the scope for corruption' through 'technology enabled e-Governance' that would minimize the discretion in the citizen–government interface and 'rationalization and simplification of the tax regime'. On the issue of black money, the manifesto laid down the promise 'to set up a Task force for dealing with the issue and recommend amendments to existing laws or enact new laws'. It asserted that the process of 'bringing back black money that belongs to India, will be put in motion on priority'.

INFLATION: This was another major issue that the BJP highlighted both in its public meetings as well as its manifesto. Just days before the first phase of the election, in April 2014, Modi said, 'When I speak of Congress free India, I speak of freeing India of the misgovernance of the Congress in the last 60 years. India has not seen the kind of corruption that it saw in the last 10 years. It means freedom from dynastic politics, misgovernance and price rise. Congress now symbolises all these things.'[50] He talked about neutralizing the effect of rising prices and said the BJP's priority would be to provide a real-time databank for agricultural produce with the use of modern technology.[51] In the manifesto, the BJP proposed several measures to combat inflation, including putting in place strict measures and special courts to stop hoarding and black marketing and unbundling Food Corporation of India (FCI) operations into procurement, storage and distribution for greater efficiency. The BJP included in its manifesto a Price Stabilization Fund and promised to evolve a single 'National Agriculture Market'.

TAXATION: At an event organized by Baba Ramdev, yoga guru and businessman, in January 2014, candidate Modi supported the idea of initiating deep reforms in the tax system. He noted that, 'The present taxation system is a burden on common man. There is a need to reform it and introduce a new system.' For his part, Ramdev had called for the 'abolition of all kinds of taxes' and promoted the idea of a single 'Banking Transaction Tax'.[52] Led by Arun Jaitley, the BJP focused much energy on decrying 'tax terrorism' under the UPA. This was a euphemism for the coercive practices of tax authorities that India's tax-paying class bemoaned.

During the campaign, Jaitley famously demanded that the slab below which income was tax-exempt go up from Rs 2 lakh to Rs 5 lakh.[53] This popular demand targeted middle-class voters. The other important promise was related to the enactment of the goods and services tax. The multitude of indirect taxes in India needed streamlining, and while the UPA tried on various occasions to amend the Constitution to enact the GST, it faced political hurdles, not least from Narendra Modi in his capacity as chief minister of Gujarat. But the GST was a major part of BJP's tax plank during the 2014 elections. The BJP also promised to 'rationalize and simplify' the tax code.

AGRICULTURE: With almost half the workforce engaged in agriculture and related activities, no political party could afford to ignore this sector. Rural distress, farmer suicides and the vagaries of nature have made this sector a major political hot-button issue. With that in mind, Modi reached out to farmers in a big way by promising to rework the formula for calculating minimum support prices (MSPs). While many economists made the case that high MSPs under the UPA had contributed to inflation, especially of food prices, Modi promised farmers a defined profit margin. During his April 2014 speech in Hazaribagh in Jharkhand, he said, 'We will change the minimum support price. There will be a new formula—the entire cost of production and 50% profit. It will not only help farmers but this step will also not allow anyone to loot farmers.'[54] This formula was first mooted during UPA1 by M.S. Swaminathan, an agricultural scientist known for his contribution to India's Green Revolution. Nevertheless, this became a powerful rallying cry for Modi's campaign.[55]

The BJP promised to increase public investment both for agriculture and rural development and said that it would take steps to increase profitability in agriculture, and 'ensure a minimum of 50% profits over the cost of production, cheaper agriculture inputs and credit'. It promised to introduce the latest technologies for farming and high-yielding seeds and to link MGNREGA to agriculture. For the farmer community, it said it would put in place welfare measures for older farmers (aged sixty plus), small and marginal farmers and farm labourers. The BJP also promised to 'implement a farm insurance scheme' to take care of crop loss due to unforeseen natural calamities and work with the states to 'set up seed culture labs in each district and regional agriculture innovation labs'. With a promise to reform the Agricultural Produce Marketing Committee (APMC) Act, the manifesto ended on a high note by announcing that it would adopt a 'National Land Use Policy', which would look at the scientific acquisition of non-cultivable land, and its development.

INDUSTRY/MANUFACTURING: While Modi frequently spoke of the equal importance of agriculture, manufacturing and services, his ambitions for manufacturing were high. In a speech to students of Delhi's Shri Ram College of Commerce (SRCC), Modi argued that manufacturing deserved special focus. In his view, the world considered India as a 'huge market where they can dump their products'. Instead, he spoke of the need to 'make our manufacturing sector efficient so that we can convert the world into a market and begin dumping our products there'.[56] Modi wanted more indigenous defence manufacturing, looser labour laws and greater ease of doing business as a way to create more jobs.

In a bid to shift India's global economic standing, from being a market for the global industry to becoming a 'Global Manufacturing Hub', the BJP in its manifesto said it 'will attempt to move towards a single-window system of clearances both at the Center and also at the State level through a Hub-spoke model'. It indicated that it would 'set up World class Investment and Industrial regions as Global Hubs of Manufacturing'. Along with this, the BJP promised to 'set up a task force to review and revive our MSME sector (Micro and Small Medium scale Enterprises); enabling it with better access to formal credit and technology for modernisation'. Similarly, to boost manufacturing, BJP promised to initiate steps for 'interest rate rationalisation and have a clear tax policy to remove uncertainty and create investor confidence'. The manifesto spoke of increasing public spending on R&D and to incentivize R&D investments by industry to improve the manufacturing sector's competitiveness. The manifesto also promised to strengthen trade facilitation to ensure easier customs clearances and visas for business travel.

FOREIGN DIRECT INVESTMENT: The BJP was careful about positioning itself on FDI. In April 2014, Modi indicated that FDI policy required a review—not only for retail but for all sectors. There were concerns in the BJP about how small traders, the party's reliable vote bank, would react to its position on FDI. At the same time, the BJP was careful not to hurt Modi's reformist credentials. The rhetoric, however, targeted the domestic audience when Modi spoke of the need to 'protect the manufacturing sector' because without protection, 'our youth's future will be destroyed'.[57] Barring the multi-brand retail sector, BJP indicated that it would allow FDI in sectors that need funds for job and asset creation, infrastructure and acquisition of niche technology and specialized expertise. The BJP committed to protecting the interest of small and medium retailers, small- and medium-sized enterprises (SMEs) and those employed by them.

EDUCATION/SKILLS: India has made major progress in improving literacy rates as well as enrolment ratios in schools. In spite of that, the education sector requires major reforms.

Access to quality and affordable education remains limited. Without good-quality education, India's growing youth population finds it increasingly difficult to land decent jobs. Reforms of the education sector were a high-priority area, and Modi and the BJP addressed this critical issue regularly. While campaigning in Karnataka in 2013, Modi addressed students on the occasion of the Golden Jubilee celebrations of Jawaharlal Nehru Medical College, a part of KLE Academy of Higher Education and Research, in Belgaum. 'A society that does not give importance to education cannot progress,' he said. 'Let there be any government, it must have a vision to make India shine in the field of education. Whenever we have entered a *Gyaan Yug*, India has led the way. The 21st century is also a century of knowledge.'[58] While promising to set up prestigious institutions such as IITs, IIMs and AIIMS in every state, Modi lamented that access to such institutions was limited. According to him, it was unfortunate that decades after Independence, there wasn't sufficient focus on education and skill building. He wanted students around the country to do all they could to make India innovative and competitive.[59]

In its manifesto, the BJP promised to make every effort to ensure 'equality of opportunity in access and success' to all learners. BJP's education plan was 'to review and revise education system; the salary structures associated with the teaching staff and most importantly, address the shortfall of faculty and related issues in the country'. The BJP proposed to double public spending on education to 6 per cent of the GDP, and involve the private sector to further enhance this. Under the scheme 'Quality education for all', it proposed to take steps such as school performance audits under the flagship 'Sarva Shiksha Abhiyan' (SSA) and universalization of skill development, especially in rural and tribal areas. In higher and professional education, the BJP proposed to set up a mechanism for close interaction between industry (including SMEs), academia and the community.

The BJP promised to restructure the University Grants Commission (UGC) and transform it into a Higher Education Commission, thus expanding its current role as just a grant-distribution agency, as well as to revisit the Apprenticeship Act to facilitate youth to 'Earn while they Learn'. The BJP promised to set up a National Commission on Education to report in two years on the state of education and the reforms needed for the sector's development. Based on the report, the BJP sought to implement a National Education Policy to meet the changing needs of the country with respect to quality education, innovation and research.

The manifesto also included a section on developing India as a 'Knowledge Powerhouse' and to take up skill development on a mission mode, at an unprecedented scale. For this, the BJP promised to launch a 'National Multi-skill Mission', run short-term courses focusing on employable skills and also set up 'Centres of Excellence' in various sectors in partnership with industries. The manifesto promised to promote vocational training on a massive scale. To increase employability, it emphasized the development of soft skills and spoke of introducing a national programme on foreign languages and a national programme for digital empowerment through computer literacy, especially for the youth.

HEALTH/SANITATION: In an interview to ETV in April 2014, Modi outlined his ideas on improving the health sector. 'We are stuck on health insurance. But health assurance is needed. We think of diseases but not of health. We should change our focus. Preventive health care should be our priority.' In his view, clean water would help reduce diseases and educating children about hygiene, including Gandhi's emphasis on cleanliness, could yield results. He talked about the need to have medical colleges in every district so that students from those districts could become doctors in villages.[60]

In its manifesto, the BJP's overarching goal for healthcare was to provide 'Health Assurance to all Indians and to reduce the out of pocket spending on health care'. It proposed to initiate the 'National Health Assurance Mission', with a clear mandate to provide universal healthcare, and set up medical and paramedical colleges to make India self-sufficient in human resources. Among its many promises, the BJP listed the initiation of the New Health Policy, a National Mosquito Control mission, universalization of emergency medical services (108 services), and integrated courses for Indian System of Medicine (ISM) and modern science and Ayurgenomics.

The manifesto also stated that 'Population stabilization would be a major thrust area and would be pursued as a mission mode programme'. The Swachh Bharat programme was announced for the purpose of creating an open-defecation-free India. To support this, the BJP promised to set up modern, scientific sewage- and waste-management systems and introduce sanitation-ratings measurement and ranking of cities and towns on 'sanitation' as well as rewards for the best performers.

LABOUR FORCE: In the manifesto, the BJP's agenda began with the promise to protect 'the interests of labour in the unorganized sector'. For this, the BJP said they would issue identity cards to the unorganized-sector workers and provide them with good-quality health and education services. The party proposed steps to improve skills through appropriate training programmes. For organized-sector labour, the BJP proposed to 'encourage industry owners and labour to embrace' the concept of 'Industry Family' (a concept in which industry owners and labourers bond as a family, to increase efficiency, skill development and upgradation, productivity, appropriate wages and perquisites, and security). The BJP also promised to extend access to modern financial services to workers (with a promise of 'considering the option of setting up a dedicated Workers Bank'). There was also a promise to strengthen the pension and health–insurance safety nets for all kinds of workers.

INFRASTRUCTURE: During the election campaign, Modi focused much attention on the infrastructure sector. His tenure as chief minister saw significant improvements in the power sector. In his view, 'If we want to industrialize, electricity is the first necessity.' He also laid out ambitious proposals for renewable energy. After inaugurating a solar power plant in Neemuch, Madhya Pradesh in February 2014, Modi noted, 'With eastern part of the country rich in water resources, it is a heaven for hydro power generation; also, our coasts are fit for wind energy. Similarly, our plains such as Gujarat and Rajasthan are fit for solar energy generation. If the planners had thought of these factors and formed a policy India wouldn't be so dependent on energy imports.'[61]

Piyush Goyal, then a member of Parliament and BJP's treasurer, wrote about India's 'infrastructure deficit in terms of roads, railways, power and ports'. The BJP intended to address this 'deficit' on a 'fast-track basis'.[62] As an example, Goyal shared plans for constructing a 'diamond quadrilateral of bullet trains', which was in line with Modi's ambitious ideas during the campaign. Other campaign promises dealt with housing for all and electricity for all, in addition to ramping up road building and related infrastructure.

For major improvements in the infrastructure sector, the manifesto promised to expedite work on freight corridors and industrial corridors and connect remote states with world-class highways and rail lines. The BJP also planned to modernize existing and operational airports and build new ones to push for low-cost air travel in India. The manifesto proposed the evolution of an economic model of port-led development—modernize existing ports and develop new ones—stringing together the Sagar Mala project. For next-generation infrastructure, the BJP promised to set up gas grids and a national fibre-optic network up to the village level. The BJP manifesto mentioned specific initiatives in key infrastructure sectors—roads, railways, water, energy and housing. A major promise included the development of a comprehensive 'National Energy Policy' and the expansion and strengthening of the National Solar Mission.

Citing the increasing trend of 'water stress', the BJP indicated that the party was committed to accord high priority to water security. It promised to launch the 'Pradhan Mantri Gram Seenchai Yojana' and a multi-pronged water strategy for reducing farmers' dependence on monsoon rains. To improve the state of potable water, the BJP promised to facilitate piped water to all households and set up desalination plants for drinking-water supply in coastal cities. Lastly, it also included the ambitious river inter-linking project in its manifesto.

On the housing front, the BJP said it would roll out a massive low-cost housing programme—houses equipped with basic facilities like toilets, piped water supply, electricity and proper access; and also, innovatively structure the programme to work seamlessly with various existing programmes, while adding the missing links. At the same time, the BJP would encourage the development of the overall housing sector, through appropriate policy interventions, credit availability and interest subvention schemes.

TOURISM: To push tourism, the BJP committed to initiate a mission-mode project to create fifty tourist circuits that are affordable and built around themes like: a) Archaeological and Heritage, b) Cultural and Spiritual, c) Himalayan, d) Desert, e) Coastal, f) Medical (Ayurveda and Modern Medicine), etc. The manifesto proposed to start a 'specialized course in tourism' for capacity development. It also promised to accord high priority to the safety and security of tourists.

As we shall see in the next part of the book, the Modi government kept some of these promises and failed to keep others. However, an inability to keep all promises is not, at least in my opinion, a failure. That is the story of all governments, and not just in India. If governments kept all promises, their agendas would probably have been less ambitious. It is good to set the bar high, show people the possibilities and then make a genuine effort to try and deliver. However, in Modi's case, the expectations were sky-high even though the manifesto comes across largely as standard fare. The reason for this may be that the electric election campaign included a lot of promises that stuck in the public's minds even as some key ideas did not make it into the manifesto. For example, while campaign rhetoric included the provision of tens of millions of jobs, any specific job creation numbers were missing in the manifesto.

In any event, let's go back to our story and see how things turned out as PM Modi took charge on 26 May 2014.

3

The Policies and Programmes

'The curious task of economics is to demonstrate to men how little they really know about what they imagine they can design.'[1]— Friedrich von Hayek

According to some observers, PM Modi's victory in 2014 ushered in the dawn of a traditional right-of-centre alternative to the left-leaning, 'socialist' consensus that had governed India's economy since Independence.[2] Achieving high economic growth, reining in fiscal deficits and curbing inflation, curtailing 'wasteful' subsidies, promoting land and labour reforms, reviving India's manufacturing sector and creating jobs at a massive scale, privatizing public-sector enterprises (PSEs), cutting regulations, improving tax administration, further opening the economy and promoting exports—all these were part of PM Modi's economic plank.[3] While the first wave of market reforms were enacted in the early 1990s, second-generation reforms had stalled since then. Many felt that PM Modi could push that agenda forward.[4] This development-oriented package had great appeal among millions of young and aspirational Indians.

With expectations rocketing after the BJP's thumping victory in the Lok Sabha elections, attention shifted quickly to Modi's economic agenda. Voters were seeking quick results, and with 282 seats out of 543, Modi had the political capital to follow through on his economic transformation agenda. However, some astute observers did not foresee the radical change that many were expecting. Speaking to the *New York Times*, Eswar S. Prasad, a professor at Cornell University in Ithaca, said that Modi 'has a fairly clear idea of what he wants to accomplish, and he does not look for ratification from the market'.[5] In line with Modi's image as a decisive leader, Prasad noted that, 'One could argue that in a country where there are far more words than actions thrown around, that this is far more preferable: a man who acts.'[6]

There was also a sense that Modi's team would be different and less beholden to the so-called 'Lutyens' elite', a reference to the nexus of Delhi's politicians, businessmen and members of the media. Swapan Dasgupta, then a pro-BJP journalist and later a member of Parliament, said, 'He [Modi] has brought in lots of people who have risen from local politics, perhaps a little technocratic. People not from the Anglophile elite, maybe.' It is a different matter that Dasgupta himself was a member of that Anglophile elite. Still, the air in Delhi was rife with expectations of major change.

In tracing the Modi government's economic policy framework, there will be opportunities to discuss issues that are not typically part of economic development. For example, the high-profile sanitation campaign, Swachh Bharat, is not about economic development per se but its success can support the country's socio-economic progress. However, for now, we begin with traditional areas of economic development. On the macroeconomic front, the UPA regime's last two years were very challenging. Panagariya, writing on the Modi government's four-year anniversary, noted, 'Growth had plummeted to 5.9 per cent during the last two years of the outgoing government, down from a nine-year average of 8.2 per cent. During the same two years, inflation had averaged 9.7 per cent.'[7]

As we shall see later, growth under the UPA, even during its second term, turned out to be higher than the numbers suggested here, but inflation and high fiscal and current account deficits were indeed a problem under UPA2. Dealing with broad macroeconomic challenges was of fundamental importance for the new government. Before we get to what the Modi government did, a little background can provide some context for its actions. I find that while we spend a lot of time discussing high fiscal deficits and inflation under the UPA, we don't talk enough about the origins of such challenges. Understanding those challenges has lessons for policymakers and also provides the context for the Modi government's policy agenda.

A working paper by two economists at the Asian Development Bank (ADB) provides a balanced perspective of the UPA's policy response to the GFC.[8] The paper notes that as the sub-prime mortgage crisis first surfaced in the United States in late 2007, India was in a comfortable situation since its banking sector was less integrated with international financial markets. In fact, the RBI was raising interests until August 2008 in an effort to cool the economy down. It was not until the collapse of Lehman Brothers in September 2008 that India felt a real hit. The ADB paper points out that 'External credit flows suddenly dried up and the overnight money market interest rate spiked to above 20% and remained high for the next month.'[9]

The severity of the crisis was such that the US stock market lost US$8 trillion in market capitalization within a few months. However, stock markets in emerging economies fared even worse. Between June and December 2008, the US S&P (Standard & Poor's) 500 dropped 36 per cent. In the same time period, stock markets dropped by even more in China (48 per cent), Brazil (49 per cent) and Argentina (51 per cent). The Indian stock market dropped 41 per cent. Currencies fell as well, including the rupee, which dropped 13 per cent.[10]

The financial crisis turned into a broader economic collapse, with demand falling in advanced economies and international commodity prices and emerging markets' industrial production crashing. The International Labour Organization (ILO) predicted that the crisis would cost over 50 million jobs.[11] The IMF had to constantly revise its estimate of global growth. In the ten months starting July 2008, the IMF reduced its global GDP growth forecast for 2009 four times—from 3.9 per cent to 2.2 per cent, then 0.5 per cent and, finally, in April 2009, 'for the first time in 60 years, the IMF predicted a global recession with negative growth of 1.3% for world GDP in 2009'.[12]

Given this global picture, there was bound to be an impact on India. As discussed earlier, the banking system remained relatively immune in the beginning. However, while the banking sector may have been less integrated, the rest of India's economy was more integrated with the global economy. This integration was a result of the 1991 reforms and progress since then. The reversal of foreign institutional investor (FII) flows was an early sign of trouble. The ADB paper notes, 'Against a net inflow of US$20.3 billion in FY2007–2008, there was a net outflow of US$15 billion from Indian markets during FY2008–2009.'[13] The markets were spooked. Equity markets lost US$1.3 trillion of market capitalization 'from an index peak of about 21,000 in January 2008 to 8,867 by 20 March 2009'. Trade, which was booming until then, started trending into negative growth territory. While India's exports as a share of GDP were only about 22 per cent in those days, their import content was relatively low. This meant that the 'multiplier effect' on the economy was 'quite large'.[14]

The Indian government's response was twofold—fiscal stimulus and monetary stimulus. In the budget presented in February 2008, the first UPA government proposed a slew of expansionary policies. This included increased outlays for MGNREGA, a massive farm-loan waiver, an increase in salaries through the seventh pay commission, and increases in farm and fertilizer subsidies. This was in addition to already elevated MSPs for rice and wheat. This fiscal stimulus was not only about combating a deteriorating economic environment due to the unfolding crisis but also likely because of a political calculus associated with the 2009 Lok Sabha election.

The stimulus increased the Central government's fiscal deficit from 2.7 per cent of the GDP in FY2007–08 to 6.1 per cent in FY2008–09. The government also announced three stimulus packages in December 2008, January 2009 and March 2009, which focused on infrastructure spending, reduction in indirect taxes and incentives for exporters. Together, these three packages amounted to 2 per cent of the GDP. While this was a substantial stimulus to shore up the economy in light of global headwinds, it was still small compared to the fiscal stimulus provided by the United States and China. The fiscal stimulus between 2008 and 2010 amounted to 10 per cent of the GDP in the United States.[15] In China, the government's fiscal stimulus package was massive at 13.4 per cent of the GDP.

Governments around the world announced a fiscal stimulus because the threat of an economic catastrophe was real. In its October 2008 World Economic Outlook (WEO), the IMF painted a grim picture. 'The world economy is now entering a major downturn in the face of the most dangerous shock in mature financial markets since the 1930s.'[16] Following the IMF's announcement, several central banks, including those in the United States, Germany, United Kingdom and China, announced cuts in interest rates. In India, as in many other parts of the world, inflationary pressures took hold in 2007 and 2008. In June 2008, inflation topped double digits. However, the RBI had earlier put high interest in place to curb inflation. By April 2009, the change in the wholesale price index (WPI) had dropped to a mere 1 per cent. This allowed the RBI to shift gears and focus on growth. The RBI cut the cash-reserve ratio and slashed the repo rate by 425 basis points within a matter of months.[17]

While the post-crisis stimulus did help the Indian economy maintain fast growth, it contributed to the slowdown later. The Economic Survey of 2012–13, prepared under the leadership of then chief economic adviser, Raghuram Rajan, argued that while external factors can partly explain the slowdown in the economy in 2012 and 2013, domestic causes also played a part. According to the survey, 'The strong post-financial-crisis stimulus led to stronger growth in 2009–10 and 2010–11. However, the boost to consumption, coupled with supply-side constraints, led to higher inflation. Monetary policy tightened, even as external headwinds to growth increased. The consequent slowdown, especially in 2012–13, has been across the board, with no sector of the economy unaffected.'

This background is important to understand the policy framework adopted by the Modi government starting May 2014. The campaign rhetoric had been scathing about fiscal and current account deficits, inflation, stalling of investment projects and a slowdown in growth. On the economic front, the objective was to ensure macroeconomic stability, pursue rapid growth, lower deficits, curb inflation, build infrastructure and create jobs. In many ways, that is what people expected and, as with most governments, the Modi government started off well. There aren't many unbiased accounts of how the Modi government's economic policy framework evolved. However, we can piece together a view by relying on writings of the less partisan supporters and critics of the government. In addition, perspectives of international organizations and scholarly journals can help us further understand economic policymaking in India.

An early indication of the Modi government's policy platform is recorded in the October 2014 issue of the 'India Development Update', a World Bank publication.[18] 'The reforms pace has gained momentum. The authorities' focus on efficient and effective implementation has been borne out in actions to expedite decision making and clearance procedures for large projects.' The government enacted reforms in a number of areas including deregulation of diesel prices, labour laws and simpler regulatory compliance, especially environmental clearances. The government also raised FDI limits in a number of sectors.

A new Expenditure Management Commission to rationalize public spending was set up and the erstwhile Planning Commission found itself on the chopping block. The NITI Aayog, an economic advisory body that was more like a think tank, was set up under the leadership of Arvind Panagariya. The Modi government also launched a high-profile effort to reverse the Land Acquisition Act, which the BJP had lent lukewarm support to in 2013. This last measure requires more detailed treatment because I believe it had an adverse impact on the overall economic performance of the Modi government. However, first we need to understand the other policies devised in the first year of the Modi government.

While every government pursues some reform measures, not all become part of the public discourse. It is difficult to find a comprehensive list of reforms in one place. However, the 'India Development Update' of April 2015 does a good job of documenting reforms under consideration at that point in time. It reviews reform measures in nine major policy areas— monetary policy, fiscal policy, financial-sector reforms, trade and capital markets, energy, infrastructure, railways, labour and land, ease of doing business, and FDI. A key reform during that time included the monetary policy framework, which set the RBI a consumer price index (CPI) inflation target of 4 per cent with a (+/-) 2 per cent band by the end of 2016–17.

In the financial sector, the government launched the Pradhan Mantri Jan Dhan Yojana (PMJDY) with an aim to vastly improve access to financial services. The government allowed dilution of its shareholding to 52 per cent in PSBs as a means for bank recapitalization and introduced the Benami Transactions (Prohibition) Bill to curb black-money transactions. In the trade sector, one of the initiatives included a new gold-monetization scheme to replace an existing gold-deposit scheme. On the fiscal side, the government decided to bring down the corporate tax rate from 30 per cent to 25 per cent over time. The government also divested 10 per cent of its share in Coal India Limited and 5 per cent of its share in the Steel Authority of India Limited (SAIL).

Discussion on the GST continued while service tax plus educational cess were set at 14 per cent. On the expenditure side, the government set its sight on expanding the direct-benefits scheme through Aadhaar, the unique identity programme. The government also launched a combination of social security and pension schemes in the form of the Pradhan Mantri Bima Yojana, Atal Pension Yojana and Jeewan Bima Yojana. In the energy sector, the sharp decline in crude prices enabled the government to deregulate diesel prices quicker than anticipated. The government also developed procedures for coal-mine auctions in line with a Supreme Court order. On the infrastructure front, the government set up a National Industrial Corridor Authority and a new institution (3P India) to support the mainstreaming of public–private partnerships (PPPs).

In railways, the government announced an ambitious plan of capital investments and major improvements in operational efficiency. It also introduced land and labour reforms. To make land acquisition less cumbersome, the government introduced an ordinance to ease the 'consent clause and impact assessment requirement for developmental projects related to industrial corridors, PPP projects, rural infrastructure, affordable housing and defense'[19]. In addition, the President approved labour reforms in Rajasthan, which was a way for the government to ease into this politically fraught area.

On the FDI front, the government increased caps in defence and railways and also eased procedural requirements in a dozen sectors. Finally, in terms of ease of doing business, the government introduced 'Make in India', an initiative to make India an international manufacturing hub. The introduction of a government-to-business (G2B) single-window portal called eBiz enabled integration of eleven government services. In addition, the Micro Units Development and Refinance Agency (MUDRA), a refinancing institution for MSMEs, was launched, as well as the proposed enactment of a bankruptcy law and the National Skills Mission to improve the employability of India's burgeoning youth population.[20]

In its first year, the Modi government identified many important tasks, announced key measures and implemented some needed reforms. However, it isn't as if other governments do not have a full plate of work when they are in power. For example, the 'India Development Update' of October 2013 notes, 'The reform momentum has picked up in the last year with authorities putting forth a number of important reform initiatives. These reforms include a major expansion of social protection coverage with the passage of the NFSA, a new Land Acquisition Bill that replaced more than 100-year-old legislation, a new Pension Bill that allows foreigners to invest in Indian pension fund companies, a Banking Laws Bill that allows for new banking licenses, a Companies Bill that replaces sixty-year-old legislation and increases transparency and corporate accountability, and the raising of ceilings and/or FDI-easing reforms in a number of sectors.' In 2013, the UPA government was on the ropes and it still went on with the business of governance. That is what governments do. That is what the Modi government also did. At the same time, as was the case with other governments, the Modi government also brought in its own style of functioning. That style had implications for governance.

Centralization in the name of efficiency

Panagariya's recollection of the early part of the Modi government documents efforts at 'improving governance and efficiency'. He observes that 'deep paralysis' affected the last few years of the Manmohan Singh government. Large infrastructure projects stalled due to lack of systematic coordination between ministries as well as 'inordinate delays in environmental clearance'. After coming into office, Modi 'directly intervened to speed up clearances and decision-making'. According to Panagariya, who was a key member of the government after taking over as the vice chairperson of the NITI Aayog, Modi regularly presided over meetings with bureaucrats from different ministries to make policy and project decisions.

The government also focused on simplification and digitization of clearances for businesses. The goal was to improve India's standing in the World Bank's Ease of Doing Business (EODB) report. While this style of functioning, in which the prime minister took a personal interest in boosting the efficiency of his government, was consistent with Modi's style as CM of Gujarat, it was a relatively new concept in the corridors of power in Delhi. There were numerous reports around that time that indicated that even senior ministers were not in charge of their ministries because Modi effectively controlled their ministries by working directly with bureaucrats. This push towards centralization of authority and decision-making sometimes took seemingly extreme forms. Prakash Javadekar, a minister, on his way to the airport to attend an international conference, reportedly returned home after receiving a call asking him to change into something more appropriate than the jeans he was wearing. The prime minister's office (PMO) called to ask, 'Are you aware that you are a central minister?'[21] Such stories are not important in themselves. What is more important is to understand if the decision-making structure helped or hindered India's development. This will become clearer as we go deeper into Modi's tenure. For now, it would suffice to keep this at the back of our minds.

The general expectation was that Modi's policy framework would be truly transformational. As I pointed out in Chapter 2 of this book, some observers heralded Modi as the second coming of Margaret Thatcher. Many expected big-bang reforms such as those related to land, labour and privatization of inefficient public-sector entities. However, not only did Modi fail to meet such expectations, his government came under attack for largely sticking to the policy framework adopted under the UPA. In fact, the Congress party would often accuse the Modi government of not only making U-turns on poll promises but also simply renaming UPA-era policies and claiming them as its own. In December 2014, the Congress published a booklet showcasing twenty-five instances in which the Modi government had reversed course on a stand that the BJP had previously taken.[22] These instances were from a variety of policy areas, including economic policy.

Political rhetoric aside, it was undeniable that there was a lot of policy continuity. This should not have been totally unexpected, given that there is broad consensus that economic growth and a certain amount of welfare spending are important for India's progress. However, many economists and analysts believed that a government unshackled from coalition politics and with a decisive mandate could unleash the much-needed second-generation reforms. This did not happen and I believe it impacted the policy framework during the remainder of Modi's term. The opposition parties accused the Modi government of being defined by three characteristics: 'a U-turn on promises, "renaming and plagiarizing" Congress-led United Progressive Alliance programmes, and taking decisions to benefit "friendly corporate houses"'.

A fight over land: A strategic blunder

This was also a time when the BJP was preparing ground for amending important parts of the 2013 Land Acquisition Act. Finance minister Jaitley had called the 2013 law 'tough' and felt that it needed changes to simplify land acquisition for ease of doing business.[23] While the law minister Sadananda Gowda had indicated in November 2014 that the government would not bring in an ordinance to amend the 2013 law, just a few weeks later the government announced that it would introduce changes into the land act by promulgating an ordinance. The government's move provoked huge opposition. Voices against the ordinance included that of Anna Hazare, the leader of the India Against Corruption movement that had instilled an adverse narrative about the Manmohan Singh government.

Without getting into the details of the ordinance, it was clear to me at that time that the Modi government was making a political blunder that would hurt it as well as the economy. My logic was relatively straightforward. The 2013 law reformed a British-era law from 1894, criticized for a variety of reasons, including for being coercive and disproportionately against the interests of poor landholders. The 2013 law sought to create a mechanism requiring consent as well as fair compensation, rehabilitation and resettlement of those selling land. Investors were worried that the law would make it much harder to acquire land within reasonable cost and time. Concerned about investor sentiments, PM Modi plunged headlong into trying to undo the 2013 law. However, the new law took effect only in January 2014. We had not seen the law in action for even one full year. There may have been some merit to arguments against the 2013 law but in terms of prioritization, the Modi government's timing was terrible.

As the Modi government pushed hard on changes to the land law, opposition became just as fierce and entrenched. The PM had little choice but to expend his political capital on this fight. In March 2015, he took to his regular radio address, *Mann ki Baat*, to castigate those whom he accused of spreading 'so many lies' about the land-acquisition ordinance. Modi argued that his government had to bring in changes to address certain 'lacunae' in the 2013 law, which he indicated had been 'enacted in a hurry'. He went on to assure farmers that his government was committed to improving their lives and that he would not betray their trust. The prime minister used his oratory to full effect with an impassioned plea in which he said, 'Rumours are being spread that Modi is bringing the law to reduce compensation. I can't even think of committing such a sin . . . Such misinformation is being circulated for political reasons. You have to guard against it.'[24]

However, it was not just the opposition parties that were crying foul. A range of rights activists and even some of BJP's allies expressed concern that the land-acquisition ordinance was likely to anger farmers and labourers. As a consequence, the BJP was increasingly isolated on this issue.[25] Despite PM Modi's considerable efforts, the 2013 law remains on the books. Many analysts argued that in a country that is overwhelmingly poor and where land is a sensitive issue, a pro-business tag could damage PM Modi politically. This experience may have led to a shift in PM Modi's policymaking.

A bit of showmanship contributed to Modi's loss in his first big fight as prime minister. Showmanship plays no small part in politics. Candidate Modi demonstrated this amply when he routinely flaunted the BJP's election symbol, the lotus, on election days during the 2014 campaign. Many accused him of flouting election laws and regulations but he went ahead nevertheless, and he won. However, showmanship can also sting sometimes. In a famous episode, Modi donned a pinstriped suit during then US President Barack Obama's visit to India. The gold pinstripes on the suit bore a repetition of Modi's full name: Narendra Damodardas Modi. The suit created a huge buzz in India and around the world. In fact, the *Wall Street Journal* carried a piece titled: 'Narendra Modi's Suit and Its Message to Obama'.[26]

Source: Indian Express

While Modi's supporters were ecstatic, the Opposition latched on to a narrative of Modi's pro-business reputation, especially when it turned out that the suit cost Rs 10 lakh (about US$15,000 at the time), an astronomical figure for a country where millions live in poverty.

Rahul Gandhi, then vice president of the Congress party, who was until then trying to recover from his party's defeat in 2014, landed a big blow when he mocked Modi's government as a government of the well-heeled. Rahul Gandhi's aggressive speech in Parliament in April 2015 coincided with increasing resistance to Modi's land–acquisition ordinance. Gandhi roared, 'Your [Modi's] government is ignoring problems of farmers, not listening to labourers. It is the government of industrialists. *Yeh to suit boot ki sarkar hai* [it is a government of the well-heeled]'. He went on to say, '60% people are farmers and labourers. The PM will gain politically if he changes sides [from rich to poor]. You are hurting farmers and they will hurt you'.[27] It did not help Modi that 2015 was a drought year and reports of rural distress were widespread.

In August 2015, the government abandoned efforts to pass legislation to formalize changes brought in through the land-acquisition ordinance. Critics felt that this was the 'biggest political failure of his premiership'.[28] Swaminathan Aiyar, an economist, wrote, 'The land acquisition fiasco reveals him [Modi] as frightened and indecisive, happier retreating than fighting to the finish.'[29] Pratap Bhanu Mehta, one of India's foremost columnists, wrote, 'Instead of clarity there is confusion,' and, 'You get the sense there is no coherence to the economic narrative. It will swirl with the wind, not giving confidence to anyone.'[30] Industrialists were dismayed and there was broad agreement that Modi's image as a decisive leader had suffered a loss. This setback was to have consequences for economic policymaking as Modi would try to burnish his image as a pro-poor, pro-farmer leader.

Banking-sector NPAs: A confounding omission

The Economic Survey 2013–14, which was published towards the end of the tenure of the UPA government, had this to say about the banking sector: 'During 2012–13, the deteriorating asset quality of the banking sector emerged as a major concern, with gross nonperforming assets (NPAs) of banks registering a sharp increase. Overall NPAs of the banking sector increased from 2.36 per cent of total credit advanced in March 2011 to 3.90 per cent of total credit advanced in March 2014 (provisional).' The Economic Survey pointed out that the growth slowdown and high debt levels in key sectors such as textiles, construction, chemicals, steel and telecom were leading to higher NPAs.[31]

The RBI's *Financial Stability Report* published in December 2013 also lists five sectors—infrastructure, iron and steel, textiles, aviation and mining—as 'stressed' sectors. The Economic Survey noted, 'Public sector banks (PSBs) have high exposures to the "industry" sector in general and to such "stressed" sectors in particular.' Finally, a working paper published by the RBI had this warning for policymakers: 'Going forward, asset quality could come under greater strains, given the weakening economic backdrop and global headwinds, impinging on the soundness of banks and macro financial stability.'[32]

Raghuram Rajan was the chief economic adviser before he became the RBI Governor. In both positions, he focused attention on problems in the banking sector. There were others who were also raising an alarm. The World Bank (and other international agencies) was closely tracking the growing NPA problem. The World Bank's 'India Development Update' (April 2013) clearly noted mounting problems in the banking sector. According to the World Bank, 'Slowing economic activity and rise in non-performing loans affected credit expansion.' The bank noted 'increased risk aversion' in the banking sector as well as a 'deterioration' in asset quality.

In the October release of the Update, the World Bank again warned, 'The deteriorating asset quality has exacerbated risk aversion among banks, and has likely played a role in the slowing in credit growth.' The bank noted that gross NPAs could cross 4 per cent by March 2014. By the time of publication of the 'India Development Update' in October 2014, the bank seemed caught up in the sunny mood of the time and noted, 'Financial sector stresses have plateaued . . .'

Of course, the World Bank hedged a bit by also indicating that the financial sector's overall health 'will need to be watched closely'. Gross NPAs stood at 4 per cent at the end of the fourth quarter in FY2014, which the bank noted was higher than at the end of FY2013.

Despite repeated warnings, the Modi government seemed unperturbed by the problems emerging in the banking sector. When I was working at the World Bank during the financial crisis precipitated by the collapse of Lehman Brothers, one thing that everyone talked about was how banking was the lifeblood of economic activity and we had to do all we could to make sure that the banking system did not grind to a halt. Stressed assets create blockages in the banking system and, unless fixed, can stall the system and undermine its ability to perform at a high level. This is a basic lesson of economics, one that the Modi government ignored initially. Its top priorities instead were to focus on micromanaging decision-making in the hope of improving efficiency and reversing the 2013 land law.

By some accounts, Jaitley was more sanguine about the NPA problem due to a belief that the investment cycle would revive because of confidence in the new government and that stalled projects could come back on line due to various efforts, including those of the PM himself.[33] This was a gross miscalculation, which has cost India dearly and dealt a severe blow to hopes of transforming the country's economy. While the enactment of the Insolvency and Bankruptcy Code (IBC) in 2016 is a crucial reform, its impact on the NPA crisis will not be immediate.

In 2014, the banking sector's gross NPAs stood at about Rs 2.4 lakh crore. This was also roughly the amount needed for India's listed banks to meet Basel-III norms. According to the Bank of International Settlements (BIS), 'Basel III is an internationally agreed set of measures developed by the Basel Committee on Banking Supervision in response to the financial crisis of 2007–09. The measures aim to strengthen the regulation, supervision and risk management of banks.'[34] In his first budget in July 2014, Jaitley had this to say about the banking sector: 'Financial stability is the foundation of a rapid recovery. Our banking system needs further strengthening. To be in line with Basel-III norms there is a requirement to infuse Rs 240,000 crores as equity by 2018 in our banks. To meet this huge capital requirement, we need to raise additional resources to fulfill this obligation. While preserving the public ownership, the capital of these banks will be raised by increasing the shareholding of the people in a phased manner through the sale of shares largely through retail to common citizens of this country.'[35] Specifically, on NPAs, Jaitley said, 'The rising Non-Performing Assets of Public Sector Banks is a matter of concern for the Government. Six new Debt Recovery Tribunals would be set up at Chandigarh, Bengaluru, Ernakulum, Dehradun, Siliguri and Hyderabad. Government will work out effective means for revival of other stressed assets.'[36]

The notion that NPA problems would go away, by focusing on stalled projects and improved decision-making, could have resulted from one of two possibilities. The first is that the new political leadership was simply not aware of the impact of stressed banking-sector assets on broader economic activity. The other possibility is that the incoming government did not receive a proper briefing by officials in the finance ministry and RBI.

Since Raghuram Rajan was the Governor of the RBI and had made a big deal about problems in the banking sector and also about how banks were 'evergreening' stressed assets, it is inconceivable that he would not have adequately briefed Messrs Modi and Jaitley. That leaves us with the possibility that Modi's priority was to work with officials in different ministries to improve decision-making and efficiency while Jaitley was figuring out the intricacies of the finance ministry. Mind you, the BJP did have in Arun Shourie and Yashwant Sinha veteran politicians who were well versed with India's economy. However, Jaitley, a lawyer with no significant experience in economic policymaking, was Modi's man for the job. In hindsight, I am not certain that was a wise choice for someone wishing to transform the Indian economy. However, the other problem here is that Modi's vision of transformation may not really have been the one which many mainstream economists might call 'transformational'. Perhaps therein lies the rub.

Demonetization: A decisive self-goal

One of the biggest initiatives of the Modi government was the massive currency swap, also known as demonetization, which the prime minister himself announced on live television on 8 November 2016. Modi informed the country that he was targeting illicit wealth (also known as black money), corruption and counterfeit money by scrapping 500- and 1000-rupee notes. The banknotes declared illegal represented over 86 per cent of the cash in circulation. At the time, there were various estimates of the quantum of black money, some upwards of 20 per cent of India's GDP. Black money is money earned either through illegitimate means or through legitimate means but on which people avoid paying taxes.[37] The stated idea behind demonetization was to keep illicit cash out of the monetary system, thereby imposing a large, one-time cost on holders of black money. Many top economists and analysts were sceptical of the initiative's efficacy, though it did find some backers as well.[38]

Modi justified demonetization on three grounds. First, he wanted to target the stock of black money, often stored in high-denomination currency that found its way into investments in real estate and precious metals. Second, Modi cited a high proportion of counterfeit notes in the economy, which he argued were detrimental to India's economic health. The RBI, in its 2015–16 Annual Report, indicated that two-thirds of all counterfeit notes were in the form of Rs 500 and Rs 1000 notes.[39] The third reason given was a belief that such a vast currency exchange would rein in terrorism.

The actual decision to demonetize high-denomination notes was kept a secret. There was frenzied speculation that even Finance Minister Jaitley was unaware of the decision until the last moment. In December 2016, the then power minister Piyush Goyal tried to put an end to this speculation by saying that Jaitley knew about the decision.[40] However, in response to a Right to Information (RTI) query in 2017, the finance ministry refused to disclose whether or not the PM consulted Jaitley before announcing the decision.[41]

Modi's announcement drew a mix of disbelief, excitement, confusion and chaos. The RBI was in charge of day-to-day implementation but the going was anything but smooth. News reports indicate that within the first month of Modi's announcement, the RBI issued at least fifty notifications related to the initiative's implementation.[42] Indians were lining up outside banks and ATMs to either deposit the discontinued currency notes or to withdraw cash. However, constantly changing rules about what people could or could not do with their money created much confusion and chaos. For example, the initial ATM withdrawal limit was Rs 2000. On 19 November 2016, the limit had to go up to Rs 4000, but it ended up at only Rs 2500.

In another instance, the RBI capped withdrawals from Jan Dhan accounts at Rs 10,000 per month. However, many of these accounts were in urban areas, where other bank-account holders could withdraw up to Rs 24,000 per week. The government was concerned about money laundering through Jan Dhan accounts but inconsistencies such as these created much confusion.[43] The draconian nature of demonetization culminated in an ordinance that criminalized the holding of old notes post 31 December 2016. Initially, the government proposed a four-year jail term and a Rs 10,000 fine for holding old Rs 500 and Rs 1000 notes. Fortunately, the final version of the ordinance dropped the jail provision.[44]

In the immediate aftermath of demonetization, the government started shifting the rationale for the initiative. With opposition to the note ban building up and reports of growing public distress, Modi sought to recast the initiative as a way of remaking India into a cashless society or at least a 'less cash' society. In his first radio address post demonetization, Modi urged young people to become 'soldiers of change' and help turn India into at least a 'less cash' society.[45] He exhorted the youth to help the older generation to learn about forms of cashless payment. Modi said that young people had 'an invaluable opportunity to serve the motherland' and urged them to 'spend some time, an hour or more, every single day, to teach this technology to at least 10 families who may not know it'. Those complaining of standing in long queues received a lesson in nationalism. Soldiers did not mind standing at the border to protect the country, why then could people not make small sacrifices to ensure demonetization's success? The people fell in line.

In one speech, Modi cast the fight as one on behalf of the poor against the rich. Speaking in Ghazipur, Uttar Pradesh, he said that his government stood 'for the poor, the villages and the farmers'. 'India has no shortage of wealth but where is this wealth stored that is a problem. There is little where it is supposed to be, and it is hoarded at places where it should not be.'[46] He added, 'It is the power of your vote that the poor is sleeping peacefully and the rich is running around the bazaar to buy sleeping pills.'[47] Despite the death of over a hundred people who collapsed in lines waiting to collect or deposit cash, and in spite of huge disruptions to the informal economy, Modi did not suffer politically. In fact, demonetization yielded early gains, especially in the form of a stupendous victory in the Uttar Pradesh state election in March 2017.

Demonetization generated much debate both in political circles and outside. The Congress party led the Opposition's charge against the initiative. Former prime minister Manmohan Singh launched a most memorable attack. On 24 November 2016, the mild-mannered leader rose in Parliament and trashed demonetization as 'organised loot and legalised plunder'. A target of many attacks when he was leading the country, Singh got an opportunity to make a scathing political attack, backed by a mainstream economics perspective, of which he himself was an adherent. His speech, laced with convincing arguments, served sobering warnings of what was to come. In talking about demonetization's objectives, Singh said simply, 'I do not disagree with these objectives. But what I do want to point out is that in the process of demonetisation, monumental mismanagement has been undertaken.'

Manmohan Singh also warned those who acknowledged the short-term costs of demonetization but supported it for its long-term gains. To them he said, 'I am reminded of what John Keynes said once: In the long run, all of us are dead.' The initiative had had a disproportionate impact on the informal economy, he said, where 90 per cent of Indian workers make a living, and warned of dire consequences for agriculture and small industry. He went on to predict that 'the GDP of the country can decline by about two percentage points as a result of what has been done. This is an underestimate, not an overestimate.'[48]

While most economists and independent observers were sceptical of demonetization's ability to achieve its stated goals, it had its share of supporters. Jagdish Bhagwati, Vivek Dehejia and Pravin Krishna took on demonetization's critics in an op-ed and noted, 'This policy has created considerable confusion among commentators, some ill-informed, some politically motivated.'[49] They argued that the money that would flow back into banks would attract a 50 per cent tax should depositors not be able to account for it. Of course, the money that would stay out of banks would essentially disappear from the system, leading to an effective 100 per cent tax on such currency notes. They estimated that the government could claim success if it generated Rs 1 lakh crore as a result of keeping illicit money out of the banking system and taxing that portion which entered the banking system. Compared to Rs 2.5 lakh crore in annual tax collections, this seemed like a good outcome—that is, if demonetization yielded such amounts, which we will come to later.

On counterfeit money, they argued that demonetization would not affect the current stock of notes as much as it would affect future flows, provided new notes had enhanced security features. As we learnt later, the government introduced new Rs 2000 notes, which some television reporters rushed to greet as marvels with chip technology. Sadly, there was no chip technology and the Rs 2000 note seems like a poor cousin of the old Rs 500 and Rs 1000 notes. As we shall see in Chapter 4 of the book, counterfeiting did not stop. Bhagwati, Dehejia and Krishna also acknowledged the limitations of stopping the creation of future flows of black money. For this they pointed to a strategy proposed by Harvard economist Kenneth Rogoff: 'The slow replacement of high denomination notes by lower denomination ones—is essentially aimed at eliminating flow accumulation of black money in the future.'

Surjit Bhalla, a prominent columnist and a long-time supporter of the prime minister, was critical of 'mainstream' economists who opposed demonetization. From Bhalla's perspective, 'The fact that no good economist would approve of DM ex-ante, does not necessarily mean that the same economists would not approve of it ex-post, like self. Thinking out of the box is not demanded of economists, but is certainly demanded of courageous political leaders.' Bhalla felt that Modi was not getting enough credit for 'boldly going against his own core political support base—a path where very few political leaders have gone before.' Bhalla wrote about two leaders who, in his view, were the only ones in the last 150 years that went against their 'core political base while formulating policies'. These leaders according to Bhalla were Lyndon Johnson (Civil Rights Act) and Nelson Mandela (Truth and Reconciliation Commission). Modi was following that path, according to Bhalla.[50]

There were other voices of support, including the usual band of corporate cheerleaders and supportive opinion writers, but, for the most part, economists roundly criticized demonetization. Amartya Sen called it Modi's 'Napoleon moment'. In his view, 'Demonetisation is a gigantic mistake, both in terms of its objective of dealing with corruption as well as the objective of one rapid jump of getting into a cashless economy.'[51] Another Nobel Laureate, Paul Krugman, said, 'I understand the motivation, but it is a highly disruptive way to do it. I hardly see significant long-run gains, but there certainly are significant, although temporary, costs.'[52]

Many analysts in India were simultaneously outraged and puzzled. Mihir Sharma, a business columnist, referred to the shifting goalposts of demonetization when he noted, 'What started as a "surgical strike" on black money is now called the dawn of a cashless society.'[53] Sharma was an early sceptic and wondered, like many of us did, if Modi had even consulted experts before embarking on this huge initiative. In a column he wrote, 'You have to wonder if Modi truly sought expert advice, or relied once again on a small and trusted set of politicians to determine policy. India's simply too big and complex for shock and awe.' It later emerged that Modi had consulted Anil Bokil, head of an obscure non-governmental organization, Arthakranti.[54] It also emerged much later that Raghuram Rajan had advised against demonetization when he was Governor of the RBI. In his book, *I Do What I Do*, Rajan writes, 'Although there may be long-term benefits, I felt the likely short-term economic costs [of demonetization] would outweigh them, and felt there were potentially better alternatives to achieve the main goals.' He goes on to admit, 'I made these views known in no uncertain terms.'[55]

Chapter 4 of this book discusses the impact of demonetization. However, for now, I want to narrate a personal experience of how PM Modi had fired the imagination of many people who felt that demonetization would transform the Indian economy, especially its payments system. In December 2016, I was on NDTV's programme, *The Big Fight*. One of the panelists was a young technology buff who was working on a government-led digital-payments initiative. As a student of economics, I was hard-pressed to find anything positive about demonetization. I certainly did not buy into the idea that demonetization would soon create a cashless or even a 'less cash' society. I believe that economies evolve over time and quick fixes are unlikely to succeed. However, our young friend, the techie, was convinced that by the end of 2017, 70 per cent of payment transactions would be digital. Astonishing as this claim was, I was impressed by how sure the young man was about it and by his lack of concern about making rash claims on national television.

Make in India: Manufacturing or marketing?

PM Modi invested a lot of time into the Make in India campaign. His full-throated support to this initiative was a departure from earlier efforts, which lacked such marketing. The previous government had also tried to shore up the share of manufacturing in the overall economy by enacting the National Manufacturing Policy (NMP) in 2011. The NMP set a target of creating 10 crore jobs in a decade and boosting the share of manufacturing to 25 per cent of the GDP.[56] PM Modi not only reaffirmed such targets in 2014, but promoted a sense of urgency in meeting them. By 2022, the government aimed to boost manufacturing's share in the economy to 25 per cent and add 10 crore new jobs to the existing 5 crore in this sector.[57]

Modi's focus on the manufacturing sector was part of mainstream thinking in India. With countries like China growing rapidly on the back of labour-intensive manufacturing, Indian policymakers have long felt the need to improve the share of manufacturing in the economy. As the World Bank noted in 2014, 'Improving manufacturing performance in India is a necessary condition for high growth and job creation.' India's manufacturing sector accounts for about 16 per cent of the GDP. For decades, the share of manufacturing in the GDP has remained below 20 per cent. As noted by the World Bank, this is low compared to the level of manufacturing's share in other comparator countries (e.g., China, Indonesia, Korea and Malaysia).[58] The relatively weak performance of the manufacturing sector was partly responsible for a growth slowdown under UPA2. Many felt that by boosting manufacturing, growth would rebound and job creation would get a fillip. Not everyone was convinced by Modi's Make in India programme, though. The arguments of sceptics make for interesting reading. But it is useful to understand the components of the Make in India initiative before we get to the policy debate.

Modi's Make in India pitch was multifaceted. He spoke of the need for investors to not treat India as a market, given the low per capita incomes here, but as an investment destination. FDI should stand for 'First Develop India', he said, and urged industrialists to not leave India because of pressure from government agencies. The government, Modi argued, would help preserve investor capital, promote ease of doing business, implement easy and effective governance, develop a skilled labour force and also invest in modern infrastructure. The goal was to make India the best investment destination in Asia.

Much fanfare accompanied the announcement. Hundreds of journalists, diplomats, business leaders and politicians attended the launch. The biggest industry leaders were present, including Azim Premji of Wipro, Mukesh Ambani of Reliance, Cyrus Mistry of Tata, Kumar Mangalam Birla of Birla and Yogesh Deveshwar of ITC.[59] One industry leader after another spoke about the need for India to focus on labour-intensive manufacturing and the desirability of the Make in India initiative. As with Modi's Vibrant Gujarat summits, this was a well-choreographed event. The PM successfully created a lot of awareness about the importance of manufacturing to India's economic prospects. So far, so good.

The immediate impact of the Make in India campaign was very positive. Within a day of the announcement of the initiative, Standard and Poor's upgraded India's rating from 'negative' to 'stable'.[60] FDI recovered sharply and billions of dollars poured in, making India one of the hottest investment destinations in the world. In 2014–15, almost US$31 billion worth of FDI came into India, which was a 27 per cent increase compared to the previous year. In 2015–16, FDI rose 29 per cent to hit a record US$40 billion.[61]

It is undeniable that the initiative did attract a lot of attention, both in India and abroad. However, as we shall discuss in the next part of this book, while high on ambition, the Make in India programme has not resulted in any significant change in the manufacturing sector's contribution to the economy. To understand why, it is useful to get a sense of the debate around the time of its launch.

The Opposition attacked the Make in India initiative for being 'old wine in a new bottle'. Former commerce minister, Anand Sharma, argued that the government was misleading the public into believing that past governments neglected manufacturing. According to Sharma, 'Such a claim militates against the facts in public domain and tantamount to deliberately hiding institutional, policy and governance reforms of last few years.'[62] The Congress position was that the idea that manufacturing is important and that India should be creating more jobs in this sector is not new. The real issue is how to go about doing it. However, there were few takers for the Congress position at that time. The campaign initiated in Delhi was to soon spread to other parts of the world, notably the United States where Modi received a 'rock-star' welcome during his visit in 2014.[63]

More than political opposition, or fawning support from Modi supporters, what was remarkable at the time was the scepticism coming in from other quarters. Notably, Raghuram Rajan, then the Governor of the RBI, struck a discordant note by arguing that instead of Make in India, there was a need to 'Make for India'. In a sharp critique of Modi's pet initiative, Rajan argued that an incentive-driven, export-led growth or an import-substitution model were not appropriate for the times. He felt that global economic conditions were not very conducive to accommodating another 'export-led China'.[64]

After facing charges of 'export pessimism', Rajan went on to clarify, 'I am counselling against an export-led strategy that involves subsidizing exporters with cheap inputs as well as an undervalued exchange rate simply because it is unlikely to be as effective at this juncture.'[65] He also cautioned against 'picking a particular sector such as manufacturing for encouragement simply because it has worked well for China'. From his perspective, India is developing differently and at a different time than China and that 'we should be agnostic about what will work'.[66] This critique is something to keep in mind as the book progresses towards Chapter 5, which lays out ideas for the future.

Rajan was not the only sceptic, though. There were many others. One of the earliest critiques came from the *Economist*. While the magazine acknowledged the overall necessity of strengthening the manufacturing sector as well as the marketing effort of the launch event, it laid out some concerns. It also criticized some of the business leaders who were 'sycophantic' in Modi's presence.[67] Mukesh Ambani reportedly gushed about being 'blessed with a leader', the 'unique leadership quality of a prime minister, a man who dreams and he does', and one who motivated a billion Indians to 'dream and do'.[68] According to the *Economist*, Yogesh Deveshwar was 'even more craven, thanking "the Almighty" for the leadership "given to us" in Mr. Modi, for "your astuteness, your wisdom . . . Sir, I'm profoundly inspired by the boldness of your vision and the simplicity with which you have communicated."'[69]

In those days, such praise for Modi from business leaders, politicians and others was not unusual. However, the *Economist* warned that strong leadership, as ascribed to Modi, may not be enough in this case. It pointed out that while Modi correctly argued for a skilled workforce, he shed little light on improving the underlying education sector. While Modi spoke of improving needed infrastructure, he didn't spell out where the money would come from. In short, the magazine argued, more details and real reforms were necessary to back up the rhetoric.

Echoing such concerns, Radhicka Kapoor, an economist with the Indian Council for Research on International Economic Relations (ICRIER), a Delhi-based think tank, noted, 'While the PM has acknowledged that India is indeed a difficult place to do business due to the large number of regulatory bottlenecks and has set a target of elevating India's ranking by 85 rungs in the World Bank's Doing Business survey, he has not outlined a specific strategy to achieve this goal.' Kapoor added, 'It will take a lot more than a flashy new website, a new lion symbol and catchy phrases to make India a manufacturing powerhouse and create productive jobs for India's rapidly-expanding workforce.'[70] Pankaj Chandra, professor of production and operations management at IIM Bangalore, clarified the challenge. He noted, 'The world over, manufacturing has changed. Modern manufacturing is about science and technology, R&D, new processes, innovation, skills and quality. If we can't do all this, I don't think the Make in India project will work.'[71]

Agriculture: A lost opportunity

During the 2014 election campaign, PM Modi made an effective case for reforms, and proposed seamless integration of agricultural products, from farms to dining tables. The transformation of the agriculture sector, which employs 49 per cent of the labour force and accounts for over 17 per cent of the GDP, is key to sustained poverty reduction and tangible improvements in living standards. Modi was keenly aware of the political importance of the sector. In October 2013, he exhorted farmers to donate their farming implements to help build a monument to Sardar Patel, India's 'iron man' and an early pioneer of the Satyagraha movement, especially a farmers' agitation in Kheda, Gujarat, where he was Mahatma Gandhi's chief lieutenant.[72] Asking farmers for contributions for Patel's statue was an 'ingenious and innovative' way for Modi to connect with the politically important constituency.[73]

Ashok Gulati, one of India's foremost agricultural experts, has written frequently about problems in the agriculture sector. He has tracked the BJP's promises to India's farmers and monitored policies adopted by the Modi government. In reviewing the policy implementation of the promise of 'cost plus 50 per cent remuneration' to farmers, Gulati has written about how the government did not move on its promise till 2018, four years after taking office. Even so, the cost base on which farmers are to receive a 50 per cent profit margin is contentious. There are two cost benchmarks and the government contemplated the use of one that was 38 per cent below the one that farmers were expecting.[74] The Modi government used input costs as opposed to the higher comprehensive costs to determine profit margins for farmers. That created resentment and if we see farmers agitating on the streets, perhaps it is because their high expectations are likely to remain unmet.

To facilitate the FCI's transformation, the government set up a High-Level Committee (HLC) in 2014 to recommend a course of action to improve this critical institution's operations. In 2015, the HLC recommended four key steps to revitalize the FCI's operations. According to Gulati, the four areas are: (i) rationalizing the FCI's procurement operations, (ii) reducing the population covered under the NFSA from 67 per cent to 40 per cent, increasing grain entitlement of beneficiaries and gradually introducing cash transfer in the public distribution system (PDS), (iii) outsourcing the FCI's grain stocking and movement operations, and (iv) introducing direct cash subsidy to farmers and deregulating the fertilizer sector. Since then, however, the government has sat on the report and the FCI reforms have not taken shape.

While Gulati was critical of the government's efforts in strengthening the agriculture sector, M.S. Swaminathan, one of India's top agricultural scientists and a pioneer of the Green Revolution, has been more supportive. In a much-publicized article, he praised the Modi government for implementing several recommendations of the National Commission on Farmers (NCF), of which he was the chairman.[75] Specifically, Swaminathan wrote, 'The recent announcement of a remunerative price based essentially on the recommendation of NCF is a very important step to ensure the economic viability of farming.' Referring to unending farmers' agitations, Swaminathan was of the view that '. . . a major demand is the waiving of loans and implementation of the NCF recommendations on MSP [minimum support price]. Both these problems are now receiving attention and appropriate action.'

While the Modi government was quick to take credit, many observers were surprised and did not buy Swaminathan's endorsement.[76] Ajay Vir Jakhar, head of the Punjab Farmers Commission, tweeted on 6 August 2018: 'Doubt if @msswaminathan wrote this [the article]; seems like an advertorial . . . something fishy . . . either way, I disagree.' Gulati had already indicated that the cost basis for MSPs was lower than what Swaminathan had himself recommended. Just a few days after his article was published, Swaminathan lent support to agitating farmers when he sent a note to the All India Kisan Sabha (AIKS), a left-wing association of farmers. He wrote, 'The Kisans'/farmers movement across the country is justly demanding the implementation of the recommendations of the NCF. It is time to ensure a genuine implementation of the recommendations of NCF, with priority to three components. First, a minimum support price or MSP based on the formula of C2+50 percent. Second, a favourable procurement policy to ensure that farmers actually receive the MSP and third, increase mass consumption through the effective implementation of the Food Security Act.'[77]

After two successive droughts in 2014–15 and 2015–16, the Modi government announced the launch of the Pradhan Mantri Fasal Bima Yojana (PMFBY), an insurance scheme that revamped an existing one that had proven inadequate. The PMFBY fixed low premiums for farmers who signed on the programme, enhanced insurance coverage to include the cost of cultivation and targeted 10 crore hectares covered under the scheme. That means the PMFBY would cover 50 per cent of the gross cropped area by 2018–19, which, while below China's 70 per cent, would be a major improvement over current coverage.[78] Economists like Gulati were cautiously optimistic about PMFBY when they lauded improvements in insurance coverage but warned that implementation by states as well as speedy disposal of insurance claims would matter greatly in assessing the performance of this scheme.[79]

Reforming agricultural markets has been a long-felt need. The Vajpayee government suggested a model APMC (Regulation) Act 2003. Many states adopted some version of the model APMC Act but the agri-market remained largely unreformed. Fragmented markets, highly insufficient infrastructure, high intermediation fees and rent seeking were perennial problems that could not be adequately addressed by successive governments.[80]

The Modi government, as with other governments, wanted to hit the sweet spot of reducing consumer prices of agricultural commodities even as farmers received remunerative prices. Keeping in mind the failure of the Vajpayee-era reforms, the government focused on creating a unified national agriculture market (NAM). The government launched NAM in 2016 with a Rs 200 crore budget and provided incentives for *mandi* (agricultural markets) to join the NAM platform. To support these changes, the government brought in the Agricultural Produce and Livestock Marketing (Promotion and Facilitation) Act (2017). The government shifted its priority from regulation under the APMC Act to facilitation under the new APLM Act. According to Gulati, this set the 'right tone for agri-marketing reforms'.[81]

In addition to these programmes, the Modi government also introduced soil health cards, a village irrigation scheme (Pradhan Mantri Krishi Sinchai Yojana, or PMKSY) and initiated work on an ambitious US$87 billion project to link rivers as a means for reducing the threat of droughts and floods. To what extent has the Modi government transformed the agriculture sector through these measures? That will be the focus of Chapter 4 of the book. What is important to note here is that it has followed up on key election promises and introduced a host of programmes. However, as with other governments, the implementation of laws, policies and programmes will be the ultimate arbiter of Modi's performance.

At this point, I would simply observe that the agriculture sector today does not look very different from the one that Modi inherited. As we should expect from all governments, there are improvements in some areas even as performance has deteriorated in some others. When Moody's, the international credit rating agency, upgraded India's sovereign rating from Baa3 to Baa2, former BJP leader and finance minister Yashwant Sinha quipped, 'Explain the change of rating from Baa3 to Baa2 to a farmer in Vidarbha.'[82] That was in 2017. In 2018, the Moody's upgrade may seem even more incomprehensible to a farmer in Vidarbha.

Tax reforms amid problems of implementation

RETROSPECTIVE TAXATION: One of the most high-profile tax issues to come up during the UPA tenure was retrospective taxation.

As with many other problems, the last two years of the UPA regime saw investor concern over an amendment to the Income Tax Act of 1961, which allowed the government to assess taxes on companies, going back many years. Foreign investors were particularly upset about this amendment and the UPA government came in for harsh attacks for undermining investor confidence at a time when the Indian economy was going through a difficult phase. In an interview to ANI, a news agency, candidate Modi seemed to reject the idea of retrospective taxation. In response to a question on the amendment, he said, 'Anywhere in the world, even in Gujarat, if changes things retrospectively [sic], then nobody will have confidence. Breach of trust is the biggest problem which should never happen.'[83]

While Pranab Mukherjee, the finance minister responsible for bringing in the amendment, defended it on account of protecting the country's fiscal interests, it appears that the senior leadership of the UPA, including Sonia Gandhi, Manmohan Singh and P. Chidambaram opposed the amendment.[84] They feared an adverse impact on foreign investment. Even so, the retrospective amendment remained on the books during the UPA regime and while the BJP did not promise to repeal the amendment in its manifesto, Modi and the BJP dropped enough hints that the law would go.

According to Panagariya, given the concerns around retrospective taxation, 'One of the early acts of the government was to assure these investors that no new cases under the law would be opened up.' The Modi government also decided to not pursue those cases initiated under the UPA regime and in which the courts had decided in favour of defendants. This, Panagariya argues, has resulted in a much more conducive investment climate as evidenced by growing FDI in India.[85] The amendment continues to haunt companies such as Vodafone and

Cairn Energy, with the opportunity cost running to hundreds of millions of dollars.

At the time of writing this book, Cairn Energy was in arbitration court contesting seizures by Indian tax authorities. Meanwhile, the Modi government is planning to seek Britain's assistance under a UK–India bilateral tax treaty to recover dues from Cairn. A tax official said, 'Once we exhaust local remedies— that is, selling Cairn's entire residual shares in Vedanta—we plan to seek the UK's administrative assistance under the bilateral tax treaty provisions to recover the dues.' The company is seeking US$1.3 billion in restitution for losses stemming from the IT case.[86] In this context, it is unclear why Modi, despite a huge political mandate and popular support for deep reforms, could not repeal the retrospective amendment, which would seem like low-hanging fruit to most observers.

DIRECT AND INDIRECT TAX REFORM: In 2009, the then finance minister, P. Chidambaram, had proposed a DTC to replace the Income Tax Act of 1961. That proposal did not make it through Parliament. Despite other attempts, there was little movement on reforming the tax code. However, with Modi and BJP making a lot of noise about 'tax terrorism' in the run-up to the 2014 election, there was an expectation that a BJP government would overhaul the direct tax system. There was already a broad consensus for reforming the indirect tax system. The Congress party manifesto included promises for overhauling both types of tax systems and the BJP also made similar promises. Yet, the Modi government's reforms to the direct tax system are incremental at best. The government did reduce the lowest personal tax rate to 5 per cent from 10 per cent, to incentivize more people to become part of the tax base. Also, corporate tax rates came down to 25 per cent from 30 per cent for companies with a turnover of less than Rs 500 crore. However, these

changes are a far cry from a major overhaul of the Income Tax
Act. In its last year, the Modi government has circulated a draft
DTC for comments. However, it is unlikely that this will move
through Parliament before the 2019 election.

On the indirect-tax front, the GST represents a major tax
reform for which the Modi government could have received
a lot more credit than it did. It took three governments and
over fifteen years to negotiate this important constitutional
amendment. Modi was a key opponent of the GST when the
UPA proposed it. In fact, when opposition members reminded
Modi in Parliament that he had been an opponent of the GST,
he countered by admitting that he doubted the GST and had
'discussed it with Pranab Mukherjee many times'. He went on
to say, 'As Prime Minister, having the experience of a Chief
Minister, I could easily address the concerns on GST.'[87]

At the stroke of midnight, on 1 July 2017, Modi rolled out
the GST in a special session of Parliament. It was a ceremony
that sought to evoke memories of Parliament's session on
India's Independence Day in August 1947. Modi termed the
new tax 'Good and Simple Tax', and referring to concerns
about inadequate preparation for implementation, suggested
that minor hiccups would dissipate with time. He quipped,
'Even eyes need to adjust to new spectacles.'[88] It was clearly
a big deal. As Panagariya puts it, 'For the first time in India's
history, any given commodity or service is subject to a single tax
rate nationally.'[89] While the GST replaced many different state
and central taxes and allows for freer movement of inter-state
commercial traffic, its structure and implementation have drawn
criticism. In a prescient attack, Rahul Gandhi tweeted on 30
June 2017, 'A reform that holds great potential is being rushed
through in a half-baked way with a self-promotional spectacle.'[90]

While the slogan for it was 'One Nation, One Tax', the
GST that was introduced had multiple 'rates of 5, 12, 18 and 28

per cent, apart from a zero rate on articles of mass consumption, a 3 per cent rate on bullion and a "sin" cess on articles such as tobacco products'.[91] Crude and its products remained outside the ambit of the GST, despite the fact that they account for a third of all tax revenues. In addition, the compliance burden seemed extraordinarily high, with many businesses initially having to file three GST returns per month.

Early on, the GST's technology infrastructure could not keep up with the volume of transactions, and the government once again seemed unprepared for the scale of reform. It was demonetization redux and gave another major opportunity to the government's critics to paint it as incompetent. Yashwant Sinha said that the GST 'would make a fine Harvard University case study of everything that was wrong with the rollout of a tax reform'.[92] The World Bank called the GST one of the most 'complex' taxes in the world because of 'higher tax rates and large number of tax slabs'. In fact, the World Bank noted that India's 28 per cent tax rate was the second highest among 115 sampled countries.[93]

As in the case of demonetization, the government announced multiple and frequent revisions of taxed items and the tax rates. There were many inconsistencies as well as inexplicable treatment of certain goods and services that contributed to a confused rollout. For example, the GST for eating in air-conditioned restaurants was initially 18 per cent and in non-air-conditioned restaurants, it was 12 per cent. Over time, the GST Council has brought down these rates. Among the hardest hit were exporters who suffered due to inadequate working capital as delays affected GST refunds. Overall, there was an impression of inadequate planning and execution of the GST's rollout. It was another major blow to Modi's image as a decisive and efficient administrator, which he had cultivated since his tenure as Gujarat's chief minister. Given the huge scope of the GST, its botched roll-out had major implications for the economy, as we shall see in Chapter 4.

Fuel subsidy reform: Making the most (too much?) of an opportunity

When Modi took over in 2014, petroleum subsidies accounted for one-quarter of India's Rs 2.6 lakh crore (US$42.4 billion) subsidies budget.[94] As crude prices touched record highs in the last few years of the UPA regime, higher subsidies kept pump prices relatively low. The UPA government decontrolled petrol prices in 2010, and stated its intention to liberalize diesel prices over time.[95] In addition, the government allowed oil-marketing companies to increase diesel prices by Rs 0.5 per month. At the time, IMF economists estimated that at that rate, India would eliminate diesel subsidies by 2014.

While in the Opposition, Modi had indicated that he would cut back on fuel subsidies. The first budget presented by the government left them untouched.[96] However, as international crude prices started declining rapidly, the Modi government fully decontrolled diesel prices by January 2015. That left only subsidies for kerosene oil and cooking gas. For the latter, the government has been increasing prices regularly. The total subsidy and under-recovery on petroleum products, which stood at Rs 1,46,339 crore in 2013–14, came down to about Rs 24,933 crore in 2017–18.[97, 98]

There has been much debate on the Modi government's fuel price policy. The drastic decline in international crude oil prices allowed the Modi government to eliminate much of the subsidy burden. However, the government made a conscious effort to not pass on the benefit of lower crude prices to consumers. By regularly increasing excise duties, the government managed to mop up billions of dollars of revenue, which helped its fiscal consolidation efforts. In 2018–19 alone, excise duties and additional taxes will yield the government Rs 2.5 lakh crore. That is 77 per cent more than what it collected five years ago.[99] Recent increases in international crude prices are now creating the challenge of lower revenues for the government even as consumers are beginning to show frustration with high fuel prices in an election year.

Many economists lauded the government for not passing along the benefit of lower crude prices to consumers. On the one hand, this policy helped improve the government's fiscal situation and on the other, higher prices helped suppress demand for dirty fossil fuels. As demands for cuts in fuel taxes grow, many have suggested that the government resist this pressure. In an op-ed in September 2018, Swaminathan A. Aiyar acknowledged that the effective tax rate on petrol in cities like Delhi and Mumbai was close to 100 per cent but argued that there was ample justification for maintaining these taxes. Citing the polluting nature of fossil fuels and their weight in India's import basket, Aiyar warned that at a time when investors were pulling money out of India, fiscal slippages could make matters worse.[100]

The government is keenly aware of the contribution of high fuel taxes. In 2013–14, the government collected Rs 88,600 crore in excise duties. In the five years to March 2019, the government's estimated excise duty collection exceeds Rs 10 lakh crore.[101] While most analysts, including those who disagree with many of Modi's policies, are supportive of the government's fuel price policy, I have disagreed with it to some extent. I believe that the government should have struck a balance between its own finances and those of consumers. With more disposable income, consumers could potentially help grow the economy, which is another way to reduce the fiscal deficit ratio.

Besides, I am not convinced that more revenues in the hands of the government is a good thing. The quality of government spending is dubious and, at a time when the economy was recovering from the blows of demonetization and the GST, a little bit of help for consumers could have had a salutary effect on the economy. In any event, the government made its choice and fuel prices are at record levels. Is the government saving money to cut taxes closer to the time of elections? That is a real possibility. There have been instances when fuel price changes appeared connected to state-level elections. The political impulse to curb prices at the pump is strong indeed, especially when it might yield dividends at election time.

Privatization remains a pipe dream

People expected a 'minimum government, maximum governance' establishment to either close down notoriously inefficient PSEs or privatize them. However, the Modi government has proven to be similar to its predecessors when it comes to reducing the role of the public sector in certain areas. This is not how the government's supporters view the situation, however. In reviewing its performance, Arvind Panagariya claimed, 'After a lag of more than a decade, the government has initiated a programme of closure of sick PSEs and privatization of those PSEs that do not serve a public purpose.' According to Panagariya, 'More than a dozen PSEs are now in advanced stages of closure'. On the privatization front, Panagariya blames finance ministry bureaucrats for slowing down the process, including in the high-profile Air India case. According to him, it is 'only a matter of time that outright sales of PSEs will be seen taking place'.[102]

Writing in the *Wall Street Journal*, Sadanand Dhume observes that the government's privatization record has 'acquired a farcical cast'. While noting that the government quietly shelved the much-hyped Air India privatization (no buyers came forward), Dhume points to the forced purchase by the Life Insurance Corporation (LIC), a PSE of IDBI, another state-owned bank with an extremely high ratio of NPAs. Making his disappointment clear, Dhume argues, 'In effect, India's privatization programme has become a dodgy accounting exercise in which one government-owned entity buys stakes in another rather than an attempt to streamline the economy by selling unproductive assets to private bidders.'[103]

In a similar vein, Mihir Sharma points out that in India, 'privatization doesn't necessarily mean what it does in the rest of the world. Successive governments have preferred the term "disinvestment"—meaning the reduction of the state's stake in big, strategic companies.'[104] While the idea behind such disinvestments is to reduce government control and interference in operations and to bring in some market discipline, the reality is that the government continues to exert influence on such companies. The government's pressures on large PSEs can have dramatically bad results. For example, Oil and Natural Gas Corporation Limited (ONGC), a huge oil exploration company, saw its cash reserves fall by 90 per cent within the course of one year. Part of the reason for this sharp decline was the government's decision to sell its stake in Hindustan Petroleum Corporation Limited (HPCL) to ONGC. In the process, the government received a huge dividend, which helps with meeting fiscal-deficit targets. Unfortunately, loss of cash reserves means ONGC has fewer opportunities to do what it really should be doing—oil exploration. The government's policy with respect to PSEs can have far-reaching impacts, as we shall see later on.

Progress in financial inclusion

With the advent of modern banking, credit became a necessity but it wasn't always accessible or affordable for everyone.

Specifically, the poor and marginalized have suffered systematic exclusion from modern banking services. This is not specific to India but the need for greater financial inclusion is clear. To address issues related to exclusion, the Modi government launched an ambitious programme to bring banking services to the excluded masses. It launched the PMJDY in 2014 with the objective of 'uncomplicated access to financial services (like Banking, Savings & Deposit Accounts, Remittance, Credit, Insurance, Pension) for anyone, rural or urban, who wishes to access them'.[105]

Another financial inclusion scheme is the Pradhan Mantri MUDRA Yojana (PMMY). The goal of MUDRA is to 'fund the unfunded'. Launched in 2015, the PMMY finances micro and small-scale entrepreneurs in three categories—Shishu (loans up to Rs 50,000), Kishor (up to Rs 5 lakh) and Tarun (Rs 10 lakh). Sixty per cent of all loans under the PMMY are for Shishu entrepreneurs. All commercial public and private banks need to participate in the scheme. Borrowers do not need to set aside collateral for the funds they borrow.[106]

As a general idea, financial inclusion is not a new one. In fact, even the concept behind the PMJDY is not new. Several initiatives over the years have sought greater financial integration in the country—Regional Rural Banks (1975), National Bank for Agriculture and Rural Development, or NABARD (1982), Chit Funds (1982), and Narasimham I & II Committees (1990s).[107] Researchers Prakhar Misra and Kadambari Shah at IDFC Institute have traced the advent of modern financial inclusion in India to the former RBI Governor Y. Venugopal Reddy who, in the Annual Policy Statement of 2005, 'fervently voiced alarm on the exclusion of vast sections of society from the formal financial system'.[108] Misra and Shah point out that Venugopal Reddy's concerns were taken forward through the *Report of the Internal Group to Examine Issues Relating to Rural*

Credit and Microfinance (Khan Committee), which recommended that banks develop 'a basic, "no-frills" account with relaxed norms and elbow room to avail banking facilities'.

In 2010–11, the UPA government launched the Swabhimaan campaign to mainstream banking services in rural areas, specifically villages with a population of over 2000. Despite these efforts, 7.5 crore households out of about 25 crore households (30 per cent) remained without access to formal financial services.[109] When the Modi government came in, the Swabhimaan campaign morphed into the PMJDY. The PMJDY showed early promise, with millions of new bank accounts started around the country. India ranked first in the Brookings Institution's 2015 *Financial and Digital Inclusion Project Report and Scoreboard.* Within three years, the government created about 25 crore Jan Dhan accounts. However, a fifth of these accounts remained dormant and some PSBs tried to game the system by making small deposits in order to show that they had met their targets.

Even so, the PMJDY did succeed in at least one objective— to create accounts for millions, and these could help in implementing other government schemes such as Direct Benefits Transfer (DBT). At this point, a quote by PM Modi comes to mind. Speaking on the third anniversary of the launch of the PMJDY, Modi said to his *Mann ki Baat* audience: 'There is now an air of prudence. He [a poor person] is now beginning to understand that the money can be of use for his children. The money can be used productively in the days to come. Not just this, when a poor person sees a RuPay Card in his pocket, he finds himself to be equal to the privileged people and feels a sense of dignity.'[110] Modi's penchant for hyperbole has not diminished. As one can expect, poor people do not feel like privileged people as a result of the PMJDY. In fact, initial assessments apart, more detailed results relating to the PMJDY, which I will discuss in Chapter 4, indicate a mixed record of achievement.

The PMMY has proven to be more contentious than the PMJDY. While the scheme is supposed to support MSME entrepreneurs, there have been concerns about its goals and scope. Some have argued that its objectives are similar to those of the NABARD and the Small Industries Development Bank of India (SIDBI), which can lead to confusion. Others point to the risk of high NPAs due to lack of collateral associated with these loans. However, given the high NPAs in traditional banking, the NPA issue for MUDRA loans is still within the comfort zone.

An interesting critique of the MUDRA scheme comes from V. Anantha Nageswaran, columnist and financial consultant. Nageswaran argues that the design and implementation of the PMMY are critical. He says in a 2015 column, 'If the outcomes are all about the quantum of loans disbursed, then it is no better than a *loan mela* and no better than an entitlement.'[111] Interestingly, Nageswaran is of the view that while MSMEs deserve support, the goal should be to make them grow bigger and not remain MSMEs.

The Annual Survey of Industries (ASI), 2013–14, points out that in the formal sector, larger units are 'deploying the most capital, providing the most jobs, wages and emoluments and generating the most output'.[112] Only 2 per cent of factories covered by the ASI survey generate a net value added (NVA) of over Rs 50 crore. These factories 'employ a quarter of the total employed in factories, provide 40% of all emoluments; generate half the total output from factories and 71% of NVA.'[113] Nageswaran is alerting us to the policy implications of resource allocation that incentivizes businesses to stay in the MSME realm as opposed to growing bigger and gaining the ability to contribute more to the economy. Nageswaran points to an International Finance Corporation (IFC) study from

2013, which shows that as firms age, they employ more people. However, India appears to be an exception to that rule.[114]

Miles to go in education

India's efforts to improve access, equity and quality of education at the primary, secondary and tertiary levels remain a work in progress. India has made great progress in universalizing primary education. However, it has been evident for some time that progress on learning outcomes has not kept pace. Furthermore, as the World Bank has noted, secondary-school education has become a 'new bottleneck'.[115] Towards the end of the UPA's tenure, India still accounted for one-third of all illiterate people in the world and enrolment rates for grades 9–12 were about 40 per cent. Of those enrolled in secondary school, 15 per cent dropped out and about a third failed in their examinations.[116] While we focus a lot of attention on higher-education institutions such as IITs, IIMs and medical institutes such as AIIMS, there is a big chunk of young people who are simply not part of the education system. Access and participation at all levels of education for all socio-economic and ethnic groups are improving. However, inequality persists in the kinds of educational facilities and the availability of modern techniques of education.

Although most children now go to primary school, the gap in the quality of education a typical student receives vis-à-vis what is imparted at better institutes is vast. Even students in the well-performing states of Himachal Pradesh and Tamil Nadu ranked towards the bottom of the global scores in the Programme for International Student Assessment in 2009. In fact, students from India's best-performing states had reading and mathematics scores that were closer to those of students from Kyrgyzstan than the average of OECD students.[117]

With this background, and with so much evidence to indicate that improved education outcomes can contribute significantly to socio-economic development, the BJP's promises during the election campaign were hopeful. The Modi government announced its intention to overhaul education policy, which flowed from the second National Education Policy of 1986. While previous governments modified the 1986 policy in 1992 and 2005, the Modi government wanted a complete overhaul, at all levels of education and across the rural–urban divide.[118] In 2015, the ministry of human resource development (MHRD) announced the initiation of a consultation process that would culminate in the development of a New Education Policy (NEP).

Unfortunately, the MHRD found itself mired in controversies such as those related to the death of scholar Rohith Vemula of Hyderabad University and freedom-of-expression disputes at JNU. The T.S.R. Subramanian Committee, appointed by former HRD minister Smriti Irani, submitted a draft report in 2016. The MHRD held stakeholder consultations and, after a new minister, Prakash Javadekar, came in, rejected the draft report and disbanded the committee. A new committee under former ISRO (Indian Space Research Organization) chief, K. Kasturirangan, was set up. That committee initiated its work in July 2017. After receiving four extensions, the fate of the NEP remains uncertain.[119]

The BJP had also committed to increase funding for education to narrow the gap with countries such as China. In India, there exists a political consensus for such an increase. Both the BJP, and the opposition Congress party, have supported increasing expenditure on education to 6 per cent of the GDP. Modi also promised the setting up of IITs and IIMs in all states, transforming the UGC, revival of the Sanskrit and Madrasa system and more. While the government lost valuable time in

its first two-plus years, it took some initiatives in the second half
of its tenure.

The government brought in the Indian Institutes of
Management Act (IIM Act) to ensure greater autonomy for
these institutions. Recent initiatives also included RISE or
Revitalizing of Infrastructure and Systems in Education, which
would earmark Rs 1 lakh crore over four years to improve school
infrastructure, open schools for scheduled tribes and promote
programmes for teachers. The Central Board of Secondary
Education (CBSE) restored Class X board examinations. The
government also decided to start seven new IIMs and six new
IITs among other top schools in a move to improve access to
rigorous management and technology education.[120] The prime
minister led a public awareness campaign aimed at narrowing
the gender gap in education. Among the objectives of the *Beti
Bachao, Beti Padhao* initiative is the need to reduce the education
gender gap. While at age fourteen, boys and girls attend school
at relatively similar rates, the gap is perceptible at age eighteen,
when 32 per cent of girls drop out.

While the government has improved its record on education
in the last year and a half, major transformation remains elusive.
For example, reforms of the UGC and the All India Council
for Technical Education (AICTE) are still under discussion,
and controversy erupted over the Institute of Eminence scheme
because of the inclusion of Jio Institute, which at the time existed
only on paper. Of course, enhancing education spending to 6
per cent of the GDP is not happening any time soon. The issue
of education quality, as opposed to access, in Indian schools and
colleges remains a looming problem too.[121]

Dinesh Singh, former Delhi University vice chancellor, had
mixed reviews to offer for the government's initiatives, especially
as far as higher education is concerned. While Singh welcomed
the autonomy granted to IIMs, he felt that the government could

'decentralise the kind of control they have on higher education that is exercised across India by a handful of central agencies'. In a telling critique, he noted that 'much as they [BJP] criticised the Congress, they have blindly followed a tradition which even the Congress had discarded namely creating a central policy for education. Which policy created Harvard or Cambridge? They haven't tried to understand the real issues.'[122]

Skill India: Old problems persist

Data from the OECD puts the skills shortage in India—measured as a percentage of firms (with ten or more employees) that have difficulty finding qualified employees—at 61 per cent. If that is not worrying enough, the Economic Survey 2014–15 noted that the skilled workforce in India is a mere 2 per cent of the total. In response to increasing worries and disquiet over unemployment, PM Modi, on 15 July 2015, celebrated as the first World Youth Skills Day, launched Skill India, a programme that included the introduction of the National Skill Development Mission, National Policy for Skill Development and Entrepreneurship 2015, Pradhan Mantri Kaushal Vikas Yojana (PMKVY) scheme and the Skill Loan scheme. The government describes Skill India as a 'Mission to create convergence across sectors and States in terms of skill training activities'.[123] The programme aims to train 40.2 crore people by 2022. How these schemes impact employability is a question for the future.

The PMKVY is the centre piece of Skill India. The government allocated Rs 1500 crores to the PMKVY and aimed to skill 24 lakh youth across India. The trainees received financial incentives through the National Skill Development Corporation (NSDC) and the scheme overshot its target in its first year. In 2016, the government launched PMKVY 2.0

with an objective of skilling over 1 crore youth by 2020. A budgetary allocation of Rs 12,000 crore was set aside for the programme.

However, the Sharada Prasad Committee, set up by the skill development ministry to review the performance of various sector skill councils, came out with negative reviews of the PMKVY.[124] The committee noted that 'no evaluation was conducted of PMKVY 2015 to find out the outcomes of the scheme and whether it was serving the twin purpose of providing employment to youth and meeting the skill needs of the industry before launching such an ambitious scheme'.[125] In various stakeholder consultations, the committee reported that 'all of them said in one voice that the targets allocated to them were very high and without regard to any sectoral requirement. Everybody was chasing numbers without providing employment to the youth or meeting sectoral industry needs.'[126]

In keeping with some of his other initiatives, Modi's Skill India leveraged an existing UPA initiative— the NSDC. However, Modi's Skill India failed to note either the NSDC's drawbacks or that skilling is merely the end point of employability, the first step being education. Thus, Skill India suffers from similar issues as its predecessor, like the back-breaking task of coordination between multiple departments or bureaucratic stumbling blocks and the continued challenges facing the education sector.[127]

While it is true that Modi's orchestration lends a sense of urgency to the cause of skilling, the unmistakable top-down approach severely impedes the flexibility of the programme to change in the face of shifts in demand, both nationally and globally.[128] The need for industries to actively participate and lead Skill India has thus been recognized as a likely solution to this, and some progress has been seen on this front in terms of Corporate Social Responsibility (CSR) participation from corporates, though the quality of training has remained an issue.[129] As if Skill India did not face enough challenges already, an *India Today* investigation revealed that the scheme was targeted by middlemen who indulged in corrupt practices to siphon money meant for genuine trainees.[130]

Healthcare remains in the doldrums

In the last few decades, India has made significant progress in achieving improved health outcomes but there remain deep-seated problems related to the quality and opportunity of healthcare. According to the World Bank, 'From 1991 to 2013, life expectancy at birth increased by more than seven years, the infant mortality rate fell by half, the share of births in health facilities more than tripled, the maternal mortality ratio fell by about 60 percent, and the total fertility rate fell to almost replacement level.'[131]

Progress in healthcare is undeniable. However, as noted in the World Bank's latest Systematic Country Diagnostic (SCD) for India, national averages mask important differences across states and social groups. For example, eight states accounting for 50 per cent of India's population witness '71 percent of infant deaths, 72 percent of under-five mortality, and 60 percent of stunting'.[132] The SCD notes that for scheduled tribes, infant mortality rates are 26 per cent higher than for the rest of the population while maternal mortality is an astonishing 63 per cent higher. There is a link between poor health outcomes and educational attainment. For instance, the SCD notes that stunting (low height-for-age) is a marker for 'cognitive impairment'. In India, stunting affects 39 per cent of children under five. Sixty per cent of children in poor households suffer from stunting. This makes them highly unprepared for classroom learning. Why is that important? The SCD indicates that, 'Reductions in stunting could increase GDP by 4–11 percent in India.' That is no small matter.

However, there are a number of reasons for the dismal state of India's health sector. Public expenditure on health is very low by international standards while out-of-pocket expenses are high. As a share of the GDP, public-health expenditure in India has hovered around 1 per cent while it is close to 3 per cent in China.[133] After the UPA government launched the NRHM in 2005, public-health expenditure increased. However, the private sector continues to dominate healthcare services, even in rural areas.

Towards the end of its tenure, the UPA government converted NRHM into the National Health Mission (NHM) to ensure more public expenditure on health in both rural and urban areas. Unfortunately, however, the quality of health services, as with education, remains poor. A study published in the *American Economic Review* found that in rural Madhya Pradesh, for instance, 'the cost per patient interaction was at least four times as high in the public sector, without commensurately higher outcomes.'[134] The World Bank SCD notes that, as in education, access to healthcare is not an issue. However, it is the quality of care that people receive that matters. The World Bank found that, '80 percent of children suffering from viral diarrhea would be incorrectly given antibiotics and less than 25 percent of the poor who are suffering from hypertension even know that they have this condition.'[135]

After coming to power, the Modi government has continued several UPA-era schemes after rebranding and recalibrating them.[136] But, it also introduced new initiatives such as Mission Indradhanush, a booster immunization programme for 201 districts with low coverage. This programme helped immunize over 2.5 crore children against seven life-threatening diseases. According to a government survey, 'The first two phases of Mission Indradhanush led to a 6.7 per cent annual increase in immunisation coverage as compared to the 1 per cent increase in the past.'[137]

The other major scheme launched by the Modi government was a repackaged version of the UPA-era Jan Aushadhi Yojana. Now called the Pradhan Mantri Bhartiya Janaushadhi Pariyojana (PMBJP), the scheme aims to provide low-cost drugs, especially to the poor and disadvantaged, through the government's own stores. Unfortunately, this scheme suffered due to 'improper implementation and a scam-tainted handling agency.'[138] Apparently, the scheme was considered important enough to be reportedly run directly through the PMO. Also, according to a government official, the acronym PMBJP is a not so subtle way of helping the ruling party, the BJP, gain politically. The specific quote attributed to the unnamed official was: 'In the run-up to next year's Lok Sabha elections, it is one of the most important schemes for the NDA. The acronym for the scheme was finalised as "PM BJP" after we received instructions from the PMO. The name itself shows how important the scheme is for the government and the PM himself.'[139]

The most ambitious health intervention is Ayushman Bharat, the National Health Protection Mission (NHPM), which aims to provide health-insurance coverage to 50 crore Indians. In some ways, the NHPM is the Modi government's answer to the UPA's NRHM. The NHPM, initially launched in 2016, sought to provide insurance coverage of Rs 1 lakh to those covered. However, the scheme failed to take off. In the final year of his tenure, Modi announced a dramatic scaling up of the scheme. Ayushman Bharat will provide up to Rs 5 lakh a year in hospital expenses to those covered by the scheme. The government would pay premiums to private insurers. Patients can seek treatment at any health facility—public or private—that has joined the scheme.[140]

While the PM has touted this scheme, also dubbed 'Modicare' by his supporters, as 'the world's biggest health-insurance plan', early details suggest that as with other initiatives there is a lot that will depend on implementation. For example, the government set aside about US$300 million (0.01 per cent of the GDP) as the scheme's first year budget. On the other hand, the *Economist* magazine notes that the government is offering 'bargain basement' prices to hospitals that sign on to the scheme. For example, the government would offer US$550 for inserting a cardiac stent.[141] This suggests a long period of negotiations between the government, insurers and healthcare providers can come up with a sustainable financial model. Keeping these types of challenges in mind, the *Economist* sums it up well: 'The one thing everyone knows about insurance is, read the fine print.'[142]

Progress in infrastructure even as gaps persist

India suffers from chronic deficiencies in infrastructure. Despite substantial progress in building national highways, rural roads, airports and ports, power stations and railway lines, there is still a lot more to do. According to the Global Infrastructure Outlook, an initiative of the G20, India will need US$4.5 trillion in infrastructure investment by 2040.[143]

Based on current projections, India faces a funding gap of about US$500 billion over this period. Beyond financing, infrastructure development requires much stronger state capacity in the form of laws, policies, institutions and programmes. In 2014, when the BJP took over the reins of power, the investment cycle had stalled and the government made a conscious choice to increase public spending on infrastructure as a way of making a fresh start.[144] However, as government officials themselves have noted, infrastructure development is a function of funding as well as capacity development, both of which have improved over time.

The sharp decline in crude oil prices over the first three years of the Modi government's tenure helped create the fiscal space to increase public investment at a time when private-sector investments were sluggish. As we shall see, the Modi government did use this opportunity to shore up infrastructure investments. However, as one would expect, there is much more to do. While infrastructure is a broad area, I will focus on three key aspects of it: roads, power and housing.

ROADS: The Modi government's big push came in the roads sector. Highway construction picked up sharply and even the rural-roads sector received a boost after a slowdown in the last few years of UPA2. The government announced the Bharatmala Pariyojana, which aims to create forty-four new national corridors and connect some 550 districts through trunk roads, with 'special attention' to connecting backward and tribal areas, tourist or religious areas, border and coastal areas, and trade routes. Having earmarked a whopping Rs 5.35 lakh crore for its implementation, Modi also hopes to generate employment through this programme.

On rural roads, the government often claimed that the flagship PMGSY constructed roads at a faster pace under the Modi government than under the UPA. However, the record indicates that under the Modi government, the PMGSY constructed roads at a clip of 134 km per day in 2017–18, which is the highest under the current government, whereas, under the UPA, in 2009–10, the PMGSY achieved almost 164 km/day of road construction. Having said that, it is also a fact that in the last few years of UPA2, it slowed down considerably and picked up after the Modi government took over.[145]

POWER: Being the fastest-growing economy, demand for power is only going to increase over time. According to India's draft National Energy Policy, energy demand in 2040 will be 4.5 times higher than it was in 2012 (NITI Aayog, n.d.). The government focused on a few major initiatives to help alleviate problems in the power sector. First, the prime minister made a public commitment to electrify about 18,000 villages that remained without an electric connection at the time he took office. For this purpose, the government launched the Deen Dayal Upadhyaya Gram Jyoti Yojana (DDUGJY).

Many, including I, have pointed out that past efforts had electrified 97 per cent of villages before Modi took over. The UPA government had electrified over 1 lakh villages during its two terms under the Rajiv Gandhi Grameen Vidyutikaran Yojana (RGGVY). What surprised me was that in talking about these 18,000 villages, the Modi government would make it seem like the other lakhs of electrified villages did not exist. When the government officially declared all villages electrified, the message it wanted to send out was that it deserved credit for 100 per cent of the work.

As the PM has also noted, 100 per cent electrification does not mean all households receive electricity. Millions of households remain without power even though their villages receive electricity. As of April 2018, less than 8 per cent of all newly electrified villages had all households connected. The government aims to electrify all households (under the Pradhan Mantri Sahaj Bijli Har Ghar Yojana—Saubhagya, a US$2.5 billion project) by March 2019. This would be a tremendous achievement. However, analysis of government data indicates that the target pace of implementation as of early 2018 is slow and meeting targets is unlikely.[146]

A challenge beyond this one will be to ensure a reliable power supply. This requires a lot of work with distribution companies, which have been under stress for years. The power sector's debt levels stood at Rs 4.8 lakh crore in 2018.[147] To address the problems of DISCOMs (distribution companies), the Modi government launched the Ujwal DISCOM Assurance Yojana (UDAY). Its objectives included: improving operational efficiencies of DISCOMs, reducing cost of power, reducing interest costs of DISCOMs, and enforcing financial discipline on DISCOMs. However, they have not yet seen the operational turnaround the government expected.[148] As the latest Economic Survey noted, 'UDAY is not a panacea for addressing fiscal situations though it has had a significant impact on addressing the structural issues attached with the power sector.'[149]

Modi has also promoted energy-efficient programmes like the National LED programme (Unnat Jyoti by Affordable LEDs for Al, or UJALA, and Street Lighting National Programmer, or SLNP come under it) and for pushing electric vehicles. While Modi has heavily promoted solar, recent moves to increase tariffs on the import of solar equipment from China and Malaysia will likely hurt the target of producing 175 GW of renewable energy by 2022. As of now, of India's set capacity of 344 GW, 70 GW is renewable (22 GW being solar). According to the ministry of new and renewable energy, 'Solar energy capacity has increased by over 8 times from 2.63 GW in 2014 to 22 GW and the wind energy capacity increased by 1.6 times from 21 GW in 2014 to 34 GW.'[150]

HOUSING: Modi's biggest contribution to affordable housing is the Pradhan Mantri Awas Yojana (PMAY) launched in 2015. This is the first step towards fulfilling Modi's election promise to provide low-cost (pucca) housing, fully equipped with water, electricity and toilet facilities. Originally intended only for economically weaker sections and low-income groups, the scheme now includes middle-income families as well. The upper limit for loans with interest benefit (Credit Linked Subsidy Scheme, or CLSS, of 3–6.5 per cent) increased to Rs 12 lakh. The carpet area for these houses also went up by 33 per cent.

In the past three years, 54 lakh houses received sanction under this scheme (though latest data shows only 16 per cent completion rate). A closer look at the PMAY shows that the government revised the target housing numbers twice already (and quietly so), from 1.8 crore to 1.2 crore and to 1 crore. Along with the PMAY, support from the National Housing Bank is another way to increase the share of mortgage contribution to GDP (currently a mere 9 per cent).[151] With the Real Estate Regulation Act (RERA), the government hopes to see more transparency in the real-estate sector and increased activity, especially since NPAs and demonetization hit the sector hard. Though there had been an announcement of a Model Tenancy Act and National Rental Housing Policy, their introduction is unlikely for now.

Trade policy is regressing

As discussed in Chapter 1, the 1991 reforms helped liberalize external trade. Since that time, we have seen trade as a share of the GDP grow rapidly. In 1990–91, merchandise trade as a per cent of the GDP stood at 13.1. By 2008–09, this ratio increased to 43.5 per cent. Policies such as import substitution, industrial licensing and reservation of some products for small-scale industries had kept India's export competitiveness in check.[152] In recent years, India's merchandise exports have declined sharply as has the ratio of trade to the GDP (28.7 per cent in 2017–18, as per World Development Indicators). Nevertheless, there is broad consensus in India that it must become a major trade player if it has to sustain high growth and lift living standards.

In its early years, the Modi government made it a point to show a willingness to remain open to trade and investment. Modi's foreign visits showcased India as a partner in commercial relations. Even when other countries started giving in to populist, anti-trade rhetoric, India positioned itself as being open to doing business. A key factor in India's stance was PM Modi's

Make in India initiative. As is now well established, modern manufacturing has thrived on well-connected, global supply chains. It was in India's interest to maintain a robust, pro-trade policy framework. And that is precisely what happened in the early years of the government.

Recent events seem to have cast a shadow on this story, though. Rising protectionism and incipient trade wars involving the United States and China have led to major challenges for emerging markets such as India. In early 2018, PM Modi went to the World Economic Forum (WEF) and declared that India was open for business. Within a month of that speech, his government raised import duties to their highest level in three decades.[153] Of course, there is context to this since the United States imposed tariff hikes on steel and aluminium, hurting exporters such as India.

As Arvind Panagariya pointed out in a column that railed against India's protectionist turn, the 2018–19 budget sought to return India to the old days of import substitution. In fact, as Panagariya notes, the government appointed a task force to cut 'imports of items that India can produce at home'.[154] Panagariya is careful not to blame the political leadership for this import-substitution impulse. From his perspective, 'bureaucratic forces have regrouped to return India to import substitution'.[155] While I am sympathetic to Panagariya's impassioned defence of free trade, I find complaints about Indian bureaucrats unpersuasive. One can't write paeans to Modi's successes and then claim that failures result from a 'decisive' and 'bold' leader being steamrolled by India's pliant civil servants.

Be that as it may, the instinct to build barriers to open trade has brought together both critics and admirers of Modi. Mihir Sharma, writing in the context of negotiations related to Regional Comprehensive Economic Partnership, or RCEP, a major trade deal, argues that there was a real chance that India's 'obstructionism' could lead to its exclusion from the pact. India's concerns about RCEP are not entirely without logic. Even so, Sharma notes, there appears to be fear of competition in India. In the RCEP case, while India may not be in an ideal situation, Sharma believes that staying out of the pact reinforces a tendency towards the old days of protectionism. As it is, tariffs have gone up on 400 products in the last two years.[156]

As with Panagariya, Sharma makes a strong plea for an open India: 'An India that retreats from the turnpike of world trade to the dirt road of autarky is one that will be poorer in both the medium- and long-term.'[157] Warnings have also come from outside the country. AEI's Sadanand Dhume cautioned, 'Historically, high tariffs bred corruption as rival businessmen lobbied politicians to manipulate duties. The tariffs also inflicted shoddy and needlessly expensive products on Indian consumers.'[158] Richard Rossow at the Center for Strategic and International Studies (CSIS) issued a stark warning, 'India has taken a dramatic protectionist turn. The scale of India's protectionist leap is surprising and likely to elicit a strong response from the United States and other major trading partners.'[159]

When Modi took office, most of us did not think of this as the type of transformation India needed. Many have tried to keep track of all of the BJP's reform proposals and election promises. As expected, the government delivered on some proposals, others are a work in progress, while still others remain untouched. The CSIS, a Washington DC think tank, provides an interesting accounting of such reforms. CSIS tracked thirty reform proposals and categorized them by degree of difficulty.[160] Of these thirty, the Modi government had completed nine, while seven were incomplete. The remaining fourteen reforms were at different stages of implementation. Of the ten reforms listed as 'difficult' to achieve, only two had reached completion at the time of writing this book. But that's the way things go when it comes to economic stewardship—some things are easier to implement, while other things take longer. That's how I see the work of previous governments and in that sense, Modi has continued a tradition that is fairly mainstream in international development. Having said that, it is now time to focus on the impact of the Modi government's policies and programmes. How did the economy and citizens fare? For that we turn to Chapter 4.

4

The Results

'The difficulty lies not so much in developing new ideas as in escaping from old ones.'—John Maynard Keynes

For any government, it is important to demonstrate that it can back its words up with action and, more importantly, results. When PM Modi took office, especially with a reputation for being an effective manager, there was a belief that his government's tenure would be transformational. Frankly, that is what Modi conveyed before becoming prime minister and also during these last fifty-five months. The BJP coined the slogan 'New India' and frequently promoted hashtags like #TransformingIndia on social media. As I mentioned in Chapter 1, on 16 May 2014, I too felt that perhaps India had reached an inflexion point. Like most Indians, I was convinced that this time it would be different: we had a government led by a political party that had sufficient numerical strength to form a government on its own, a leader with a formidable reputation of leadership and administrative acumen, with only a battered Opposition to contend with. Modi could do anything, it seemed. Perhaps Modi was right:

he would do in sixty months what others had not done in sixty years.

As a member of the Congress party, I was depressed that we had lost so badly. At the same time, I felt that perhaps the country needed a fresh direction. With millions of poor people, and with massive problems in agriculture, health, education, skills, jobs among others, I too was watching the situation with a degree of anticipation as to how things would unfold. Mind you, as a member of the Opposition, I was not about to give up on holding the government accountable. I did not want to be critical for the sake of being critical. What I was concerned about was the cost of Modi's development politics. I see the RSS and the BJP as having an agenda that is antithetical to the fundamental tenets of the Indian Constitution. So, I was concerned that if Modi and team did really well in development terms, it could be at the cost of irreparable damage to India's social fabric.

With this thought lingering in my mind, I went to meet a senior Congress leader and expressed my concerns to him. Surprisingly, I found the leader to be rather nonchalant. He allayed my fears and said, and I am paraphrasing, that the UPA had been in power for ten long years and fatigue had set in. He also spoke of a degree of arrogance that had crept in, especially among some ministers. His view was that the BJP should now shoulder the burden and that the Congress needed to take a breather. I received a jolt. Here we were, saddled with the worst defeat in history, and this leader was talking about the BJP shouldering the responsibility of dealing with the country. He took it a step further. He said that the BJP would unravel on its own because 'they don't have the experience', and that Modi's centralization instincts would not suit a big and diverse country such as ours. I must admit that I left that meeting feeling somewhat dejected. It was almost as if some of our seniors had given up. But this idea that the BJP might falter on its own stuck with me. It provides useful context to understanding the performance of the Modi government.

The other thing I have tried to keep in mind is my training at the World Bank, with which I have been associated since 1995. When I joined the World Bank's Operations Evaluation Department (now called Independent Evaluation Group), I began learning about measuring results. Our job was to assess the World Bank Group's performance at the project and country levels. I also saw the World Bank evolve its approach to evaluation by insisting that we should not only be concerned with 'inputs' that are associated with development programmes, but also ascertain how our support was producing 'outputs' and ultimately helping our clients (typically governments) achieve 'outcomes' and 'impacts' in the service of their citizens. So, it was not enough that the World Bank gave money to developing country governments. We had to assess proper utilization of funds, and if that really helped improve people's lives. If we use that kind of framework, I would argue that we focus not only on *saaf niyat* (good intentions), as the BJP and PM Modi have been arguing of late, but on achievements instead. For instance, as a policy matter, did demonetization work and what was its impact, regardless of the intentions of the government? This is the framework I want to use for this part of the book that deals with the Modi government's performance.

One more thing. We must understand that India's Central government is not the only one responsible for India's economic development. State governments play a very important role in this process. Of course, the private sector, corporates as well as small businesses, millions of self-employed people and a billion plus consumers—they all play a part. However, to the extent that the Central government has an outsized role in the stewardship of the economy, and that is the premise of this book as well as Modi's prime-ministership, we will assess the Indian economy's performance over these last five years in this specific context.

If the economy does extremely well and is genuinely transformed, PM Modi will claim credit and he shall receive it. At the same time, if the country's economic performance is below expectation, the government should expect to receive blame. Again, I want us to remember that we are looking for a transformation of the Indian economy under PM Modi. From Modi's perspective, his inheritance was meagre and he pursued his promise of transformation through a set of policies and programmes, some of which were grand in scale. It is time to understand if the results meet the high bar set by the prime minister himself.

As any student of economics will tell you, a review of macroeconomic indicators is as good a way as any when assessing the performance of an economy. People are familiar with terms such as economic growth, fiscal deficit (or surplus), current account deficit (or surplus), inflation, etc. Once we complete a review of these overarching results, we can focus on specific sectors such as manufacturing and agriculture as well as results of key government initiatives and schemes. These types of indicators can help us determine the effectiveness of policies and programmes implemented by the government. Of course, we are also interested in the outcomes and impacts of the government's policy framework, which will lead us to a discussion on job creation, health and education, and overall quality of life.

Incrementalism versus big-bang reforms

The growth of economic output has become a fairly mainstream concept. Economic growth is necessary for reducing poverty and improving living standards. I will discuss the 'quality of growth' or if the growth is inclusive later in the book. However, GDP growth rates do bring praise or opprobrium to governments. I would frequently share the economic growth numbers achieved under the UPA when I would defend that government's record. In the days prior to the 2014 election, I felt that India had done relatively well and achieved historically high growth rates. Of course, economic growth was relatively low in the last two years, and that is where the narrative against the UPA government took hold.

In the Modi government's first year, India's macroeconomic situation appeared to stabilize. To assess how things changed after the Modi government took over, it is useful to review the government's Economic Surveys of 2013–14 and 2014–15. The Economic Survey, released just before the annual budget presentation, shows a retrospective view of the economy's performance, whereas the budget is a forward-looking document that establishes the government's revenue and expenditure priorities. By looking at these two documents, one gets a sense of how things changed in the course of that first year. However, it is also important to keep in mind that for all changes, we need to understand what is driving the change, and that is where we get a sense of the stewardship of an economy.

In the 2013–14 Economic Survey, the government reported that economic growth had slowed in 2012–13 and 2013–14 to 4.5 per cent and 4.7 per cent respectively. According to the survey, 'Sub-5 per cent GDP growth for two years in succession was last witnessed a quarter of a century ago in 1986–87 and 1987–88.'[1] As I write this, I must admit I was not aware of this fact. In any event, growth had slowed considerably. The Economic Survey went on to indicate, 'India's growth declined from an average of 8.3 per cent per annum during 2004–05 to 2011–12 to an average of 4.6 per cent in 2012–13 and 2013–14.'

However, India was not alone in this slowdown. The survey said, 'Average growth in the emerging markets and developing economies including China declined from 6.8 per cent to 4.9 per cent in this period (calendar-year basis).'[2] Another worrisome issue was the 'slowdown in manufacturing growth that averaged 0.2 per cent per annum in 2012–13 and 2013–14'.[3] Beyond a slowdown in economic growth, other indicators of economic health were not exactly rosy. The fiscal deficit ended up at 4.5 per cent of the GDP in 2013–14 while the current account deficit was 1.7 per cent of the GDP. Inflation, measured in terms of the WPI, was 6 per cent in 2013–14, coming down from higher levels in earlier years. Food price inflation averaged 12.2 per cent in the five years leading to 2013–14. That was one of the biggest knocks against the UPA government. The 6 per cent inflation in 2013–14 was still relatively high and above the 'comfort zone' of policymakers.

In November 2015, about two years after the 'Fragile Five' designation, Milan Vaishnav of the Carnegie Endowment of International Peace (CEIP) had this to say about how things had changed: 'In the two years since India was added to the ignominious "Fragile Five" club, it has engineered a remarkable reversal of fortune.'[4] In 2014–15, India's economic growth stood at 7.4 per cent and the fiscal deficit was contained at 4.1 per cent of the GDP.[5] Vaishnav noted that the IMF's World Economic Outlook had certified India as the fastest-growing economy, China and other emerging markets had 'cooled off', inflation had been reduced sharply and the current account deficit was expected to be about 1 per cent of the GDP.

Clearly, the macroeconomic situation had improved, but there are two points that Vaishnav raised in his policy brief that merit attention. Before that, however, we need a small digression on the calculation of GDP growth and how the 7.4 per cent growth rate mentioned above was not comparable to the 4.7 per cent achieved in 2013–14.

In January 2015, the Central Statistical Office (CSO) changed the methodology for calculating GDP. There were two main changes. First, the base year for estimating national accounts aggregates such as GDP changed from 2004–05 to 2011–12. This is a normal change and occurs periodically. Second, the CSO shifted to calculating economic output at market prices as opposed to the previously prevalent factor costs. Also, as economies evolve, some products and services become less important while others gain prominence in output calculations. This was in line with international practice and was unobjectionable. However, the CSO only provided estimates of economic output under the new methodology from the year 2011–12 and not prior to that. This meant that it was impossible to compare the GDP growth of the Modi years with economic performance during most of the years of the Manmohan Singh government. This issue has been very controversial and I have written extensively about it. However, for now we will confine ourselves to what the new methodology indicated about growth in the much-maligned last two years of the UPA's tenure. The 2014–15 Economic Survey showed that growth in 2012–13 was 5.1 per cent and in 2013–14, it was 6.9 per cent (since then, the CSO revised these rates to 5.5 per cent and 6.4 per cent).

The Economic Survey reported these revised growth figures in the following manner: 'The economic scenario presented by the new series (with 2011–12 as base year) reveals that there was perceptible improvement in some of the macro-aggregates of the economy in 2013–14, which got strengthened in 2014–15.'[6] Vaishnav also noted that the Modi government inherited an improving economy. In pointing to the recovery in India's economic trajectory, Vaishnav suggests, 'In truth, India's stabilization programme began in the waning months of UPA's tenure when then-Finance Minister Palaniappan Chidambaram and Reserve Bank of India (RBI) Governor Raghuram Rajan championed a series of remedial steps to get India's economic house in order. The BJP government, for its part, reaffirmed this commitment to stabilization.'[7]

The 2014–15 Economic Survey provides further evidence of a recovering economy towards the end of the UPA's tenure. While growth was recovering, the fiscal deficit and inflation had shown a significant downward trajectory and the current account deficit was a mere 0.7 per cent of the GDP in the final quarter of 2013–14. The manufacturing sector grew at 6.2 per cent and 5.3 per cent in 2012–13 and 2013–14, respectively. The services sector was responsible for much of the recovery in 2013–14, 'trade and repair services, rail transport, communication and broadcasting services and miscellaneous services achieved double-digits/close to double-digits growth during the year'.[8] The survey also notes that 'agriculture and allied sectors—including crops, livestock, forestry and logging, and fishing—picked up growth in 2013–14'. This was partly due to an 'exceptionally good year' in terms of rainfall that year.[9]

The popular narrative in India is that the Modi government inherited an economic mess and in an astonishingly quick time, the new government's efforts led India to become the fastest-growing (large) economy. As indicated in the government's own reports, that is simply not true. However, macroeconomic performance did improve during Modi's first year. Growth picked up to above 7 per cent, the fiscal deficit declined to 4.1 per cent of the GDP, inflation slowed sharply to below 5 per cent and the current account deficit ended up close to 1 per cent of the GDP. These improvements are indisputable. However, one big factor that aided the Modi government's record was a stroke of good fortune.

Vaishnav argues, 'While it would be churlish to deny the Modi government credit for macroeconomic stabilization and resuscitating the investment cycle, it would be equally shortsighted to dismiss the role of relatively benign global economic conditions.' These benign conditions included a historic collapse in global crude prices, which had a major positive impact on growth, fiscal deficit and inflation. Vaishnav also puts India's relative growth performance in context by noting that India's peers were not doing as well at the time. Brazil was contracting, Russia's economic growth was 'negative' and China's shift from investment to domestic consumption was slowing its economy. The challenges faced by India's peers made its own 'economic success shine even brighter in comparison'.[10]

Why is crude oil that important? Crude oil is the biggest portion of India's import bill and its prices impact economic growth, the fiscal and current account balance as well as inflation. According to the Economic Survey 2014–15, 'Since June 2014 (until the end of FY2014–15), India has experienced a very favourable terms-of-trade shock as a result of a 50–55 percent decline in the price of crude-oil and other commodities.' The downward trend in crude oil prices continued in 2015–16 when in January 2016, oil prices fell below US$28 per barrel.[11]

So, how did the decline in crude prices help the Modi government? An analysis by the *Mint* newspaper showed that 'almost the entire reduction of about 0.6% of the gross domestic product (GDP) in India's fiscal deficit between FY14 and FY16 could be attributed to the sharp fall in crude prices'.[12] The current account balance improved. The government liberalized diesel prices sooner than anticipated on account of this sharp decline. However, instead of passing on the benefits of lower crude prices to consumers, the government retained much of the gain through progressively higher excise duties on petroleum products.

The difference in crude prices during the Modi government's tenure and that of the UPA, especially UPA2, is telling. Between 2011 and 2014, crude prices averaged US$108.5 per barrel. Between 2015 and 2017, crude prices averaged only US$59.3.[13] This obviously helped the economy improve and led the Opposition to remark that the Modi government was 'lucky' to have taken over to harvest an oil bonanza. To this, the prime minister remarked, 'Ok, let's accept that I am lucky but you have saved money. If Modi's luck is benefitting the people, what can be more fortunate? If because of my good luck, prices of petrol and diesel get reduced and common man saves more, then what is need for bringing someone who is unlucky?'[14]

Writing on this remarkable turn of events, Harish Damodaran, a columnist, noted in a February 2015 article, 'In 2012–13 and 2013–14, the total under-recoveries to state-owned oil marketing companies on sale of petroleum products—which has to be borne by the Centre either directly as subsidy or lower dividend revenues—amounted to Rs 161,029 crore and Rs 139,869 crore, respectively. But today, there are no under-recoveries on diesel

(Rs 92,061 crore and Rs 62,837 crore in the two years), even as
the Centre has de-controlled prices of this fuel.'[15] With oil imports
soaking up less foreign exchange, Damodaran and other analysts
expected the rupee to gain and the RBI to have more breathing
room for interest-rate cuts, which could help push growth rates
higher. At least that is how it was supposed to be.

Milan Vaishnav's early review of the Modi government's
performance had two especially interesting points. The first was
about not only giving the new government credit for an improved
economy but also acknowledging that the economy was already
recovering under the UPA government. The second interesting
point noted by Vaishnav and many other economists and analysts
was the absence of 'big bang' reforms by the Modi government,
at least until that time. Vaishnav notes, 'Many observers have
been surprised by how cautiously the government has proceeded
on the economic reform front, given the government's unique
electoral mandate and Modi's campaign promises that he would
administer "bitter medicine" to the country by taking tough
economic decisions to right India's economic affairs.'[16]

At the time, it was indeed puzzling for many, including some
of Modi's supporters and well-wishers, to see that the government
was pursuing what Vaishnav called 'creative incrementalism'. Let
us first turn to some of the commentary on this big-bang-versus-
incrementalism approach to get a sense of how much this mattered.

As discussed earlier, Modi's rhetoric and reputation led most
observers, though not all, to think that big-bang reforms were
imminent. What are big-bang reforms? If the 1991 reforms liberalized
trade and eliminated the worst excesses of the infamous Licence Raj,
subsequent reforms were about gradual changes in a number of areas.
However, after the high-growth period under the UPA government,
especially its first term, the need for deeper reforms was clear. Some
of the reforms that economists and commentators, especially on the
right, had been pushing included privatization of inefficient, loss-

making PSUs, broad subsidy reform, far-reaching labour reforms, and radical changes in the tax code (both direct and indirect).

It would be disingenuous to argue that Modi did not accomplish anything or that there were no reforms. That is because he did accomplish reforms in some areas. However, his record has been far from transformational. As late as August 2018, Sadanand Dhume of the AEI summed it up in this manner: 'When Narendra Modi became India's prime minister in 2014, he styled himself as a business-friendly politician with a Thatcherite zeal for "minimum government". As he gears up for next year's general election, Mr. Modi sounds more like a tub-thumping Latin American populist.'[17] Modi's ardent supporters do not share this harsh assessment, but it isn't as if analysts such as Dhume wished anything but success for the prime minister.

In the early years of his tenure, Modi went especially slow on reforms and his incrementalism clearly annoyed some of his well-wishers. Writing just a few months after Modi took office, Bibek Debroy complained in an article that the 'promised redesign of governance was about revamping systems and institutions, not repopulating them with those who are now the favoured few. This requires shock therapy, not halting and incremental steps.' He went to lament, 'NDA is nothing but UPA with better implementation. But the campaign message didn't quite ring that way.'[18] The government recruited Debroy as a member of the NITI Aayog, the successor institution to the erstwhile and much-maligned Planning Commission.

Surjit Bhalla, a columnist and long-time Modi supporter, expressed dismay when instead of reforms, the Modi government seemed to back away from key World Trade Organization (WTO) agreements. He seemed apoplectic in noting, 'India is making itself a laughing stock in the eyes of the world community (perhaps it does not matter) by violating agreements it made just six months earlier when it made the WTO accept its unreasonable demands.'[19] Bhalla would later become a member of the Prime Minister's Economic Advisory Council (PMEAC).

In the early months, even Panagariya was concerned about the government's trajectory. He wondered if the 2015–16 budget will spell out 'the government's policy vision and reform strategy clearly or will it be yet another document by the same finance ministry bureaucrats that chooses continuity over growth and jobs for the masses'?[20] Panagariya, also a Modi supporter, became NITI Aayog's first vice chairperson. Interestingly, and I am not a conspiracy theorist, these three articles all came out in July 2014. Clearly, those on the right were anxious to see much more progress and quickly.

Not everyone was this impatient and not everyone believed that big-bang reforms were imminent. Days before Modi's victory in 2014, Sadanand Dhume hosted a Google Hangout with three experts on India's economy—Vivek Dehejia, Mihir Sharma and James Crabtree.[21] The topic was 'Can Narendra Modi be India's Thatcher?' The subtext was to debate if he would usher in major reforms. Dehejia was of the view that expecting Modi to be like Thatcher would be 'too much to expect' while Sharma felt that Modi has 'not yet built the constituency for reform'. Crabtree thought that Modi 'may start out moderately but may become more radical as he shows signs of political capital to change the country'.

This relatively sobering analysis ultimately proved correct when the government itself made clear that big-bang reforms were unlikely. Arvind Subramanian argued that it was 'unreasonable' to expect big-bang reforms in what he called 'frustratingly vibrant democracies such as India—with a dispersed power structure across the Centre, the states and different institutions'.[22] The Economic Survey of 2014–15 argued with a degree of finality, 'Big Bang reforms as conventionally understood are an unreasonable and infeasible standard for evaluating the government's reform actions.'

Instead, the Economic Survey argued, 'India needs to follow what might be called "a persistent, encompassing, and creative incrementalism" but with bold steps in a few areas that signal a decisive departure from the past and that are aimed at addressing key problems such as ramping up investment, rationalizing subsidies, creating a competitive, predictable, and clean tax policy environment, and accelerating disinvestment.'[23] If there was any doubt left, Modi himself put paid to the idea in an interview to the *Wall Street Journal* in which he is quoted as having said, 'When I came to the government, I used to sit down with all the experts and ask them to define for me what is "big bang"' for them. Nobody could tell me.'[24]

It appears that Modi did not see his political capital the way many of us saw it. I, for one, was certain that transformation was around the corner given Modi's sweeping victory, the massive defeat of my own political party, his oratory and genuine popularity, as well as his stature as the undisputed leader of the BJP. All this meant that Modi could potentially do the kinds of things that few leaders would dare try. In fact, in India, bold experiments have almost always occurred during times of crisis. Here was a unique opportunity to flip that script by enacting transformational reforms in the midst of political stability. Modi could craft a legacy that few Indian leaders could even dream of.

Unfortunately, that was not to be.

I won't lie. To some extent, I am relieved that Modi chose the path of incrementalism because I did not want India to have fond memories of a leader who I believe to be fundamentally out of step with values that nourish India's social fabric. At the same time, I couldn't help but hope for a better future for the hundreds of millions of Indians who are less fortunate than I. The secret is out: Despite serious reservations, I wanted Modi to succeed in transforming the Indian economy. I also hoped he would rein in the worst impulses of his political support base that were damaging to the country. It is true that I publicly opposed the Modi government but in the initial part of his tenure, I was hoping against hope that he would truly bring achhe din and promote *Sabka Saath, Sabka Vikas* (with everyone and for everyone's progress).

As we shall see, my scepticism won out and the record of the Modi government has been anything but transformational. I don't think even his supporters would contest that. His tenure has been transformational in one respect: the country is more divided than ever, regressive forces are ascendant and our institutions are increasingly under attack. That is not the kind of transformation people had signed up for.

It is not my contention that Modi has failed completely on the economy, or that he has enacted no reforms or that he has had no positive impact on people's lives. In fact, he has succeeded in some areas, pushed through some reforms and made improvements in many areas. However, that is not remarkable in itself. Other governments also have a record of accomplishments. Recall from Chapter 1 that Pandit Nehru's tenure saw a vastly improved economy compared to the pre-Independence era, the Green Revolution took shape during Indira Gandhi's tenure, the first major growth spurt occurred in the 1980s under Rajiv Gandhi, P.V. Narasimha Rao presided over the 1991 structural reforms, A.B. Vajpayee promoted disinvestment and other reforms, while Manmohan Singh introduced major welfare policies including MGNREGA and the Food Security Act.

To be sure, these other prime ministers, and the ones whose tenures were shorter, all helped build India. They also made mistakes. That is how development takes shape—a mix of progress and some missteps. The question before us is, whether or not Modi was exceptional and transformative, and if he has done in sixty months what others did in sixty years. That was his vision, and this book would be incomplete if I did not present evidence that can help us assess his performance using his own standard. To do so, I will review progress against socio-economic indicators, followed by a review of results of key policies and programmes. I will also include a brief assessment of two major initiatives—demonetization and the GST. Finally, I will conclude by assessing how successful the Modi government has been in creating jobs for India's burgeoning youth population.

Economic growth

The size of the economy and its growth rate have both become matters of debate. However, the evidence is clear on a few issues. India is still some distance away from sustained 8–10 per cent growth that the government often talks about.[25] Also, economic growth under the Modi government has been below the rate achieved under the UPA government. The Economic Survey comprehensively describes the state of India's economy at the end of the fiscal year 2017–18.[26] According to the survey, the Indian economy crossed 8 per cent growth in 2015–16 and then decelerated in the past two years. This was the only year in which the economy broke the 8 per cent growth barrier. According to the IMF's latest World Economic Outlook, India's growth in

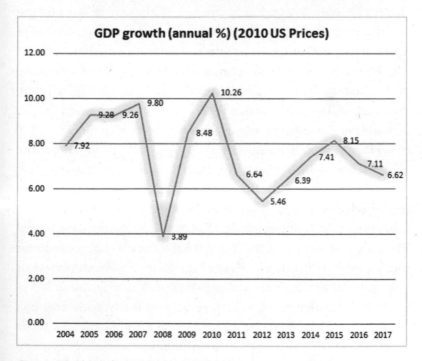

Source: *World Development Indicators, World Bank*

Modi's fifth year is likely to be only 7.3 per cent and in the first year of the next government term, the growth is likely to be 7.4 per cent.[27] This despite the fact that the economy grew at a surprising 8.2 per cent in the first quarter of 2018–19, which was the highest in nine quarters.[28]

After the release of the new GDP methodology, the economy grew at 6.4 per cent in 2013–14, which was the last year of the UPA government. Continuing the recovery, the economy grew at 7.4 per cent in 2014–15 and 8.2 per cent in 2015–16. However, in the subsequent two years, the economy grew more slowly at 7.1 per cent and 6.6 per cent. What happened? The 2017–18 Economic Survey makes important observations about India's growth. It notes that in the first half of 2017–18, India's economy temporarily 'decoupled' from the global economy— India's growth slowed just as the rest of the world was picking up steam. According to the survey, the main reasons for slower growth 'lay in the series of actions and developments that buffeted the economy: demonetization, teething difficulties in the new GST, high and rising real interest rates, an intensifying overhang from the TBS (twin balance sheet) challenge, and sharp falls in certain food prices that impacted agricultural incomes'.[29]

Having said that, India's GDP data has been under the scanner ever since the CSO changed the methodology for calculating economic output in 2014–15.[30] Most analysts were surprised after the publication of the new GDP series. Even the government's chief economic adviser, Arvind Subramanian, and the then Governor of the RBI, Raghuram Rajan, cast doubt on the new CSO data.[31] According to the *Economist* investors 'roundly disbelieve India's growth figures'.[32]

One issue that remained a sore spot for many, including me, was the CSO's inability (or reluctance) to provide the back series of GDP, which would allow for an apples-to-apples comparison between growth rates under Modi and Manmohan Singh. In

June 2016, I wrote in the *Business Standard* newspaper, 'The CSO promised to revise the GDP data for earlier years (prior to 2011–12). From a policy perspective, this is necessary in order to compare current growth with that in the past years. But more than three years later, the CSO has still not provided it. This is unconscionable as it creates credibility problems for the data that the Indian government puts out.'

This was not just a criticism by someone opposed to the government. Many analysts worry about the lack of clarity regarding India's economic output. In that article, I shared information on how the United States Bureau of Economic Analysis (BEA) revised its GDP methodology in 2013. Unlike India's CSO, the United States BEA revised GDP data all the way back to 1929! Similarly, 'In 2016, China's National Bureau of Statistics (NBS) announced that it, too, would begin including R&D expenditure in its GDP calculation. This resulted in modest upward revision of the GDP for past years. How far back did this revision go? NBS revised its GDP data all the way back to 1952.' As far as I am concerned this is an unconscionable omission.[33]

A committee appointed by the National Statistical Commission to produce back series GDP calculations did make public a draft of its report in August 2018. This report, since then removed from the CSO's website, indicated, 'India's economy grew in double digits twice during the previous United Progressive Alliance government (UPA) under Prime Minister Manmohan Singh, 10.23% in 2007–08 and 10.78% in 2010–11.'[34] This put the government on the defensive because, as it is, the comparison with the UPA years was not favourable and most certainly not what BJP promised. With this new data out, the Manmohan Singh years looked stellar. According to a report in the *Mint* newspaper, a CSO official said that these new data points are 'indicative and experimental numbers'.[35]

The government promised to release final figures in a 'month's time'.[36] Sadly, that month has come and gone but we still don't have official GDP data that can help us definitively compare growth under the Modi government with that achieved under the Manmohan Singh government. It is unlikely we will see any definitive numbers before the election in 2019. However, many, including former finance minister Yashwant Sinha, have already made up their mind. Sinha charged the government with 'cooking up statistics and figures to hide a grim reality about the economy and country's growth rate'.[37]

Before we move on to other indicators of India's economic health, there is one GDP-related matter that merits attention. The Modi government spends a lot of time highlighting its 'achievements'. This is what most observers feel was missing in the Manmohan Singh government. While the record of the UPA government has been fairly good, the previous government did a poor job of publicizing its achievements. In contrast, the Modi government does a fairly good job of making people aware of what it has accomplished. Unfortunately, it has a knack of sometimes exaggerating or misrepresenting facts, which hurts its own credibility. One such episode, among several that I will discuss later, relates to the size of the Indian economy. In July 2018, World Bank data put India's GDP at US$2.597 trillion, surpassing France's US$2.582 trillion in 2017.[38] The Modi government was quick to claim credit for making this 'achievement' possible.

In an article at that time, I expressed disappointment with the government's unabashed claim that it had made this 'achievement' possible. My disappointment was twofold. First, I noted at the time, 'reaching this milestone is a result of cumulative efforts of many governments, but I don't expect

Chart 1

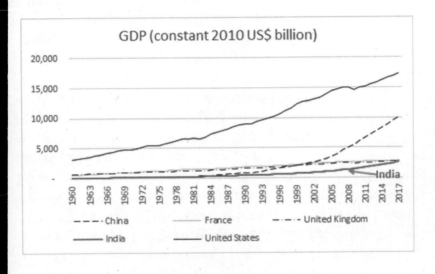

Chart 2

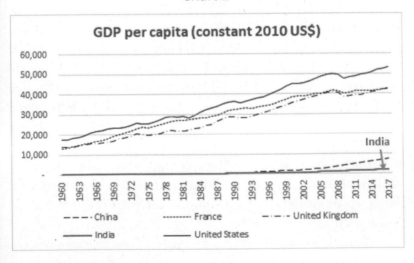

Source: World Development Indicators, World Bank

a propaganda–obsessed government to behave graciously'.[39] After all, Manmohan Singh had handed over a US$2 trillion-plus economy to Narendra Modi just as Singh had inherited a large and growing economy from A.B. Vajpayee. I shared a chart showing India's GDP over the years. That makes the point clearly.

My second disappointment was about the impact such contextless announcements have on governments as well as citizens. I argued that looking at absolute GDP numbers was misleading. 'Being the sixth largest economy is no mean feat—and surpassing France, a historically wealthy and large economy, is cause for some cheer. However, if one looks at how India's GDP translates in per capita terms, the reality is far less pleasant. With a population of over 1.3 billion, India's GDP per capita is $1,964 (Constant 2010 US$) as opposed to France's per capita of close to $42,568.' Furthermore, I found that India's GDP per capita was only about 4 per cent of US GDP per capita. To put India's struggle in perspective, India's GDP per capita in 1960 was a mere 2 per cent of the per capita GDP of the United States or France. In fifty-seven years, during which growth has been moderate to high, India's GDP per capita now is still only 3.7 and 4.6 per cent of US and French GDP per capita respectively. I ended on a note of caution: 'Excessive focus on GDP without unpacking the internal dynamics of the economy will likely lead to complacency and eventual disappointment. More troubling, our policy framework is likely to be impaired if institutions get into the mindset of "all is well".'[40]

There have been other instances of such exaggeration or deliberate attempts to misrepresent data. Former minister and senior BJP leader Arun Shourie once remarked that 'falsehood has become the hallmark of this government'.[41]

He was speaking in a different context but he was not alone in complaining about the Modi government's proclivity to indulge in 'propaganda', something which ultimately can create credibility problems for the country's institutions. Accusations of propaganda notwithstanding, official data shows that the Indian economy grew at a healthy rate of over 7 per cent per year. It is also indisputable that growth rates achieved by the previous government were, on an average, higher.

Fiscal management

Governments have a key role to play in economic development and poverty reduction. However, for a government to play this role effectively, it must have the financial resources to invest in the kinds of programmes that contribute to sustainable development. It is worth noting that the government's chief economic adviser indicated that, 'poverty reduction achieved from 2005–06 to 2011–12 was the fastest in the history of the country'.[42] This was also a period of high growth. However, the relatively high levels of fiscal deficit and inflation, and lack of large-scale job creation drew criticism.[43]

During the Modi government's tenure, the fiscal deficit retained its downward trajectory. The government can claim credit for the low fiscal deficit compared to the performance of the UPA government and it does deserve credit—to some extent. As discussed, a big part of the lower fiscal deficit story has to do with the steep fall in international crude prices. The oil windfall added about Rs 7 lakh crore (US$100 billion) to the government's coffers in its first three years.[44] Another important reason is the monetary policy stance of the RBI, which has tried to manage inflation within reasonable bounds

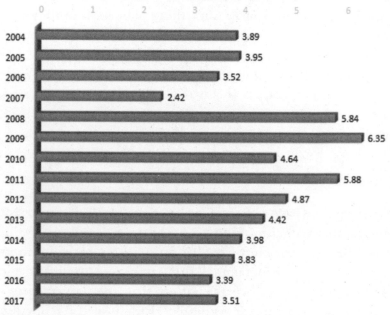

Source: *Reserve Bank of India*

by sticking to an interest rate regime that the government and its supporters oppose.

However, the government also took steps such as increasing excise duties on fuel, which helped bring in additional revenues. In fact, reports indicated that the government's revenues from fuel excise duties would exceed Rs 10 lakh crore over its five-year term with the final year accounting for Rs 2.5 lakh crore of that amount. For context, in the UPA's final year, this revenue was only Rs 88,600 crore.[45] Another tool used for fiscal consolidation was to moderate the MSPs for agricultural products. With elections coming up, the government announced a hike in MSPs, which is likely to adversely impact the fiscal deficit.[46]

It is important to keep in mind that one major way that Indian governments reduce fiscal deficits is through disinvestment—reducing government ownership in PSUs. However, deals such as the one between ONGC and HPCL discussed earlier raise eyebrows. In that case, ONGC's borrowings for the acquisition would not be part of the government's budget whereas the government's revenues would receive a boost, thereby helping achieve the fiscal deficit target for 2017–18. According to N.R. Bhanumurthy, Professor, National Institute of Public Finance and Policy, 'ONGC's borrowings to fund the HPCL deal will be like an off-budget liability for the government. It will reflect in the outstanding liability of the government, but will not be in the fiscal deficit calculations.'[47]

The Central government has managed to stay on the path of fiscal consolidation that started towards the end of the previous government's term. There has been minor slippage in terms of meeting the fiscal deficit targets over the last two years, but the government is on track to meet its medium-term target of containing the deficit to under 3 per cent of the GDP.[48]

The oil bonanza in the government's first few years also helped the fiscal situation. A report of the Comptroller and Auditor General (CAG) showed that increases in fuel excise duties contributed to more than a 50 per cent growth in the contribution of central excise revenues in FY2016 compared to FY2015.[49] Indirect tax revenues now account for 50 per cent of gross tax revenue, and 44 per cent of the indirect tax is now from central excise duties.[50] This strategy helped contain the Central government's fiscal deficit.

However, the government hiked excise duties at a time when consumer demand, especially in rural areas, was tepid because of two successive weak monsoons.[51] Would it have been better to pass on lower fuel costs to consumers, fueling demand and potentially increasing growth? That is a question researchers should focus on in future. Readers will notice that I have not discussed the GST here. Since that is an important reform, I will address it separately under the section on special themes.

International trade and current account

Over time, exports have become a big part of India's economic growth story. In 1990, exports were only 7 per cent of the GDP, whereas in China the ratio was 14 per cent. In 2013, India's exports reached a high of 25.4 per cent of the GDP (higher than China's 24.5 per cent). This ratio has come down to just under 19 per cent in 2017. China's ratio has dropped below 20 per cent.[52] It is in this context that India's export performance has drawn serious attention in recent years.

Exports have shown weakness for much of PM Modi's tenure, but this is a continuation of a trend that started in the last few years of the previous government's tenure. This is partly a reflection of weakness in global demand for product categories in India's export basket (such as engineering goods, gems and jewellery, chemicals and ready-made garments).[53] Even so, exports have grown by about 2.6 per cent over the last five years while they were growing at about 18 per cent in the five-year period from 2003–04 to 2007–08, when economic growth averaged about 8.5 per cent per annum. Clearly, global weaknesses have a role to play in this weak export performance.

External factors alone do not account for India's weak export performance. Domestic bottlenecks are also to blame. Initiatives such as demonetization and the rollout of the GST have contributed to the slowdown in exports. Agricultural exports have come down as well. Meanwhile, agricultural imports have gone up.[54, 55, 56] Sajjid Chinoy, Chief India Economist for J.P. Morgan, has pointed out that without sustained and higher export growth rates or a significant rise in domestic consumption, India's economic growth is likely to remain well below potential.[57]

Exports have revived recently, with growth at 9.8 per cent in 2017–18. However, this figure hides a deeper worry. An analysis by *Business Standard* shows that Indian exports grew by an average 22 per cent during 2004–05 to 2008–09. This growth dropped to 12.3 per cent during 2009–10 to 2013–14. However, under the Modi government, exports shrank by an average -0.4 per cent in the first four years of its tenure. Given the prime minister's desire to make India into an export powerhouse and his support for Make in India, this weakness in exports was unexpected.

More importantly, it is India's openness to trade that is causing discomfort to both supporters and opponents of PM Modi. IMF data indicates that in 2016, 'India's trade openness— the sum of exports and imports to GDP—was 27 per cent'. This compares very unfavourably to the 43 per cent achieved in 2012.[58] With the government adopting a policy framework that appears to be protectionist, India could be on a path eschewed a long time ago.

As mentioned elsewhere, Modi championed globalization in Davos at the WEF in early 2018 and warned against forces of protectionism. Shortly thereafter, India raised tariffs on a variety of products, including smartphones. This has led to much hand-wringing, including by Panagariya who has written multiple articles cautioning against the 'temptation for a return to import substitution to make a success of

Make in India'.[59] Columnist T.N. Ninan was more direct, arguing that 'the government's recent focus on protecting the home market through tariff hikes is unlikely to help exporters. Time will tell if it will serve the cause of import substitution. Even if it does, it will nudge the economy towards higher-cost production, and that is not going to help exports.'[60]

After Raghuram Rajan's departure from the RBI, Panagariya and Subramanian have also exited, marking a turning point with foreign-trained economists seemingly unwelcome in the government's scheme of things. Vivek Dehejia, himself a foreign-trained economist, wrote somewhat dejectedly, 'These departures were welcomed by nationalist outfits with ties to the ruling Bharatiya Janata Party (BJP)

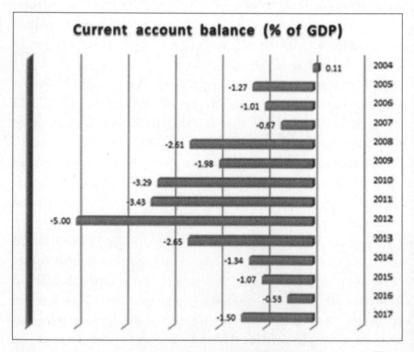

Source: Economic Survey of India, Ministry of Finance, 2017–2018

and its ideological parent, the Rashtriya Swayamsevak Sangh (RSS)—in particular, the Swadeshi Jagran Manch (SJM), which has staunchly opposed economic reforms, of labour law in particular.'[61] Time will tell if the Modi government will be able to turn the country's trade regime around. However, the pressure to liberalize further will be difficult for the remainder of his term.

As a footnote to the trade story, I want to point out that the Modi government did maintain a good current account balance for much of its term. As discussed previously, in the last quarter of 2013–14, the current account deficit was a mere 0.7 per cent of the GDP. With crude oil prices declining, India's import bill declined and that helped keep the current account deficit down. More importantly, a 'higher goods trade deficit has offset buoyant remittances from abroad and a positive services trade balance'. This has led to a rising current account deficit. Unfortunately, with oil prices firming up and a lacklustre export performance, India's 2018–19 current account deficit is likely to rise to 2.6 per cent of the GDP from only 0.7 per cent in 2017.[62] Overall, the trade story does not in any way indicate that the economy is going through a major structural shift. In fact, concerns expressed about hints of protectionism tell us that we should keep our eyes open for a different, more retrograde shift, which would serve India ill.

Inflation and monetary policy

Inflation can be a politically charged issue. However, it is very important from an economic development perspective. Relatively low and stable inflation contributes to sustainable economic development. High inflation can act as a tax on poor and disadvantaged groups. In a research paper, economists

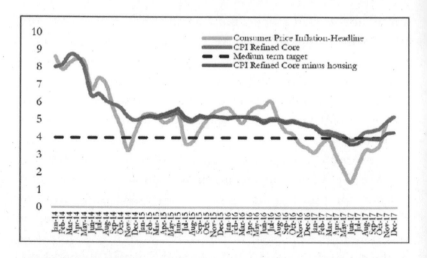

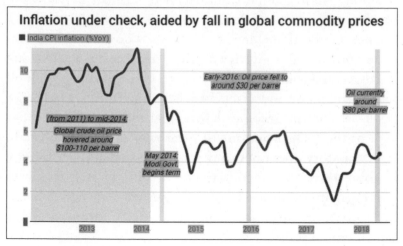

Source: Bloomberg

William Easterly and Stanley Fischer demonstrated that 'the disadvantaged on a number of dimensions—the poor, the uneducated, the unskilled (blue collar) worker—are relatively more likely to mention inflation as a top concern than the advantaged on these dimensions'.[63] They also studied the impact of changes in inflation on poverty. They found that 'high inflation tended to lower the share of the bottom quintile and the real minimum wage, while tending to increase poverty'. Readers may recall that one of the biggest challenges facing the UPA government was relatively high inflation. As the government's data indicates, there were times when India faced double-digit inflation. Around the time Raghuram Rajan took over as RBI Governor, inflation started coming down and is now well below the 5 per cent mark.

The Modi government can take satisfaction from the relatively low levels of retail and wholesale inflation achieved over the last four years. In part, this success is because of the sharp decline in global crude prices. An analysis by Bloomberg makes this point very clear, as shown in the attached chart.[64]

However, the government's fiscal policy and the RBI's monetary policy also contributed to this positive story on inflation. Low to modest increases in MSPs as well as higher taxes on fuel played a part. In addition, the RBI's relatively tight monetary policy helped keep inflation down. In this context, the government's agreement with the RBI to establish a monetary policy framework was an important reform that allows the central bank to target inflation within comfortable bounds. To implement the framework, the government established a six-member Monetary Policy Committee (MPC) in 2016. The MPC's mandate in simple terms is as follows: 'The objective of monetary policy framework is to primarily maintain price stability, while keeping in mind the objective of growth.'[65] This mandate has allowed the RBI to support a stable inflation environment, and the Modi government deserves credit for this institutional reform.

A different initiative, demonetization, also contributed to keeping inflation down. Given its importance, we discuss demonetization in a separate section. In the aftermath of

demonetization, retail inflation hit a 'two-year low' in December
2016. Reports at the time indicated that there would be a short-
term adverse impact on GDP and some signs were troubling.
For example, December 2016 saw the 'biggest monthly fall
in automobile sales in 16 years'.[66] Services and manufacturing
contracted, and there were numerous reports of fire sales across
product categories. Demonetization may have helped keep
inflation in check for a few months but, as we shall see, the
initiative undermined the autonomy of the RBI, and diluted the
positive MPC story.

Agriculture

The rural economy continues to pose challenges to the Indian
growth story. Agriculture remains extremely important for the
Indian economy. According to the World Bank, close to '49
per cent of the labor force works in the agricultural sector; the
sector uses 61 percent of the country's land and 90 percent of its
water'. It also notes the great strides Indian agriculture has made
from producing 'chronic food deficits to food surpluses and
net food exports since the early 1990s'.[67] Having said that, the
agriculture sector has suffered in recent years due to a variety of
reasons. Two successive droughts ravaged India's rural economy
in 2014 and 2015. During the 2014 election campaign, PM
Modi made an effective case for reforms, and proposed seamless
integration of agricultural products, from farms to dining tables.
However, the Modi government's tenure has not left the mark
on agriculture one would have hoped for.

In Chapter 3, I explained policy measures undertaken
by the government. However, as many experts have noted,
transformation of the agricultural sector is still far away. Key
promises remain unfulfilled. For example, Modi himself promised
on multiple occasions to make farming remunerative by offering

a 50 per cent profit margin through the MSP mechanism. His government failed to keep this promise during the first four years. In its final year, the government made what it called a historic decision to provide MSPs at 50 per cent over costs. However, as Ashok Gulati noted with a degree of angst, '. . . despite the so-called historic decision of the Modi government, the average annual increases in MSPs have been the lowest (except that of ragi) during its tenure.'[68] Gulati was comparing MSPs under UPA1, UPA2 and the Modi government.

Vivek Kaul, an economist and columnist, has pointed out that the Modi government took the cost calculation at A2+FL (input costs plus imputed family labour cost) but not comprehensive cost, 'C2', which includes imputed value of rent on land and interest on capital. The Swaminathan commission had recommended a 50 per cent margin over C2 not A2+FL, which is what the Modi government is using. Kaul notes, 'The larger point being that the 50 per cent margin over A2+FL has already been granted in the past. It has happened more than a few times in the past. It's just that it wasn't marketed as well as the Modi government does.'[69] Other economists have expressed concerns about the fiscal impact of higher MSPs but it appears that the Modi government is not beyond succumbing to political calculations.

What about other initiatives such as the PMFBY, PMKSY and the NAM? Unfortunately, the news on these initiatives is not that positive, even though these programmes use existing foundations. For example, the PMKSY is a new avatar of the Accelerated Irrigation Benefits Programme, which started in 1996 and ended in 2015. A Parliamentary Standing Committee report in 2018 indicated 'lethargic' progress on a key component of the PMKSY. According to the report, watershed development projects, which are vital for the success of the PMKSY, were lagging badly and that 'not a single one of the 8,214 projects sanctioned between 2009 and 2015 at a cost of ₹50,740 crore had been completed'.[70]

In a similar vein, the PMFBY was initially failing to pay insurance claims on time, and insurance companies appeared to be receiving huge amounts in premiums even as payouts lagged. A report in the *Times of India* noted that '17 insurance firms (5 public and 12 private) empaneled under the Pradhan Mantri Fasal Bima Yojana (PMFBY) registered a margin of Rs 15,029 crore as they paid out claims of a mere Rs 2,767 crore against the Rs 17,796 crore collected as premium'.[71]

Such news stories created a lot of anger, especially with reports of rural distress coming in from different parts of the country. Fortunately, the government tweaked the scheme to ensure more timely claims payments and it now appears to be working better.[72] The electronic National Agriculture Market (eNAM), an online trading platform, is a work in progress but its impact is likely to be modest, at least in the beginning. According to Gulati, eNAM would cater to only about '7% of the Indian farmer population, and handles only about 2% of the total value of agricultural output of the country'.[73]

Where does all this leave us as we try and understand how Modi has shaped the agricultural sector? Modi's impact on agriculture has not distinguished itself in a substantive way. This is painfully obvious when we review the performance of the agriculture sector in the past four years. Government data indicates that agricultural GDP grew at an average growth rate of 2.5 per cent per annum in the past four years. In comparison, in the last four years of the UPA government, the sector grew at an average annual growth rate of 5.2 per cent.[74]

Interestingly, investment in agriculture (measured by gross capital formation as a share of agricultural GDP) fell from 17.7 per cent in 2013–14 to 15.5 per cent in 2016–17. Agricultural exports declined from US$42 billion in 2013–

14 to US$38 billion in 2017–18. They were lower in the intervening period. Agricultural imports went up by about 50 per cent during this time.[75] Gulati notes that 'compared to 2013–14, the profitability of most major crops is down by at least one-third in 2017–18. Therefore, it is not surprising that the annual growth rate of 3.6 per cent in farmers' real incomes, achieved between 2002–03 and 2012–13, has fallen to about 2.5 per cent in the last 48 months.'[76]

I want to remind readers that even in a sector that is in the news for all the wrong reasons, India has a record of achievement that goes back a long way. I won't use the Green Revolution example again, but let me talk about irrigation in a country that is so dependent on monsoon rains. Did you know that India had more land under irrigation than any other country in the world up to 2010? India was number one for fifty years. China surpassed India in 2010.[77]

When you think of history and past mistakes, please do also think about past successes. Those who denigrate the work of past generations are likely to create more bitterness than new accomplishments. In any event, in this crucial sector that provides for millions of Indian families, the Modi government's performance is below par. Let us just say that a new opportunity to reshape agriculture will have to wait for the next government.

Industrial production and Make in India

When PM Modi launched the Make in India initiative in September 2014, expectations of a recovery in industrial production were high. To understand Modi's manufacturing push, we need some context. There are three broad categories that constitute India's GDP—agriculture, industry and services. For many years now, agriculture's contribution to the GDP has been going down (this is not unique to India), while the services sector has been going up. The industrial sector, which includes manufacturing, has stagnated despite a lot of emphasis from various governments.

Policymakers and economists have often held up East Asian–style industrial growth and job creation as a model for India. Given the requirement for creating jobs and with agriculture already employing a disproportionate share of workers, the industrial sector is an under-performer. It is in this context that PM Modi launched 'Make in India', a programme to help revive manufacturing and to create much-needed jobs. PM Modi has set ambitious targets such as growing manufacturing's contribution to 25 per cent of the GDP by 2022 and creating 10 crore manufacturing jobs. While the previous government had similar targets, they were set over a longer period of time.[78]

But things have not gone as planned, as industrial production and some key sectors have shown mixed growth and even lower growth compared to that achieved under the UPA. The index of industrial production (IIP)—which measures the growth in various sectors such as mining, electricity and manufacturing by surveying data provided by companies—has grown more slowly in the last four years as opposed to the ten-year period under the UPA. In May 2017, the government changed the base year for calculating industrial output from 2004–05 to 2011–12. Such revisions help policymakers get a more accurate picture of the sector's current composition. In any event, the average growth of IIP from June 2014 to August 2018 was 4.1 per cent for manufacturing and 4.2 per cent for the broader IIP (manufacturing is part of IIP). By contrast, manufacturing grew by an average of 7.2 per cent between May 2015 and May 2014. During the same time, IIP grew by an average 6.4 per cent, which is about 50 per cent faster than the rate achieved under Modi.

Source: IHS Markit

The IIP does not cover the entire industrial sector, but it is the most widely used indicator of the health of the broader sector.[79] On a different note, the latest Nikkei/Markit Manufacturing Purchasing Managers' Index (PMI)—a composite indicator designed to provide a single-figure snapshot of the performance of the manufacturing economy—has been expanding for fifteen months and has shown good growth in recent months. However, when you look at the PMI chart, it is clear that the growth achieved in past years was much higher.

Pollyanna De Lima, an economist at IHS Markit, which prepares reports on PMI, presented a mixed picture of trends in the indicator by noting: 'The trend for employment was particularly encouraging, with job creation at a ten-month high. Firms sought to increase their competitive edge, with marketing activity and investment in research and development, which meant business sentiment remained positive. However, goods producers see challenges and uncertainties ahead, which in turn translated into the weakest degree of optimism seen in 20 months'[80] The IIP and PMI data suggest that the news remains mixed and there is no significant break from the past growth trajectory for this sector, which remains vitally important to the prime minister's economic agenda.

One area where the PM's efforts have borne fruit is in improving India's ranking in the World Bank's EODB report. In 2014, when India ranked 134 out of 189 countries, the Modi government had indicated that it would work towards making India one of the top fifty countries in terms of the EODB report. The rankings did not budge initially but in the 2018 report, which reviews developments as of 2017, India jumped an astonishing thirty places to the 100th rank. Clearly, the World Bank had recognized improvements in the two major cities, Delhi and Mumbai, on which India's ranking is based. More recently, India jumped another twenty-three spots and is now the seventy-seventh ranked country on the 2019 EODB report.

As I wrote in an article in 2017, 'This is a big improvement, one that I have no problem in acknowledging and welcoming. Had the ranking not improved substantially, I would have been among the first to criticize the government.'[81] As I stated in that article, some caution about the rankings is important to note.

When staff at the IFC, the World Bank Group's private-sector arm, first conceptualized the Doing Business report in 2002, I was a young staff member at the World Bank. After the first few rounds, it became clear that these rankings had a signalling effect for investors and that countries were beginning to take them seriously. Sitting in meetings during the IMF-World Bank Annual Meetings in Washington DC, I would find it amusing to see government officials from a variety of countries complain to my bosses about how their countries'

EODB rankings were unfair. One of the common complaints would be about the report's methodology as well as its failure to recognize what government officials considered 'reforms'. Internally, many World Bank staff members expressed concerns about the methodology as well as the fact that governments were focusing more on improving their ranking as opposed to fixing ground realities. Over time, however, these rankings became a popular tool for nudging countries towards business-friendly reforms.[82]

When India jumped thirty spots in the 2018 report, experts at the Center for Global Development (CGD), a Washington DC think tank, were not impressed. In February 2018, the CGD wrote an assessment titled, 'A Change in World Bank Methodology (Not Reform) Explains India's Rise in Doing Business Rankings.'[83] In its assessment, the CGD noted that 'On January 12, the World Bank's chief economist at the time, Paul Romer, told the *Wall Street Journal* he had lost faith in the integrity of the Doing Business index, suggesting it was being politically manipulated.' Romer was 'rebuked' by the World Bank president and retracted his statement. However, immediately thereafter, he quit the World Bank.[84] The CGD produced a chart showing that if the World Bank followed a consistent methodology and used a fixed number of countries, India's ranking in the 2018 report would not be that different from the time the Modi government took office.

I also pointed out something else in my 2017 article. I noted that there is no question that any report that tries to capture reforms across the diversity of nations is extremely difficult to conceptualize and implement. The World Bank report acknowledges the methodological challenges of such a large exercise. Over the last several years, there have been concerns that some countries were trying to game the rankings.[85, 86]

India's thirty-point improvement in the 2018 EODB report is not unique. Russia gained thirty spots in the Doing Business 2014 report compared to the 2013 report. This came after President Vladimir Putin ordered his officials to ensure Russia improves its ranking from 118 in 2012 to fifty by 2015 and twenty by 2018. Russia was in the thirty-fifth position in the 2018 report and currently sits in the thirty-first spot, sandwiched between Spain and France, ahead of several Western European economies. But we must view this high ranking in the context of Russia's dismal 107th rank in the Heritage Foundation's Index of Economic Freedom (India ranks 130th) and 135th rank in Transparency International's Corruption Perceptions Index (India ranks eightieth).[87] This suggests that we need to look at a business environment from multiple perspectives to gain a broader understanding of what is happening on the ground.

There is one final point on the Modi government's efforts to make it easier to do business in India. The NITI Aayog prepared a report that dealt in great detail with ease of doing business in different states. With the help of a survey conducted between April 2015 and April 2016, the report, prepared by IDFC Institute, painted a less-than-rosy picture of ease of doing business in India. The report noted that 'for a majority of respondents, parameters such as setting up a business, land and construction, environment, labour,

Source: Center for Global Development.

water and sanitation, taxes, and access to finance remained the same compared with a year ago; on legal matters, they reported that things had worsened'.[88]

The government appeared to distance itself from the report. The NITI Aayog came out with a statement indicating that the report was 'meant to be a research document and its contents do not represent the views of the Government of India or NITI Aayog'.[89] The NITI Aayog took pains to clarify that the World Bank's methodology was different from the one adopted by IDFC Institute and that we should not read too much into these findings. Having said this, and going by the World Bank's EODB report, the regulatory framework for businesses has improved, at least in Mumbai and Delhi. This is cause for optimism over the coming years.

Road infastructure

Road infrastructure is critical to India's development, both in terms of how fast the economy grows as well as the geographical distribution of economic gains. During the first four years of the Modi government, there has been much progress in terms of road construction and maintenance. Of course, I am not suggesting that building a certain length of roads is the only measure of a government's effectiveness, but it is an important measure and we have data to show the kind of progress achieved under PM Modi. The other caveat is to note that

PMGSY Road Construction		
Year	Total Length (KM)	KM/Day
2004-05	15,464	42
2005-06	22,891	63
2006-07	30,710	84
2007-08	41,300	113
2008-09	52,405	144
2009-10	60,117	165
2010-11	45,109	124
2011-12	30,995	85
2012-13	24,161	66
2013-14	25,316	69
2014-15	36,337	100
2015-16	36,449	100
2016-17	47,447	130
2017-18	48,750	134

Source: Indian Express, *Public Information Bureau*

while the ministry of road transport and highways is responsible for national highways, the hugely important rural roads network falls under the ministry of rural development. Both national highways and rural roads are important and we will review data on both.

Government data indicates that the Modi government constructed about 31,000 kilometres of national highways in its first four years. This overall number compares favourably to the five-year construction achievement of 24,425 kilometres under UPA2. The government estimates that the full five-year total is likely to touch 39,000 kilometres.[90] This would represent a 60 per cent improvement over the achievement of the UPA's second term. However, there is a catch. It turns out that while the Modi government has indeed constructed highways at a faster pace, the share of two-lane highways was higher than in the case of UPA2 (76 per cent and 60 per cent respectively).[91]

The first UPA government had some landmark achievements in the road sector, including the construction of the Golden Quadrilateral highway project, which 'upgraded the quality and width of 5,846 km of highways linking four major hubs in India.'[92] The Vajpayee government conceptualized the Golden Quadrilateral. The Modi government's ambitious Bharatmala highway project is considered the second biggest roads project after the National Highway Development Project (NHDP), which was initiated under the Vajpayee government.[93] Overall, as one would expect, with a growing economy and an improving tax base, there is more fiscal space to invest in important infrastructure projects, and that is what other governments have done and the Modi government is following that tradition.

As far as rural roads are concerned, the premier initiative for building a village road network came from the Vajpayee government. In December 2000, the government launched the PMGSY. According to a government press release in April 2018, the PMGSY connected 85.37 per cent of eligible rural habitations (1,78,184).[94] The press release also included annual data on PMGSY road construction from 2011–12 to 2017–18. The data showed that PMGSY road construction had substantially increased from 85 km/day in 2011–12 to 134 km/day in 2017–18. Such press releases led PM Modi's party to claim that records were being broken under the Modi government (see tweet by official BJP handle[95]). Was 133, or even 134 km/day, a record? The short answer: No. Data from earlier years indicates that the fastest rural roads construction happened under the UPA government.[96] Have things improved since the waning days of UPA2? Absolutely. Has the Modi government's record on rural roads been far more accomplished than that of the UPA? Absolutely not.

Power infrastructure

The Modi government has emphasized a variety of improvements in the power sector—from electrifying all villages to improving the financial condition of state power distribution companies to helping spur more solar and wind power generation as a substitute for fossil fuels. Of course, India's energy mix is still fossil-fuel heavy, with 90 per cent of energy needs derived from fossil fuels.[97] However, the prime minister has set ambitious targets for solar and other renewable sources of energy, which are likely to become important for diversification of the energy mix as well as for reducing endemic pollution around the country, especially in big population centres.

The government frequently talked up three aspects of the power sector—coal production in the aftermath of the so-called UPA-era 'coal scam', reforms of the state distribution companies under the UDAY scheme and rural electrification. After the Supreme Court ordered the government in August 2014 to change the policy framework and introduce auctions of coal blocks, the government conducted auctions in 2015. A government press release in 2015 stated, 'India has hit a gold mine with the recently concluded auction of 29 coal mines in two phases. The public exchequer continues to swell on revenue from coal block auctions. The total proceeds from the coal mines auctions have crossed Rs 1.93 trillion surpassing CAG's estimate of Rs 1.86 trillion losses on account of allocation of 206 captive coal blocks without auction since 1993.'[98]

Government estimates indicated that coal-mine auctions and allotments would yield Rs 3.35 lakh crore for the states. Modi himself remarked, 'Fetching of over Rs 2 trillion from auction of just 33 coal blocks has shown that policy-driven governance can rid the system of corruption.' What these statements left unsaid was that the revenue projections were over a thirty-year period. In fact, in the first 3.5 years, the revenue yield was only Rs 5684 crore, less than 2 per cent of what most people understood to be the actual amount.[99]

Coal's significance to the power sector is immense. It accounts for 90 per cent of power generation in India. According to the ministry of power, India's installed electricity capacity was 344 GW at the end of August 2018. Coal accounted for 57 per cent of this amount. Clearly, the government was right to focus on the coal sector. The UPA government received a lot of criticism for a slowdown in this sector. However, the government's data indicates that after an initial jump in the growth of coal supply in 2014–15, it dropped subsequently and coal imports have grown because coal production has not kept up with demand.[100] This has impacted power generation as well. Overall, power generation in the country has not seen a significant uptick under the Modi government. As the chart shows, growth of power generation is not that dissimilar compared to earlier years.[101]

Generation Growth (%)

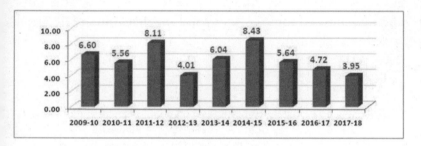

Source: Ministry of Power, Government of India

The second challenge that received much emphasis was the revival of state power DISCOMs under the UDAY. Launched in 2015, UDAY sought to revive DISCOMs, shore up demand and help resolve persistent power-sector woes.[102] UDAY, marketed as a scheme to resolve power-sector woes, suffered due to problems in the banking sector and the growth of NPAs that afflict a variety of companies, including those in the power sector. While the Modi government has managed to do well to keep the pace of power generation at a competent level, demand has not kept pace, partly because of NPA problems in the sector.

Earlier in 2018, the government celebrated reports of UDAY's success in reducing DISCOM losses. Unfortunately, the reality turned out to be more complex. For example, a report in the *Financial Express* indicated that DISCOMs under UDAY had cut their losses by 50 per cent (Rs 17,352 crore) in the year ending in March 2018. However, in the same time period, their dues to power generation companies had swelled to Rs 32,071 crore.[103] Delayed payments on the part of DISCOMs are leading to stressed assets in the power generation sector. This is fairly typical in economic development. There are so many moving parts that in spite of good intentions, good ideas and good efforts, things don't always work out well. All governments face similar situations, and sometimes things work out and at other times they don't.

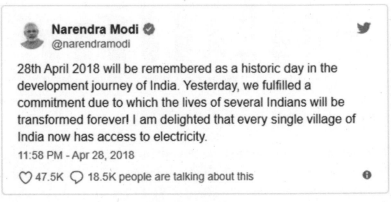

Narendra Modi ✔
@narendramodi

28th April 2018 will be remembered as a historic day in the development journey of India. Yesterday, we fulfilled a commitment due to which the lives of several Indians will be transformed forever! I am delighted that every single village of India now has access to electricity.

11:58 PM - Apr 28, 2018

♡ 47.5K   ♡ 18.5K people are talking about this   ⓘ

Source: Twitter. Accessed on 1 September 2018

This leads me to the final point in the power sector. The prime minister promised to provide access to electricity in about 18,000 villages that were without power connections in 2014. The minister of power, Piyush Goyal, launched a well-publicized campaign to ensure connectivity of these villages during the government's term. Happily, the government succeeded in meeting this objective in 2018.

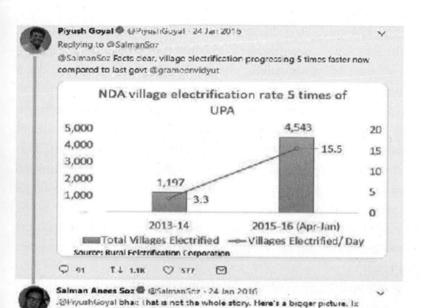

Piyush Goyal ● @PiyushGoyal · 24 Jan 2016
Replying to @SalmanSoz
@SalmanSoz Facts clear, village electrification progressing 5 times faster now compared to last govt @grameenvidyut

NDA village electrification rate 5 times of UPA

Source: Rural Electrification Corporation

♡ 91   ↱ 1.1K   ♡ 577   ✉

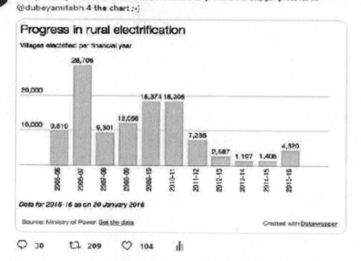

Salman Anees Soz ● @SalmanSoz · 24 Jan 2016
.@PiyushGoyal bhai that is not the whole story. Here's a bigger picture. Ix @dubeyamitabh 4 the chart ;-)

Progress in rural electrification

Villages electrified per financial year

Data for 2015-16 as on 20 January 2016

Source: Ministry of Power Get the data   Created with Datawrapper

♡ 30   ↱ 209   ♡ 104   ⅈ

Source: Twitter. Accessed on 1 September 2018

The PM celebrated this milestone with a tweet. Piyush Goyal, the BJP and many ministers celebrated this great news. However, the way the government portrayed this particular issue left a bad taste. The government conveyed an impression that past governments deserve criticism for not achieving this target in seventy years of Independence and that the Modi government deserved all the credit for 100 per cent rural electrification. This was both disingenuous and disrespectful. After all, as mentioned earlier, electricity came to over 97 per cent of India's villages before Modi became prime minister.

In fact, village electrification became a contentious issue for me personally when I engaged in an exchange with minister Piyush Goyal on Twitter. I shared with him a chart prepared by policy analyst (and friend), Amitabh Dubey. The chart presented government data on the pace of rural electrification under the UPA and the Modi government. We had a point but it was also true that the villages electrified by the Modi government and those electrified in the last few years of the UPA were the ones that were harder to work in, mostly because of their remote location. However, the way the Modi government took credit would imply that a runner who runs the anchor leg of a 4x100-metre relay race should get all the credit of a victory. In our case, the Modi government was like a runner who was running the last 10 metres but was claiming credit for winning the entire race.

Two final points are worth mentioning. First, to classify a village as electrified, power lines must connect to a minimum of 10 per cent of the households plus key public facilities. This definition prevailed during previous governments as well. That means not all households have power connections. In fact, over 3 crore households did not have a power connection when the BJP was taking a victory lap.[104] PM Modi has promised to work hard to connect all households and that would be a terrific accomplishment and I wish him well in doing that. Our fellow citizens deserve it and we now have the means to accomplish this.

The other point to mention is that Modi and the BJP have been very unfair in targeting past governments for not electrifying all rural areas before 2014. As I mention in Chapter 1 of his book, India's power infrastructure was meagre and its financial resources extremely limited for decades. The story of rural electrification in the United States should put India's achievements since Independence in perspective. After the invention of electricity in the 1880s, the United States was able to supply electricity to 90 per cent of urban dwellers by the 1930s. However, only 10 per cent of rural households had power at that time.[105] The United States completed rural electrification only in the 1960s.[106] The United States was already a major economic power at a time when India was struggling under British rule. If the United States took so much time to achieve complete electrification, I am not surprised that a poor country such as India has taken this long to achieve its electrification goals.

Investment

Finance Minister Arun Jaitley has observed that India will need two decades of investment to bridge its infrastructure gap.[107] The World Bank has quantified some of these needs. According to the bank's 2018 SCD for India, 'Infrastructure investments alone could consume an estimated US$6 trillion before 2030.' The rural–urban transition will mean that cities will have to absorb almost 1 crore residents each year for two decades. This will likely require almost US$20 billion each year.[108] The private sector will need to chip in with the bulk of that investment. However, for the time being, private-sector investment remains weak and the government has to do a lot of the heavy lifting as far as investment goes.[109] Weak private-sector investment is partly a result of stressed balance sheets and partly due to the high NPAs piled up in the banking sector, which has led to a slowdown in credit growth.

India: Gross fixed capital formation (% of GDP)

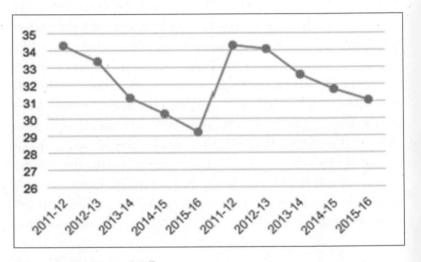

Source: Central Statistical Office

India's investment ratio (gross fixed capital formation as per cent of GDP) has witnessed a declining trend since it reached an all-time high of 35.61 per cent in the quarter ending September 2011. As reported by the Centre for Monitoring Indian Economy (CMIE), the investment ratio reached a low of 27.95 per cent in September 2017. After rising for a couple of quarters, the ratio fell again (to 28.8 per cent) in the quarter ending June 2018.[110] Along with banking, the *Economist* labelled investments as comprising India's TBS problem. As credit to industry has fallen sharply over the last few years, firms have cut back on investments and jobs. Corporate sales and earnings are weak and capacity utilization is low.

The *Economist* argues that even if credit were available, many firms may simply not borrow.[111] The CMIE analysis argues that without greater investment, there is little chance of sustaining high growth rates. The government acknowledges that without a pickup in investment, growing the economy will be a challenge.[112] However, it has so far been unable to make substantial progress on creating a more favourable investment environment, despite the initial positive sentiment created by PM Modi's focus on improving India's World Bank EODB rankings.

While it is true that the problems in the banking sector as well as weak corporate balance sheets are largely to blame for the weak investment scenario, the Modi government could have done a lot more a lot sooner to turn the situation around. To understand that, we need to discuss the situation in the banking sector. However, before doing that, let me share with you two points that are related and interesting. First, when Modi took office, there were two policy areas that garnered much attention. One was the 'policy paralysis' towards the end of UPA2. The stalling of major investment projects became a stick with which to beat the UPA government. The other issue was that there was a feeling that foreign investors needed greater confidence to invest in India. Economists consider FDI vital for India's growth and with Modi's victory, expectations of ever higher FDI flowing into India were natural. So, did the economy do much better under Modi on these two counts—project stalling and FDI?

Data released by the ministry of statistics and programme implementation (MoSPI) shows that stalled projects as a share of all projects under implementation reached double digits (11.58 per cent) in December 2013. However, for the two years following that, the Modi government was unable to reduce this ratio. In fact, project stalling grew under Modi's first two years.[113] The situation worsened in 2017 when the CMIE

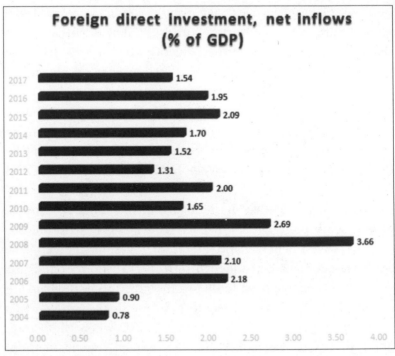

Foreign direct investment, net inflows (% of GDP)

Year	Value
2017	1.54
2016	1.95
2015	2.09
2014	1.70
2013	1.52
2012	1.31
2011	2.00
2010	1.65
2009	2.69
2008	3.66
2007	2.10
2006	2.18
2005	0.90
2004	0.78

Source: World Development Indicators, World Bank

indicated that 13.22 per cent of projects under implementation stalled in September 2017. Stalling in private-sector projects was much worse than the overall figure, with 22 per cent of those stalled in September 2017.[114]

Lack of environmental clearances is the single biggest reason for project stalling. If you recall, the BJP highlighted lack of environmental clearances as a reason for project stalling when it was in the Opposition. In February 2018, the *Indian Express* reported that 'the Prime Minister's Office (PMO) is planning to rename projects currently tagged under the "stalled" category as "shelved" or "dropped" or "abandoned" ventures, to set the ball rolling for stalled projects across the country'.[115] Recent data presented in *Mint* indicates that project stalling has declined but is still at double-digit levels (10.9 per cent in September 2018), even as new project announcements have declined and private-sector stalling is at historic highs.[116] Interestingly, this report shows that project stalling in September 2017 was 11.5 per cent. However, as you can see just a few lines above, I had indicated that a CMIE analysis (reported in an older *Mint* article) listed stalled projects at 13.22 per cent. It isn't clear how older data has improved but it could be because of the reclassification of some stalled projects so that they no longer appear as stalled.

On FDI, the Modi government has largely followed the UPA government's policies and expanded the sectors in which India allows such investment. In some cases, such as single-brand retail, the Modi government removed FDI caps. Overall, as Richard Rossow of the CSIS noted in 2017, the Modi government made thirty-seven sector reforms in its first three years, the same as the Manmohan Singh government did in ten years.[117] Some of these changes were significant while others were modest. For example, there are no restrictions in the construction and railways sector and the government approved 100 per cent FDI in defence but, as the CSIS noted, 'rejected the first and only proposal to establish 100% foreign-owned defense manufacturer in India'.[118]

Modi's early years saw a revival in FDI interest in India. In fact, of the four years in which Modi has been in power, India notched up record FDI in three straight years (2015–16, 2016–17 and 2017–18).[119] The media highlighted these records and the government basked in the adulation, as one would expect. However, I have often felt that looking at absolute FDI numbers is unhelpful in understanding the impact of FDI. Even at an estimated US$62 billion in 2017–18, which is the highest ever FDI in India, it represents only about 2 per cent of the GDP.

Speaking of which, I don't know how many people are aware that when looking at FDI as a share of GDP, the record for highest FDI inflows was set during the tenure of the UPA government.[120] While we should do all we can to attract more FDI, I feel encouraging domestic sources of investment is a much bigger priority. As a footnote to this story, the department of industrial production and promotion (DIPP) data indicates that FDI inflows grew at the slowest rate in 2017–18.[121] That is where the Modi government was not able to make much progress and that provides a good segue to the next topic— problems in the banking sector.

Banking sector

India's banking sector is in trouble. Worse, it has been in trouble for some time and its continued fragility has caused uncertainty and adverse impact beyond the banking sector. NPAs, or assets that have stopped producing income for banks, stood at 2.4 per cent of gross advances in 2009–10. As Arun Jaitley noted while presenting the 2013–14 Economic Survey, NPAs of all banks, including private-sector lenders, increased to 3.9 per cent in March 2014.[122] The government noted that the sharpest increase was in the infrastructure sector where NPAs went up from 3.23 per cent (2010) to 8.22 per cent.[123] By September 2016, this ratio stood at 9.1 per cent and as of June 2018, NPAs 'crossed 11.6 per cent or over Rs 12 trillion'.[124, 125]

It may be useful to put this latest banking-sector crisis in context. India's banking sector witnessed a crisis when NPAs touched 12.8 per cent of gross advances in 1991, before reforms helped it recover and gradually bring down the level of NPAs.[126] Over time the banking sector became more diverse, with private banks catching up in number with PSBs and foreign banks. However, in terms of asset ownership, PSBs still dominated and in 2009–10 accounted for almost 75 per cent of banking-sector assets. This was lower than the 90 per cent figure in 1991.[127]

Unfortunately, greater diversity in ownership of banking-sector assets was not sufficient to protect against a crisis. In the aftermath of the GFC, the government attempted to sustain growth through enhanced access to capital for both an expanded middle class, as well as big infrastructure projects in power, steel, oil and other sectors. PSBs were at the forefront of implementing this strategy.[128] This coincided with a slowdown in investments, as well as with a growing anticorruption movement that contributed to delayed clearances for projects. As projects stalled, banks became more cautious about lending for infrastructure investments. Credit growth in FY2016–17, at 5.1 per cent, was the slowest since 1953–54.[129] It recovered in 2017–18 and touched 10.32 per cent on an annual basis.[130]

There are no easy solutions to the banking-sector crisis. The ministry of finance and the RBI were aware of the severity of the problem. However, the problem also has significant political dimensions. The government probably did not wish to gain a reputation of bailing out big industrial houses largely responsible for bank NPAs.[131] The RBI initiated several programmes such as the Strategic Debt Restructuring process after bank balance sheet problems became public knowledge.[132] A more serious initiative came in the form of an asset quality review (AQR) in the second half of 2015.[133] The AQR helped uncover further serious problems in the banking sector. The government also announced the Indradhanush programme, which included a recapitalization programme over a four-year period, along with other ideas to help the banking sector recover.[134] However, there is considerable debate about the efficacy of the government's policy actions so far. Some experts believe India requires a transformative approach as opposed to an incremental one, but there is no consensus on what such a transformation could look like.[135]

I have long argued that the Modi government should have tackled banking-sector problems in its first year. I have laid out my case in Chapter 3 of the book and it makes no sense to repeat myself here. However, it is important to reiterate that credit flow is like lifeblood and the banking network is like arteries that carry that blood. If the arteries choke, the heart is in trouble. In essence, the banking sector choked while the government's focus was elsewhere—on land, on ease of doing business, on FDI and on politics.

The question for us is the following: Should PM Modi have invested his considerable popularity and political capital on rescuing the banking sector in 2014, instead of promoting a new land legislation or even in focusing on blaming the previous government for the NPA mess without coming up with solutions? As it is, the former Governor of the RBI Raghuram Rajan wrote in a note to a parliamentary committee that the causes of NPAs were threefold—bankers were overoptimistic, the previous government was indecisive in dealing with related policy issues and that international factors compounded the bad-loans problem.[136] Pranab Sen, a reputable economist, is of the view that the bad-loans problem was 'not just a Congress legacy' but could be traced to the Vajpayee government's decision to ask banks to lend for long-term infrastructure projects.[137]

I personally think it was a grave miscalculation to not deal decisively with banking-sector NPAs. After all, wasn't decisiveness Modi's calling card? The Modi government kicked the can down the road and allowed NPAs to fester, which acted as a drag on the economy. Some may argue that the government did bring in the IBC, as well as a Rs 2.11 lakh crore (US$32 billion) bank recapitalization programme in 2017 to reduce NPAs. However, by the time the government implemented these steps, the situation had worsened considerably. Of course, Modi's demonetization decision and a glaringly incompetent rollout of the GST also adversely affected the economy. Timely intervention in the banking sector would have helped the economy become much more resilient. I believe indecision with regard to the NPA crisis is as much if not more responsible than demonetization and the GST for creating a challenging political economy for Modi.

To give you a sense of the complexity of these issues, the RBI, in response to an RTI query, indicated that 'in the last four years of the Modi Government, loan frauds have amounted to a whopping ₹55,000 crore more than in the previous five years of UPA-II under former Prime Minister Manmohan Singh.'[138] Furthermore, Raghuram Rajan claimed in a note to Parliament's Estimates Committee that the RBI submitted a list of high-profile fraud cases to the PMO in 2016.[139] However, no action was taken by the government. Again, the politics of banking-sector NPAs will continue, but I view government inaction as a hugely important lost opportunity to steady India's economy well before the implementation of demonetization and the GST, when it was recovering.

Special theme: Summary of Central government schemes

As with other governments, the Modi government has introduced a number of schemes for the welfare of citizens. Some of them target financial inclusion (PMJDY and PMMY), others target agriculture (PMFBY), Pradhan Mantri Ujjwala Yojana, housing (PMAY) or skill development (Skill India). Modi also announced ambitious programmes such as Smart Cities and the much-hyped bullet train project. The scheme that has arguably received the most attention has been the

Swachh Bharat Abhiyan, which I did mention in the previous section. It is simply not possible to assess each of these schemes individually. However, a few points merit attention.

First, not all the schemes announced by the Modi government are new. According to an analysis by the Quint, an online news site, the Modi government renamed nineteen out of twenty-three schemes started by its predecessor, the UPA government.[140] For example, the famous Jan Dhan Yojana is the new name of an existing scheme Basic Savings Bank Deposit Account (BSBDA). Swachh Bharat Abhiyan was originally Nirmal Bharat Abhiyan while the RGGVY (rural electrification) became DDUGJY. All this should not be shocking or surprising. Governments routinely build on the work of their predecessors and that is a good thing. However, the wholesale name changing was perhaps more for BJP's politics and had less to do with substantive changes to the programmes themselves.

A vivid example of continuity in government work is MGNREGA. During a speech in Parliament, Modi called MGNREGA a 'living monument' to the failure of the UPA government[141]. The campaign against the UPA's welfare schemes had reached a crescendo during the 2014 Lok Sabha election. This anger against MGNREGA was puzzling given that the World Bank had called MGNREGA 'innovative' and a good example of 'how good governance and social mobilization can go hand in hand'.[142] Despite Modi's rhetoric, his government announced the highest ever allocation for MGNREGA in the 2017–18 budget, likely because the scheme helped to alleviate distress caused by demonetization.[143]

Second, what does it matter if a government takes forward schemes initiated by another government? Shouldn't we be more concerned about the effectiveness of those schemes? That is a reasonable proposition. The Vajpayee government devised the PMGSY (rural roads), and the Manmohan Singh government implemented it in a big way. That's the way things should be. In fact, the Modi government deserves credit for taking the UPA's Nirmal Bharat Abhiyan and giving it a very high profile through the Swachh Bharat Abhiyan.

The Jan Dhan Yojana has clearly helped bring a lot more people into the banking sector. Yes, most accounts have not seen much activity but perhaps over time, there will be economic activity through them. However, as Amitabh Dubey points out in his blog Chunauti, the Modi government inherited India's entire payments infrastructure, 65 crore Aadhaar enrolments, DBT in LPG and 25 crore BSBDA accounts that preceded the Jan Dhan Yojana. Dubey voices some frustration when he points out, 'The NDA has done a commendable job on financial inclusion, but how come it wasn't "reform" when the UPA did it?'[144]

Not everything goes according to plan, however. Some schemes have done badly and left the Modi government with a mixed record. For example, the Parliamentary Standing Committee on Urban Development released a report indicating that the government's 'six top infrastructure initiatives spent on an average just 21 per cent, or $1.2 billion, of the $5.6 billion allocated'.[145] The Smart Cities programme spent only 1.2 per cent of the funds allocated to it.[146] Another high-profile scheme, Skill India, which is at the heart of India's employment challenge, has faced considerable implementation challenges.

A five-member committee headed by Sharada Prasad, former director general of general employment and training in the ministry of labour and employment, found that Skill India was 'poorly implemented, with unrealistic targets'.[147] In its report, the committee noted that 'everybody was chasing numbers without providing employment to the youth or meeting sectoral industry needs.'[148] In a similar vein, the famous Mumbai–Ahmedabad bullet train project has not moved much even though there was a groundbreaking ceremony just prior to the Gujarat elections in 2017.[149] This is not to suggest that the Modi government is not doing its best to follow up on its promises, but development is complicated and the record of past governments needs to be seen in the same context.

Source: Twitter. Accessed on 1 September 2018

One final point on this vast topic: if one government does really well in terms of implementing something that a previous government initiates, there can be a number of factors at play. For example, when the BJP tweeted[150] that under the government's UJALA scheme, consumers bought LED bulbs at a steep discount, I had to point out that LED prices had fallen by 90 per cent since 2008 and that was the main reason for the government's ability to provide these bulbs at such a low rate. Amitabh Dubey did a deeper analysis and came away with the conclusion that the government's claims of huge savings were based on 'dodgy maths'.[151]

Ultimately, we care about the impact on people's lives. To the extent that citizens benefit, we should celebrate. That is where I want to add a note of caution on schemes that most observers may consider successful. For example, while Jan Dhan Yojana has been successful in terms of the huge number of people

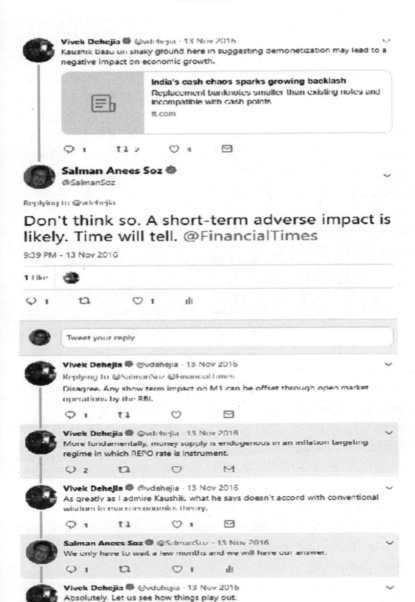

Vivek Dehejia ✔ @vdehejia · 13 Nov 2016
Kaushik Basu on shaky ground here in suggesting demonetization may lead to a negative impact on economic growth.

> **India's cash chaos sparks growing backlash**
> Replacement banknotes smaller than existing notes and incompatible with cash points.
> ft.com

💬 1   🔁 2   ♡ 4   ✉

Salman Anees Soz ✔
@SalmanSoz

Replying to @vdehejia

Don't think so. A short-term adverse impact is likely. Time will tell. @FinancialTimes

9:39 PM - 13 Nov 2016

1 Like

💬 1   🔁   ♡ 1   ılı

Tweet your reply

Vivek Dehejia ✔ @vdehejia · 13 Nov 2016
Replying to @SalmanSoz @FinancialTimes
Disagree. Any short term impact on M1 can be offset through open market operations by the RBI.
💬 1   🔁   ♡   ✉

Vivek Dehejia ✔ @vdehejia · 13 Nov 2016
More fundamentally, money supply is endogenous in an inflation targeting regime in which REPO rate is instrument.
💬 2   🔁   ♡   M

Vivek Dehejia ✔ @vdehejia · 13 Nov 2016
As greatly as I admire Kaushik, what he says doesn't accord with conventional wisdom in macroeconomics theory.
💬 1   🔁   ♡ 1   ✉

Salman Anees Soz ✔ @SalmanSoz · 13 Nov 2016
We only have to wait a few months and we will have our answer.
💬 1   🔁   ♡ 1   ılı

Vivek Dehejia ✔ @vdehejia · 13 Nov 2016
Absolutely. Let us see how things play out.

Source: Twitter. Accessed on 1 September 2018

who have opened banks accounts, researchers have found that 'the available evidence presented so far does not suggest that the precarious conditions of indebtedness that poor people of this country find themselves in has seen any signs of abating as a result of the JDY'.[152] Government schemes can be very important and they must be implemented well. At the same time, we need to ensure that they ultimately impact beneficiaries in the intended manner. This makes for a complex development framework but complexity is very much a part of how economic development works.

Special theme: The lasting impact of demonetization

I made it fairly clear in Chapter 3 of this book that demonetization was a self-goal by the Modi government. From ordinary people to experts, demonetization has come in for withering criticism. I believe that if PM Modi's electoral prospects are at all threatened in the 2019 Lok Sabha elections, demonetization's lasting impact will be partly responsible. For most economists and development experts, demonetization did not achieve its initial objectives as a weapon against corruption, black money, terrorism or counterfeit money. It also did not make a significant advance in making India less cash dependent. I will address these points next. However, for now it is useful to review the findings of an IMF study that I believe helps explain why the adverse impacts of demonetization seem to persist. I had written an article about that, and it is useful to document the main points from that piece.

While I was convinced demonetization would have an adverse impact on the economy, initially I thought it would be of a short-term nature. I recall a Twitter exchange with economist Vivek Dehejia, who was supportive of the move at the time.

Not everyone was convinced that the adverse impacts would be of the short-term variety. Economists Radhika Pandey at the National Institute of Public Finance and Policy (NIPFP) and Rajeswari Sengupta at the Indira Gandhi Institute of Development Research (IGIDR) wrote in December 2016, 'The impact of the contractionary demand shock triggered by the November 8 currency ban will gradually radiate from cash-intensive activities to virtually every sector of the economy. This will lower the GDP growth. The resurgence in growth may prove to be a challenge and may take longer than expected in an already sluggish investment scenario.'[153] In the same piece they made a point that I found evidence for in the IMF paper that I mentioned above. 'The longer the time taken to normalise the situation, the deeper will be the damage inflicted upon the real economy, and **some of the damage caused may end up being irreversible**.'[154] [Emphasis added]

The initial costs of demonetization appeared modest to some people. This was perhaps because the full extent of the unfolding crisis was unknown in the weeks following the announcement. The *Economist* reported in January 2017 that the PMI 'plunged from relative optimism throughout 2016 to the expectation of mild contraction'.[155] Investment proposals by firms fell sharply from 'an average of 2.4trn rupees ($35bn) a quarter to just 1.25trn rupees' in the quarter ending December 2016. To one expert this was a 'significant but not catastrophic' impact.[156]

Mind you, demonetization had supporters as well who were willing to overlook what they called short-term pain for long-term gain. As an example of such thinking, Rajiv Kumar, at the time a Senior Fellow at the Centre for Policy Research (CPR), wrote a piece titled 'Bye-Bye Rs 500 & 1,000 Notes: Modi's "Achhe Din" Are Finally Here'. In the article, Kumar gushed: 'This measure is a game-changer and puts the Indian economy on a radically-different trajectory. Finally, it will not be fashionable or a status symbol to wave wads of cash and flaunt ill-gotten wealth in public. Bravo!'[157] Basically, the argument was that Modi's attack on black money, financing for terrorism, printing of counterfeit notes, and the goals of formalization of the economy and a 'less cash' society were within reach. So, how did it go?

A year after demonetization, it was becoming clear that the move was failing to meet its objectives. For example, a Bloomberg analysis conducted a year after the announcement reminded us that 'a lawyer representing the Modi government informed the Supreme Court that the government believes that "about a third of the 15.44 trillion rupees of bills invalidated wouldn't come into banks", implying that Indians would rather forfeit this money rather than risk detection'.[158] Of course, as we know now, 99 per cent of the notes were returned. In the same report, Bloomberg noted, 'While detection of fake currency went up in the year ending June 30, 2017, it was "still just 0.08 per cent of total currency in circulation compared with 0.07 per cent the previous year".' Furthermore, the report observed that 'fake versions of the 2000-rupee note announced Nov. 8, 2016, have been detected.'[159]

What about financing for terrorism? There is no concrete evidence to indicate that demonetization led to a significant decline in terrorism. In fact, Prasenjit Bose, an economist, found that 'total fatalities in terrorism related violence in India have hardly seen any significant decline in 2017 (data till August 2017) compared to the two previous years, with violence in Jammu and Kashmir actually witnessing an escalation'.[160] Bose was of the view that the rise and fall in terrorist activity is determined by a variety of factors and that it could be argued that 'demonetisation has had no impact on the financing of terror, unless the finance ministry is suggesting (without evidence of course) that the perpetrators of such violence are now suddenly being able to carry on their activities free of any cost'.[161]

The Modi government added a few additional objectives to demonetization's initial ones. The finance minister made the case that there would be greater formalization of the economy, more people would become part of the tax system and that India would become a 'less cash' society.[162] Certainly, tax returns filed for 2016–17 after demonetization increased by 25 per cent. However, as Suparna Dutt D'Cunha noted in *Forbes* magazine, there were conflicting claims about the widening of the tax net. 'In May (2017), Finance Minister Arun Jaitley said 9.1 million new taxpayers were added, but in August, Prime Minister Modi said there was an increase of 5.7 million taxpayers after demonetization. Meanwhile, the Economic Survey put the number of new taxpayers at 5.4 million, or just 1% of all individual taxpayers.'[163]

James Wilson, an activist who has assiduously followed demonetization and its aftermath by writing data-packed articles, typically in opposition to the government, provides more evidence on this front. In an October 2018 article, Wilson quotes CBDT (Central Board of Direct Taxes) data to show that 'there was an 11.6% growth in the number of income tax payers in 2013–14, without any demonetisation. It then fell to 8.3% and 7.5% in next two years but increased to 12.7% in 2016–17 but again fell to 6.9% in 2017–18. So, the trend shows that there was no dramatic increase in the number of taxpayers.'[164] Wilson also notes that growth in direct taxes was much higher during the UPA's ten years (average 20.2 per cent) as opposed to the Modi government's four-year average growth of only 12 per cent.[165]

Did India become a 'less cash' society? Unfortunately, on this count as well, the answer is in the negative. Economists Vivek Dehejia and Rupa Subramanya used RBI data to show that currency in circulation as a ratio of M3 (broad money) is now approaching pre-demonetization levels. Dehejia and Subramanya argue that 'the failure of demonetisation to make India a less-cash society does not necessarily imply a complete failure of the larger digitization drive—data suggest that some components of digital payments are up after November 2016, although it is not clear if this is merely a continuation of pre-demonetisation trends or an effect wrought by demonetisation.' However, their conclusion is striking: 'Making India a less-cash society was a clearly stated goal of the Modi government. For instance, on 30 August 2017, finance minister Arun Jaitley was explicit that India is a "high cash economy" and that changing this was a goal of demonetisation. That effort has evidently failed.'[166]

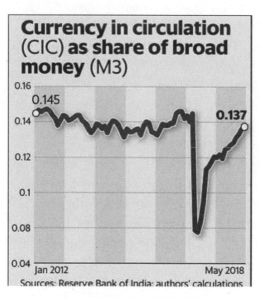

Source: Dehejia, Vivek and Rupa Subramanya. 'Demonetization Failed to Make India a "Less Cash" Society'. Livemint.com. 18 June 2018.

Of course, it is one thing to argue that demonetization largely failed to achieve its objectives and quite another to make the case that it had an adverse impact on the economy. However, even on this front, the evidence suggests that demonetization was a terrible idea. In addition to the more than hundred people who reportedly died as a result of demonetization, millions lost their jobs according to a CMIE analysis, and millions dropped out of the labour force. Those supporting demonetization contested these assertions.[167] However, let me just note that the government's own economic surveys have indicated that demonetization contributed to a slowdown in the economy.

The 2016–17 survey notes that 'GDP growth slipped from 7.7 percent in the first half of 2016–17 to 6.5 percent in the second half. Quarterly real GDP growth also shows a deceleration in the third and fourth quarters relative to the first two quarters. The slowdown in these indicators predated demonetization but intensified in the post-demonetization period.'[168] What that survey could not have predicted is that in the following quarter, economic activity slowed and the growth rate slumped to 5.7 per cent, the slowest pace in three years.[169] This vindicated economists such as Kaushik Basu, the former World Bank chief economist who had warned that due to demonetization, 'India's economic growth is bound to nose-dive'.[170]

Beyond these impacts, some economists were concerned that there would be long-term and possibly irreversible adverse impacts of demonetization. In 2017, Ajay Shah at NIPFP wrote about demonetization as a 'macroeconomic trauma'. He noted, 'Many feel that once cash is back to normal levels, life will return to normal. Macroeconomies do not work like that.'[171]

In April 2018, I wrote about the work of two IMF economists that is relevant here. Valerie Cerra and Sweta Chaman Saxena published a paper, 'Growth Dynamics: The Myth of Economic Recovery' in the *American Economic Review*.[172] In a recent blog that provides an update of the original paper, Cerra and Saxena argue against the traditional business–cycle view of recessions as 'short-term periods of negative economic growth'.[173] Basically, an economy grows along a certain trend line, moving up or down around that line. However, when an economic shock strikes, the economic output falls but, after some time, the economy recovers to its original path (*see* first chart). The Indian government and many policy experts took a similar view as far as demonetization was concerned.

However, this new study of 190 economies does not agree with the traditional business-cycle view. The study shows that 'all types of recessions—including those arising from external shocks and small domestic macroeconomic policy mistakes—lead to permanent losses in output and welfare'. This is as unequivocal as it gets when you ask IMF economists for their views on global economic matters. Even though India did not technically suffer a recession, the economy did go through a sharp post-demonetization growth slowdown. Even though the IMF study does not specifically talk about demonetization, policymakers in India must pay attention to its findings because these have great relevance for India.

Beyond the finding on permanent loss of output (*see* second chart), the study finds that economic scars from recessions and crises can have 'dramatic long-term consequences'. There is a long-held belief that poorer countries will eventually catch up with the developed world because of higher growth rates, more access to technology and greater investment opportunities. However, historical data indicates that on an average, poor countries' incomes have fallen behind and convergence is not happening. Cerra and Saxena found that poor countries suffer more frequent and deeper recessions and crises. Each time, they lose some part of the economic output permanently and, as a result, fall further behind.

The study recommends that we should be more conservative in forecasting growth after recessions and that policymakers avoid crises and severe recessions. While India did not suffer a recession, its sharp slowdown was a result of a crisis due to demonetization, a macroeconomic policy blunder. I don't believe PM Modi had any idea of what demonetization could do to the Indian economy. It appears that he neither thought through the implications of demonetization nor cared to consult experts who could have persuaded him to drop the idea. Demonetization's adverse impact is likely not over. It may have scarred the Indian economy permanently. It was self-inflicted and that is the greatest tragedy of all.

Special theme: The GST

In March 2017, eleven years after P. Chidambaram first proposed it, the Modi government steered the GST through Parliament. The GST replaces a variety of central and state indirect taxes into a single nationwide tax. According to Shailesh Kumar of the Eurasia Group, the GST was 'arguably the biggest reform of India's tax code since the founding of the country'.[174] The delay in implementing the GST was due to a lack of consensus between political parties and the state governments they controlled. One of the biggest opponents of the GST was PM Modi himself when he was chief minister of Gujarat. In his view, and he was not alone, producing states such as Gujarat and Tamil Nadu could lose revenues since taxes would now be based on consumption.

With Modi and the BJP in power, it was easier to achieve consensus on implementing the GST. The Congress and other opposition parties were already in favour of it. Many experts predicted that economic growth could go up by as much as 1.5 percentage points in the event that the GST became law.[175] A study by economists at the United States Federal Reserve Bank concluded, 'The GST would lead to real GDP gains of 4.2 per cent under the baseline assumptions, driven by a surge in manufacturing output.'[176]

Despite these positive sentiments about the GST, a thorough debate ensued. The Congress party complained that the proposed GST was too complex given that it would have multiple tax rates and a guaranteed cap on tax rates set at 18 per cent. However, the government pushed ahead with its proposal and Parliament passed the constitutional amendment and sent it to the states for ratification. Assam became the first state to ratify the new law in August 2016, while my own state, Jammu and Kashmir, ratified it in February 2018, becoming the thirty-first state or union territory to do so.

In an extraordinary move, the government convened a special session in Parliament's Central Hall at the intervening midnight of 30 June–1 July 2017 to launch the GST with pomp and show. Along with President Pranab Mukherjee, Vice President Hamid Ansari and PM Modi, two former PMs, Manmohan Singh and H.D. Deve Gowda, helped commemorate the launch of this major economic reform.[177] The Modi government deserves credit for the spectacle that accompanies what it believes to be of importance. The GST was clearly among the most important initiatives the government would undertake, and the Parliament ceremony reflected that reality.

However, the preparations behind that elegant ceremony were in sharp contrast to the apparent lack of preparation for its implementation. The complexity of the tax, with its multiple slabs, the heavy compliance burden and the breakdown in the IT infrastructure, drew howls of protest in the early days after its launch. As Arun Kumar of the Institute of Social Sciences, a Delhi think tank, notes, the GST's 'faulty design' would not ensure the expected growth dividend. Kumar talks about a variety of problems with the new tax—delayed fixing of tax rates, multiple and monthly tax returns, and the sheer volume of transactions that clogged up the GST network.

There was a lot of confusion about input tax credit and who could claim it and, as discussed earlier, multiple and high tax rates (0 per cent, 5 per cent, 12 per cent, 18 per cent and 28 per cent) caused a lot of angst.[178] By the way, as the World Bank has noted, 'Some goods receive special treatment under the GST: there is a special cess on luxury and "sin" goods. Gold is taxed at 3 per cent rate, precious stones at 0.25 per cent, while alcohol, petroleum products, stamp duties on real estate and electricity duties are excluded from the GST and they continue to be taxed by the state governments at state specific rates.'[179]

Politics also seemed to impact decisions on what tax rates should apply. During elections to the Gujarat legislative assembly, Congress President Rahul Gandhi called the GST 'Gabbar Singh Tax', recalling a notorious villain from the famous Bollywood movie *Sholay*. The government's populist instincts appeared to surface. PM Modi had coined the term 'Good and Simple' Tax for the GST. However, the tight election in Gujarat appeared to force the Modi government to reduce the GST for a number of items. Reportedly, this cost the government Rs 20,000 crore (US$3.1 billion) in revenue.[180]

The World Bank called the tax 'one of the most complex in the world', with the 'second highest tax rate' globally.[181] In its latest update on India, the World Bank makes the case that 'The introduction of GST in India is a historic reform.' It also notes, 'While teething problems on the administrative and design side persist, the introduction of the GST should be considered as the start of a process, not the end.' The World Bank also points out that 'international experience suggests that the adjustment process can affect economic activity for multiple months, the benefits of the GST are likely to outweigh its costs in the long run'.[182]

While the GST suffered from teething problems, the government pushed the narrative that GST implementation was going well. This is contrary to the facts as described by institutions such as the World Bank and individual experts. Indirect tax collections have trailed government targets, although in October 2018, GST collections exceeded Rs 1 lakh crore for the first time. Finance Minister Jaitley tweeted on the occasion: 'The success of GST is lower rates, lesser evasion, higher compliance, only one tax and negligible interference by taxation authorities.'[183]

However, as the World Bank has noted, GST collections have been lower than what the government targeted for 2018–19 and, according to some experts, the fiscal deficit target of 3.3 per cent of the GDP is unlikely to be achieved.[184] The latest information at the time of writing this book indicates that indirect tax collections increased by only 1.2 per cent in April–September 2018, much lower than the 5.6 per cent achieved in 2017–18 or the double-digit growth achieved in the previous two years.[185]

Having said that, the World Bank notes, 'Center's gross tax collection increased to 11.6 percent of GDP during 2017–18—a 2 percentage point of GDP increase since 2015–16.'[186] In an interview to the IMF's *Finance & Development* magazine, Arvind Subramanian observed, 'In principle, everyone bought into the view that it [GST] had to be simple. But . . . each state had its own political compulsions. One state was a producer of some good, and they would say, well, charge that at a lower rate. Unfortunately, politics required that we had to depart from this simple three-rate structure . . . There is still some way to go, and I'm hoping that over time simplicity will be achieved.'[187] About that, India's former chief economic adviser is absolutely correct.

It is also important to point out that the emphasis on indirect taxation in India is not appropriate. These taxes are inherently regressive. We need reforms of direct taxes such as corporate and personal income taxes. Those taxes are progressive in nature since the rates are higher for high-income individuals or entities. While the UPA government had proposed a new DTC, it didn't go anywhere. Under the Modi government, the GST was a clear priority but major reforms of direct taxes are necessary.

The Modi government did reduce corporate tax rates from 30 per cent to 25 per cent and eliminated some exemptions for corporations. However, in the 2018–19 budget, the 25 per cent tax rate applies to those businesses that had a turnover of up to Rs 250 crore.[188] We will have to see how the tax story evolves but for some years now, indirect taxes are growing as a share of tax revenue.[189] On the direct-tax side, the share of personal income tax is growing compared to that of corporation tax. The one thing I would urge everyone to do is advocate a tax system that incorporates good international practices and progressive elements that help India grow its middle class and reduce growing inequality.

Special theme: Employment and workers

Between 2010 and 2030, India's working-age population is likely to grow by 25 crore.[190] At the same time, the working-age population is likely to decline in advanced economies and in China. This is what a much-anticipated demographic dividend could look like. Policymakers have been gushing about what the future could hold for India. But, herein lies the problem. India is not creating jobs at the scale at which aspirational young Indians are joining the workforce.

The pace of employment generation has steadily decreased over the last few decades. During the period 1983–84 to 1992–93, employment increased by about 2 per cent per annum. After this, from 1993–94 to 2004–05, it slowed to 1.85 per cent per annum. During this time, the economy grew faster than in the preceding ten-year time frame. From 2004–05, the economy grew at a historically rapid pace but employment growth slowed down further.[191] After a marginal improvement between 2010

and 2012, employment growth declined sharply during the
period from 2012 to 2016. According to the Labour Bureau,
this decline in employment was perhaps the first such instance
since Independence.[192]

Most people in India are aware that each month 10 lakh people
join the labour force. What most people do not pay attention
to is that actually more people above the age of fourteen could
potentially join the labour force to seek employment. However,
the reason only 10 lakh young people start looking for work is
because India's labour force participation rate (LFPR) is low by
international standards. It is about 54 per cent, while the global
standard is around 62 per cent. By this low standard, about 1
crore additional people should be looking for jobs each year.[193]
While this shows how many new people are coming into the
job market, we also face a stock problem—young people who
enter the job market are unable to find jobs.

Another group of young people is marginally employed
or underemployed, as the NITI Aayog describes them. Using
Labour Bureau data, the CMIE estimated that at the beginning of
2016, there was a stock of 8 crore Indians who were unemployed
or marginally employed. CMIE goes on to suggest that after
the November 2016 demonetization, the ranks of unemployed
grew. This means the jobs crisis may be far more serious than
commonly understood.

Researcher Radhicka Kapoor reviews data from the Labour
Bureau's Annual Household Employment survey (not to be
confused with the bureau's quarterly employment surveys which
are based only on enterprises employing ten or more workers
in select sectors) and highlights job-creation problems from a
different perspective. Total employment fell from 48.04 crore
in 2013–14 to 46.76 crore in 2015–16. Kapoor notes, 'The only
sector to have witnessed a significant increase in employment
was wholesale and retail trade where employment increased

from 43.7 million to 48.1 million. In the manufacturing sector (both organized and unorganized) employment declined from 51.4 million to 48.1 million over the same time period.'[194]

The data presented above highlights the jobs situation in its totality. However, as alluded to earlier, India's employment structure skews heavily towards informal jobs. As the World Bank notes in its latest SCD for India, less than a fifth of the workers in India are in salaried jobs. According to the World Bank, 'India needs to create regular, salaried jobs with growing earnings rather than self-employed ones in order to join the ranks of the global middle class by 2047—the centenary of its Independence.'[195]

It is in this broad context that we should assess Modi's performance rise. Various accounts indicate that the BJP under PM Modi promised millions of jobs each year. While the Opposition claims that Modi promised 2 crore jobs per year, news reports put the figure at 1 crore.[196] Either way, Modi himself set the expectation of a roaring, job-creating economy. It is for this reason that many government schemes have targeted skill development as a crucial objective. However, despite the government's claims, the employment story now is no different from the one during the Manmohan Singh government.

An analysis by Bloomberg indicated that while India was growing fast, the link between growth and job creation is weakening'.[197] The main reason for this disconnect, according to research by Azim Premji University, which Bloomberg cites, is that there is a mismatch between skills and available jobs. The analysis indicates that unemployment remains high among young and well-educated Indians.[198] This research also indicated that nearly half of the 46.7 crore workers in 2015 were self-employed, with a third being casual workers, and only 17 per cent were regular salaried workers.[199]

The failure to create jobs is becoming the biggest political challenge for the Modi government. There are constant reports in the media about the challenging jobs situation in India. The government's response has been to latch on to questionable data on job creation to argue that India does not have an employment problem. The government jumped on a study by Pulak Ghosh of the IIM Bangalore and Soumya Kanti Ghosh of the State Bank of India, which used Employees' Provident Fund Organisation (EPFO) to show that India created 55 lakh new jobs each year.[200] EPFO data tracks formal-sector employment, and if the economy was creating 55 lakh new jobs each year in the formal sector, this would represent not only a great political victory for Modi but would also turn conventional wisdom on its head. In a television interview in January 2018, Modi claimed that 'lies were being spread' about a lack of jobs in India.[201] Modi went on to say, 'In one year, EPF (Employment Provident Fund) accounts of 70 lakh youth between the ages of 18 and 25 have been opened.'[202]

This report was debunked by Jairam Ramesh and Praveen Chakravarty who argued in a detailed rebuttal, 'It doesn't take much to realise the flaws in this analysis: New 18- to 25-year-old EPFO members do not automatically mean net new jobs in the economy; an informal job that turns formal with an EPFO registration does not mean it is a new job; cherry-picking an EPFO data point and post–demonetisation/Goods and Services Tax (GST) time frames lead to these grossly misleading conclusions.'[203] Vivek Dehejia seemed to agree with Ramesh and Chakravarty, calling their critique of the Ghosh and Ghosh methodology 'persuasive'.[204] Dehejia bemoaned the fact that 'the debate has been twisted by the authors' untenable and implausible claim that new EPFO registrations, in particular of younger workers, largely represent net new additions to employment'.[205]

For a country that needs to add over 10 lakh jobs each month, it is dispiriting to have top leaders such as the prime minister and the finance minister latch on to such flawed analysis to claim that all is well when a preponderance of the evidence points in the other direction. As Ramesh and Chakravarty concluded in their article, 'India's jobs situation is a very grim challenge that must be acknowledged, confronted and for which we must debate solutions. A serious issue such as lack of jobs for millions of youth cannot be wished away by hiding behind misleading data analysis and a media spin.' I agree with them and not simply because they are my colleagues in the Congress party. With rapid changes in technology and prospects of automation, the jobs challenge will only get more difficult as waves of young people enter the job market in the years to come.[206]

The first four parts of this book were about demonstrating that the Modi government had failed to transform the Indian economy. Mind you, lest you feel I have been overly critical of the Modi government, I have presented information that is from official sources as well as from individuals who are both supporters and opponents of the Modi government. Many of the organizations and people whose work I have quoted are independent and have nothing to do with any political organization.

It is my opinion, based on the evidence I have seen, that Modi's governance has been incremental in nature and, frankly, his accomplishments are far less impressive than most had expected when he assumed office. You may have noticed that I did not assess progress in health and education, which are vital for any economic development and employment strategy. I don't believe the Modi government has done enough in moving the needle in these two key sectors. In Chapter 5 of the book, I will discuss these two sectors and their role in creating jobs and ensuring India is set on a path of sustainable and inclusive economic development. This final part of the book has less to do with the Modi government or its accomplishments and failures and more to do with how India's economy can be prepared for an uncertain future.

5

The Future

'No economy can succeed without a high-quality workforce, particularly in an age of globalization and technical change.'[1]—Ben Bernanke (2010)

'Economic growth without investment in human development is unsustainable—and unethical.'[2]—Amartya Sen (2013)

Here comes the future

We live in a time of profound social, economic and environmental change. If not managed well, these changes can be disruptive and not necessarily in a good way. Countries around the world confront the question of how best to effectively manage these changes that are driven in a large measure by technological innovation, climate change and demographic shifts. Prosaic needs anchor these big themes—the well-being of the human race, most commonly projected through a desire to ensure a good future for the next generation. Worries about the future, especially the future of work, are dominating the discourse in international economic development. There are also worries about how unequal progress will be and if some people will be left behind. Governments and experts are grappling with these concerns even as change continues unabated.

The quotes by Bernanke and Sen touch on key themes in this part of the book. To say that technology will help reshape our future is a statement of fact. As the writer William Gibson said, 'The future is already here, it's just not very evenly distributed.'[3] No matter where we look, technology is all around us, changing how we live and work and interact with each other. It is also evolving, relentlessly, making it hard to keep up. New technologies will spur others beyond our imagination. The cycle of innovation will continue globally. It is for us in India to be ready as a nation to ensure that these cycles are virtuous and not vicious.

Along with these global trends, each country faces bread-and-butter development challenges. In India, we confront endemic problems in the agricultural and industrial sectors. Infrastructure needs are vast even as investments have slowed. The rural economy is unable to slow the migration of workers to urban areas, which remain unprepared for a large influx of people. Environmental degradation and pollution are exacting a heavy toll at a time when India's growth is enabled by fossil fuels. Of course, India's biggest development challenge is that of employment and demographic pressures. As life expectancy has increased in India, people are ageing at much lower income levels compared to the experience of advanced economies. If that was not a serious enough problem, the country's youth bulge requires a productive outlet in the form of tens of millions of decent jobs. With more young people available to support those who are retiring, all eyes are on the realization of a demographic dividend. However, lack of adequate employment opportunities threatens to become a demographic curse.

Connecting global trends to India's circumstances is a vast topic, beyond the scope of this book. However, it would be a missed opportunity to not present some broad ideas that should become part of India's development discourse. It is also important to present some principles that should serve as the basis of policy formulation in India. We can come up with sectoral visions or strategic plans, but we also need some cross-cutting principles that are good to keep in mind as we navigate increasingly complex global, national and local development contexts. The few principles presented here are not exhaustive. However, their inclusion is meant to catalyse a debate on the very need for such principles.

One of the central themes of international development is to create gainful employment for the next generation of workers. This challenge is of particular relevance to India. Reforms in agriculture or the adoption of artificial-intelligence technologies or greater urbanization, all impact the big employment question. With this in mind, we discuss employment as an overarching development challenge. To address this and other development challenges, we issue a call to action in a number of important areas. We conclude with a note on the discourse we are having in India and contrast it with what is happening globally.

Global trends

This section summarizes information from a variety of sources including assessments put forward by development institutions, consulting firms, technology companies, intelligence agencies and individual experts.

In highlighting key global trends, this part of the book emphasizes the importance of looking beyond the work of any one government. There is no beginning or end to economic development. It is a journey and we are its current travellers.

Like those who came before us, we try to leave our mark as we deal with current challenges and seek ways to build a bridge to the future, which appears both daunting and exciting. Beyond this basic framework, there is also the matter of getting a sense of how the world is evolving. India's economy does not operate in isolation. What happens elsewhere can create hurdles for India's economy, as well as opportunities that could allow India to leapfrog its current development trajectory.

There are many exciting reports on emerging global trends. As these reports note, there is a lot of uncertainty in how changes will unfold over the next few decades. However, it is useful to get a sense of the potential changes just as a way of situating ourselves in the global landscape, uncertain as it is. While technology and innovation usually dominate talk of the future, many experts use demography as a starting point. This is because we tend to think of changes from our own human perspectives. On that front, the richer countries and even Russia and China appear to be ageing. That means there will be fewer workers to support those who reach retirement age. On the other hand, in Africa and, to a lesser extent in South Asia, the population will be younger. That means the potential for a demographic dividend remains high. Of course, the caveat of a potential demographic curse is applicable to these countries. Worryingly, some countries with ageing populations are less well off. This creates a serious challenge for policymakers in these countries, many of which happen to be in Eastern Europe.

Shrinking working-age populations in advanced economies can have adverse impacts on the ability of these countries to maintain robust economic growth. Losses in productivity can create uncertainty globally because these countries have a big share of the global economic pie. China has gained a sizeable share of the global economy and may pick up some slack. However, with protectionism rising in the aftermath of the 2008 financial crisis, we need to see how robust global growth is likely to be in the coming decades compared to pre-crisis years. If global growth remains subdued, it will have implications for emerging economies such as India since a key avenue for growth (through trade) would be of limited value. To make matters worse, the liberal values enshrined in globalization are under attack around the world, and populism—of both the left and the right—may reduce opportunities for people and countries that are less well off now.

Climate change is already having a major impact globally. Predictions of severe adverse consequences, including for countries like India, are well-documented. The frequency and intensity of natural disasters are increasing and their economic costs are rising because of a variety of factors, most notably the agglomeration of economic activity around urban centres. Water stress is causing policymakers much distress and is fuelling conflicts such as the one in Syria or in the Nile Basin. Water insecurity is likely to be a key driver of future conflicts around the world. In India, states have serious disagreements over shared water resources and adapting to this reality is an urgent task.

Technology is evolving in ways that most of us would not have imagined even a few years ago. Based on experience, it is safe to assume that innovating and developing new technologies will continue unhindered and these changes will constantly reshape the world. Artificial intelligence, automation and robotics will have a profound impact on how we produce goods and services. The new Internet of things will enable connectivity of everyday-life items and provide big-data-enabled insights to businesses and consumers in ways that will be routine in the future, but which are still incipient right now. This will transform the way we live. Of course, for some of us, small changes like using Amazon's Alexa are already here. However, these are still in the early stages of development. In a similar vein, automation can transform work and likely impact employment in ways that we may not be fully able to imagine right now. We tend to focus on job losses but there could be gains as well, especially on the productivity front. Advances in biotechnology could enhance our ability to live longer and healthier. How that affects our demographic reality is uncertain. However, past predictions of a steady state for the global population may prove incorrect.

Advanced manufacturing is gaining momentum. While 3D printing is not mainstream yet, it is likely to be soon. There is already talk of 4D printing, which would allow the manufacture of products that can change their form or function. Nanomaterials and metamaterials are already finding their way into some of the products we use and this is likely to increase. The impact of these types of advanced materials on industries could be immense, and they could also have an impact on our resource base. Studying these developments could be extremely useful for countries that face resource constraints. Are these the types of materials that can help dramatically improve the well-being of their populations? It is hard to say now because some of the future technologies we read about require the suspension of disbelief from our perception of what is possible.

The preceding paragraphs show just a sliver of what is going on at the global level. There is a lot of change happening and technology is not the only thing that is changing. There are a variety of disrupters. However, technology has the capacity to help us manage the impact of all that is changing around us. As has been the case in the past, some will benefit from these changes while others will do so to a lesser extent. Some will use technologies in productive ways while others will not. It is a choice and India must make this choice as well. We face a number of critical challenges. Understanding how the future is shaping up can help us contextualize these challenges. With that in mind, let us get to India's defining national challenge—employment—and how the future may mould it. We will then discuss principles and actions that can guide India's economic policymaking with an eye to the future.

Employment—an overarching development challenge

When the next government takes over, it will have to attend to multiple challenges. Before we discuss those, however, we need to talk about an overarching challenge that is at the heart of any discussion involving India's future—employment generation. If the economy produces the kinds of decent jobs that Indian youth are struggling to find right now, the ramifications will be massive and positive. India could end extreme poverty, reduce inequality and achieve upper-middle-income country status. The table below provides the World Bank's income classification. India's gross national income (GNI) per capita in 2017 was US$1820. There is quite a distance to travel and other countries won't be sitting still. Even so, some researchers predict that by 2030, India could eliminate extreme poverty.[4] Reaching upper-middle-income status also appears to be a distinct possibility. Clearly, there is a lot at stake.

Country classification thresholds

Threshold	GNI per capita (current US$)
Low-income	<995
Lower-middle income	996–3895
Upper-middle income	3896–12,055
High-income	>12,055

Source: World Bank (as of 1 July 2018)

We should not assume, however, that growth is inevitable or that job creation will happen if there is growth. Such complacency is unlikely to yield appropriate institutional and policy frameworks because of the nature of the employment challenge. Between

2010 and 2030, India's working-age population is on course to grow by a massive 25 crore people.[5] But herein lies the problem. India is not creating jobs at the scale at which aspirational young Indians are joining the workforce. Each month, close to 10 lakh young people join the workforce.[6] Many of them hold degrees from Indian schools, colleges and universities. With a degree in hand, expectations of jobs are natural. However, there are very limited job opportunities in the formal sector, where employers often complain about the problem of inadequate skills of potential employees. Inevitably, most Indians are self-employed or work in the informal economy.

As educated youth shift away from rural areas, the availability of non-farm jobs becomes increasingly important. However, greater mechanization in India's manufacturing sector and a greater emphasis on skills and automation services could leave many without jobs.[7] Technological changes could potentially worsen India's employment scenario. Already, there are dire predictions about machines taking over jobs due to automation. Many of these are activities that millions of Indians are engaged in. ICRIER's Radhicka Kapoor has argued, 'Capital intensity of production has been increasing sharply, but recent economic growth has benefited industries which rely more on skilled workers and capital as opposed to unskilled/low skilled workers.'[8] As capital intensity grows, this will have important implications for labour and inequality.

The World Bank has predicted that 69 per cent of jobs in India are threatened by automation.[9] According to the World Bank, the kinds of jobs created in India in the last decade and a half suffer from three deficits—'a deficit in the overall number of jobs, a deficit in the number of good jobs, and a deficit in the number of suitable jobs for women'.[10] The World Bank warns, 'In a young and increasingly aspirational society, this growing jobs deficit has the potential to turn the much-awaited

demographic dividend into a demographic curse.'[11] There is
good reason to believe that jobs will be the central issue for
India in the coming years and decades. There is important work
ahead and, frankly, it can't start soon enough. Having said that,
India's next government must look at the employment challenge
as a journey. We need to create a bridge of ideas and actions
from where we are today to where we want to be in 2030 and
beyond.

Principles of economic policymaking

FIRST, DO NO HARM: This may be obvious but in a world driven
by rising populism, we need to be extra vigilant about the
implications of government policies. Depending on which side
of the ideological spectrum we find ourselves on, we could
debate the merits or demerits of any policy initiative. However,
in rare cases, there may be policies that unambiguously disrupt
economies and not in a good way. Demonetization was clearly
one such policy, even though government supporters at the
time made it seem like the greatest thing since sliced bread!

I am perfectly willing to accept that there can be
inefficiencies built into policies that create entitlements or
prolong government ownership of PSEs. However, that is not
the same as quackery masquerading as expertise, as we saw in the
case of demonetization. Future policies should always pass the
basic smell test of the 'first, do no harm' principle. If populism
makes the enactment of a patently harmful policy inevitable,
then it is incumbent on experts and those who believe in sensible
policymaking to make their voices heard and point out that their
government's proposed action is harmful to the public interest.

EMBRACE CHANGE: Change is rarely easy. However, it bears
reminding that adopting an ostrich-like attitude in the face of

clear and overwhelming change is downright irresponsible. There are plenty of experts and institutions that have sounded the alarm with respect to global advances in technology and how that might impact humans. The future of work is now a dominant development theme. Dire predictions about artificial intelligence, machine learning and robotics taking over jobs from a growing number of young people, especially in countries like India, are an almost daily news item for those of us who track international development issues.

Reactions range from dismissal of such concerns as Malthusian exaggeration to Luddite obstructionism. However, what India needs is a measured realism and an acknowledgement that innovation and technological advances (or climate change for that matter) are very much a reality that we must contend with. As with past upheavals, our generation does have the opportunity and capacity to adapt to these shifts. Instead of giving in to pessimism, we must get our heads out of the sand, remove the blinkers from our eyes and put our thinking caps on. India has a lot to gain by actively preparing for and shaping the future.

INVEST IN PEOPLE: Underinvestment in people is at the heart of India's development challenges. For far too long, sectors such as health and education have received less attention than they deserve. If Indians look back at Modi's tenure or even before that, they can testify to the fact that public discourse has little space for foundational topics such as child health, early-childhood education, malnutrition, etc. We talk a lot more about ease of doing business, enhancing India's manufacturing capabilities or growing faster than any other nation. This suggests we are seeking shortcuts and are unaware that growth by itself is not sufficient for ensuring a decent standard of living for all people.

As experience from countries around the world tells us, economic development does not happen through quick fixes. Modern manufacturing and services can't work without skilled and educated workers. Children who suffer from malnutrition or students who receive poor-quality education cannot become productive workers of future enterprises. This is just one of the many linkages between investments in basic health and education and economic activities at the broader level. Simply put, human capital development must become the core of India's development engine and an integral part of our development discourse.

REINVENT THE ROLE OF THE STATE: Modi's slogan of 'minimum government' was catchy and it conveyed a degree of unease with big government. However, as we now know, Modi's centralizing instincts have led to a government that is neither smaller in size nor more effective. Instead of coming up with an alternative slogan, we need to take a step back and see where government and its institutions stand today with respect to our changed socio-economic landscape. Taking this further, we need to understand what the future may look like and assess what our government should look like.

Clearly, as our way of living evolves and as our economic structures change, government institutions, policy frameworks and programmes must adapt accordingly. Of course, this has happened in the past although one cannot say with confidence that the government has adapted in a systematic way to changes in our socio-economic structure. The institutions that were relevant in the 1950s, 1960s or 1970s may not be relevant now. Certainly, the future is likely to look very different from our current circumstances. Have we done a good job of evolving the capacities of our institutions to keep up with our changing needs? I don't think a lot of people would answer that question in the affirmative.

More likely than not, the creation of new institutions or reforms of existing ones have been episodic and not systematic. It is difficult to argue that maintaining institutional status quo in an era of profound changes is going to help us. We need to be very open to reforming our institutions and building capacities to help deliver the promise of the future. The government's enabling role in ensuring sustainable progress is well recognized. However, the government can only perform that role if it is sufficiently stocked with appropriate skills, an ability to adapt continuously and a recognition that it is primarily an 'enabler', not a 'doer'.

A call to action

While any new government will face the pressure of delivering on election promises, especially those related to jobs, some basic and immediate challenges need attention. By addressing these challenges, and by maintaining macroeconomic stability, the next government can begin to establish a foundation for far-reaching reforms of the kind that India needs for the future. Discussing all near-term challenges is not possible here. However, there are key areas that require immediate attention and there are some rigorously debated areas that are now awaiting tough decisions.

Two introductory points before we go further: First, the challenges discussed below would be considerably worse if the macroeconomic framework was in bad shape. Fortunately, that is not the case. Overall, economic growth appears solid (though not spectacular), inflation is modest and the fiscal deficit is manageable. The rising current account deficit (driven by a large trade deficit) is a worry. However, the overall macroeconomic framework is in good shape at the time of writing this book. Second, this part does not discuss topics such as ease of doing business, rapid improvements in manufacturing or promoting infrastructure investments. These topics are critically important and they have received much attention in public policy discourse. The calls to action below are for areas where we either need immediate attention or which deserve more attention than they have received so far.

1. RESOLVE FINANCIAL-SECTOR PROBLEMS: If there is one major error of omission committed by the Modi government, it is the half-hearted approach towards the mess in India's financial sector, especially PSBs. The *Economist* presented an excellent summary of the evolution of problems in the banking sector and how these problems are manifesting themselves in non-bank financial institutions as well. In a piece titled 'India's Banking System Is Flirting with a Lehman Moment', the magazine observes that the government has failed to come to grips with 'a $100bn mountain of dud loans', mostly belonging to PSBs.[12]

Of course, these problems predated the Modi government. Tracing these problems to the 2005–12 period, when the UPA was in power, the *Economist* notes that 'state banks went on a lending bender, extending credit to dubious tycoons and to infrastructure projects'. As Raghuram Rajan has also noted, banking-sector troubles were a result of 'over optimism', 'slow growth', 'loss of promoter and banker interest', 'malfeasance' and 'fraud'.[13] Unfortunately, the *Economist* points out, 'The government has not properly recapitalised these zombies and the flow of credit from them has slowed.'

To make matters worse, non-banks such as IL&FS, a lender to infrastructure projects, defaulted on its debt of about US$13 billion.[14] Fears of a contagion in the non-bank sector, which borrows about US$250–300 billion for its financing needs, has led to a collapse in market value of these institutions. This scary situation emerged on the heels of large-scale fraud at Punjab National Bank, a major PSB that reported fraud of about US$2 billion committed by diamond merchants.[15]

As more capital flowed into India during 2012–17, and with banks flush with cash post demonetization, they have been looking for ways to lend large amounts of money. One reckless solution appears to have been financing non-bank financial institutions, the biggest fifty of which have 'doubled their debts and assets in the past five years'.[16] The magazine notes that up to US$100 billion could be coming due in the next twelve months. The *Economist* has a dire warning: 'Now panic has seized parts of the privately-run system. One bank boss says the situation is as bad as the Asian crisis of 1998 or the global crash of 2008.'[17]

The financial system is a central pillar of a modern economy. If it is in trouble, we must attend to it. Other challenges can wait. Mind you, the Lehman Brothers crisis triggered a much broader financial crisis and had a huge adverse impact around the world. Researchers at the Federal Reserve Bank of San Francisco had this to say on the tenth anniversary of the 2008 financial crisis: 'A decade after the last financial crisis and recession, the U.S. economy remains significantly smaller than it should be based on its pre-crisis growth trend. One possible reason lies in the large losses in the economy's productive capacity following the financial crisis. The size of those losses suggests that the level of output is unlikely to revert to its pre-crisis trend level. This represents a lifetime present-value income loss of about $70,000 for every American.'[18]

It doesn't appear that most people even comprehend that financial crises have very real impacts and can hurt some of the most vulnerable sections of society. Indecision in the face of a financial crisis is in itself a decision to not be bold and to risk misfortune for millions. The Fed research note on the 2008 crisis ends grimly: 'the economy is unlikely to regain this large output loss and GDP is unlikely to revert to its previous trend level.'[19]

There are many ideas for dealing with problems in the financial sector. There is a lot of international experience available to policymakers. It doesn't make sense to list all of those ideas here. However, some broad principles must be adhered to. These include greater transparency, more competition, a stronger regulatory framework and a watchdog, a reduced role of the government in bank operations, and a credible path to state decontrol.

As the *Economist* points out, 'if India does not get its financial system back on its feet, the economy will not grow fast. It is that simple.'[20] Taking that a step further, without economic growth, chances of eliminating poverty are lower, job creation becomes more challenging and giving hope to a restless population seems almost impossible.

2. SIMPLIFY THE GST: Reforming the GST will be high on the next government's agenda. Before its launch, economist and columnist Mihir Sharma noted, 'We're just a few days away from the launch of a new indirect-tax regime, the goods-and-services tax, or GST, and anxiety about its rollout is all-pervasive.' He complained that the GST was looking like an Indian wedding.[21] Speaking of the substantial technological challenges related to the GST, Sharma flagged concerns by noting, 'Internet forums usually dedicated to figuring out which sub-clauses of the Income Tax Act can safely be ignored are now overrun with posts complaining of the dread phrase: "Failed to establish connection o the server".'[22]

There are some in India who think GST implementation challenges are over. In defending the GST (and demonetization), Finance Minister Jaitley claimed that their adverse impact lasted only about two quarters.[23] There is no evidence to indicate that demonetization's impact was a two-quarter phenomenon. As discussed in Chapter 4, its impact was likely far-reaching and some of it may be permanent. In the GST's case, however, the impact could very well be short-term but international experience suggests otherwise. Let us stick with the Malaysian example, which introduced the GST in 2015.

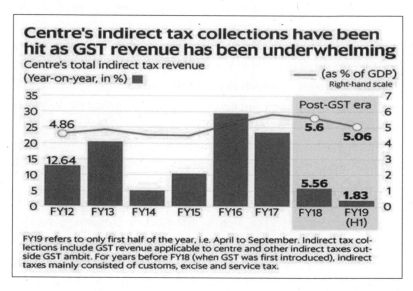

Centre's indirect tax collections have been hit as GST revenue has been underwhelming

Centre's total indirect tax revenue (Year-on-year, in %) ■   ── (as % of GDP) Right-hand scale

FY19 refers to only first half of the year, i.e. April to September. Indirect tax collections include GST revenue applicable to centre and other indirect taxes outside GST ambit. For years before FY18 (when GST was first introduced), indirect taxes mainly consisted of customs, excise and service tax.

Source: Tadit Kundu, 'How GST and Demonetisation Impacted Govt Finances', Mint, *5 November 2018.*

By all accounts, Malaysia put in a lot of time to get ready for the tax. It was also based on a single 6 per cent tax rate, making it simpler to administer compared to the five tax rates and other levies that are part of India's GST. Despite this, the Malaysian GST was deeply unpopular and the new prime minister followed up on a campaign promise and abandoned the GST and replaced it with a sales and services tax (SST) starting 1 September 2018.[24] This is not to suggest that India should replace its GST. The Malaysians may have to contend with a drop-off in revenues due to this switch.[25] The point here is that the GST needs reforms and the sooner we accomplish them, the better it will be for the economy, the government, businesses and consumers.

Before launching the GST with much fanfare, the government touted its positive impacts as a reason for implementing this tax. There was little awareness of its potential adverse impacts. As of November 2018, gross revenues from the GST crossed the Rs 1 lakh crore mark only twice since July 2017. An analysis by the *Mint* newspaper shows that the Central government's indirect tax collections took a hit because GST revenues were 'underwhelming'.[26] In the same report, *Mint* refers to an RBI study that indicated that GST implementation hindered the MSME sector's exports.[27]

What could the next government do about the GST? It depends on your attitude to policymaking. In tax-related matters, my view is similar to many who argue in favour of easing the burden on taxpayers. For instance, on the GST, Mihir Sharma has argued in favour of a 'shift in government attitudes'. Sharma believes that officials see the GST as a tool for tax compliance whereas he would prefer to ease the burden on taxpayers. 'That will automatically reduce evasion and increase revenues,' says Sharma.[28] This is an important point and if politicians and business persons speak of tax terrorism, the underlying point they are making is that of suffering under a coercive regime that relies far more on the stick than on the carrot. Of course, you can find plenty of experts who will argue the opposite.

Some believe that the 'Indian situation', as many refer to it, is one where the stick is more appropriate because of its effectiveness. Nevertheless, a few basic principles are important.

The number of tax rates should ideally be two, or preferably one, with essential commodities being tax free. The maximum tax rate should be much lower than the current 28 per cent, perhaps below 15 per cent. Personally, I see no justification for a sales tax rate that is in double digits.. There is plenty of data with the government to ascertain a reasonable rate that minimizes the hit to revenues but one that is not excessively regressive. Frankly, the current high rate structure is untenable and unnecessary.

Finally, it has always been a bit of a puzzle to understand why so many have to file monthly returns, including taxpayers who do little business. Of course, governments need revenue on a continuous basis. However, the requirement for frequent filings could apply to the biggest taxpayers. They are likelier to already have a battery of tax professionals. There is no reason to make everyone, especially small enterprises, go through the grind of filing GST returns frequently.

If policymakers are concerned that simplification may yield lower revenues, they only have to look at the early returns described above to see the impact of a complicated system. The other problem is, as the *Mint* newspaper has noted, litigation is increasing. There are more investigations by the National Anti-profiteering Authority, which was set up under the GST framework. Many felt that such an agency might become a coercive tool in the hands of the government. Some of those fears seem to be coming true and an effective GST is still some distance away.[29]

3. RECOGNIZE AGRICULTURE'S POTENTIAL: Without meaningful reforms, productivity and returns from agriculture will remain depressed. That is likely to continue a sense of desperation that pervades Indian agriculture and chances of earning a decent living from farms is unlikely to come to fruition. The government will probably be unable to keep its promise to double farm income in a sustainable manner. One of the biggest challenges of agriculture remains the declining size of farms, most of which

are small or marginal. Those considered large, above 10 hectares, are less than 1 per cent. The average farm size has more than halved from 2.82 hectares in 1970–71 to only 1.16 hectares in recent years. To make matters worse, yields have fallen, with technology and improved methods more difficult to apply in smaller farm settings.[30]

The continued reliance of so many Indians on agriculture perplexes those who don't make a living on farms. Why don't farmers leave agriculture and make a living elsewhere? Wouldn't that improve productivity? Wouldn't that improve farmer remuneration? Why focus so much on boosting farm income when we really need fewer people in agriculture? These questions fail to recognize important considerations when seen from the perspective of farmers. For example, many farmers view their farms, however small, as a security guarantee. Furthermore, in an economic environment in which decent jobs in the non-farm sector are not able to absorb the growing ranks of India's youth, it is unrealistic to expect farmers to let go of their land or profession.

A medium-term strategy should focus both on boosting farm incomes and simultaneously on creating job opportunities in other sectors. That could create a momentum for both consolidation of landholdings as well as a movement of workers from farms to other sectors. Also, boosting farm incomes may seem like a political expedient but it has great development potential. Higher incomes can lead to farmers adopting more modern techniques and create greater awareness of and access to improved practices and choices of products that are less resource-intensive. This would be particularly useful as climate change manifests with greater intensity in the future. Better-off farmers may also be able to navigate and negotiate advantageously with marketing and middlemen that are so often in the news for all the wrong reasons.[31]

Over the next decade, the agricultural sector is likely to benefit from key trends including additional demand of over 400 tons by 2025. Importantly, the increased demand for food will coincide with a changing pattern of consumption. Indians are including more fruits, vegetables and proteins in their diet. There is also greater recognition of scarce resources including land and water. This could force changes in production techniques to bring India's yields closer to levels in China, which are currently much higher.

Another opportunity for the farm sector is in reducing waste. About 60 per cent of food losses happen during transit and storage. Adoption of cold storage and improvements in logistics could unlock huge savings in the sector. Of course, as in other areas, technological disruption and innovation can create value in a variety of ways, including relevant market information, advisory services and data analytics. Creating new and improved value chains can help farmers reduce marketing costs while more robust credit and insurance facilities can greatly strengthen their ability to mitigate cost of doing business.[32] Let's hope the next government takes the steps needed to make Indian agriculture a beacon of hope and promise for the next generation of farmers.

4. MANAGE RURAL–URBAN TRANSITION: According to projections by the McKinsey Global Institute (MGI), India's urban population will grow from 34 crore in 2008 to 59 crore in 2030. MGI notes that this 'urban expansion will happen at a speed quite unlike anything India has seen before'. India will take only half the time to add the next 25 crore people to the ranks of urban India as it did the first time around.[33] This growth will increase the demand for a number of services—healthcare, education, housing, transport, recreation, along with basic public services such as water, sanitation, electricity and roads.

Agglomeration of economic activity in India's urban centres can also mean cost savings in service provision, which MGI estimates at 30 to 40 per cent compared to that in less densely populated rural areas.[34] This is the good news. Major challenges will accompany this transformation and India must plan for it. Due to underinvestment, Indian cities are unable to provide decent public services. The MGI estimates a requirement of US$1.2 trillion in capital expenditure alone over the next twenty years. This is about eight times the level of spending in recent times.[35] Funding is only one issue that policymakers have to grapple with. Reforms of urban governance structures as well as clarity in relationships between various levels of government, especially from a funding perspective, are some of the other challenges in the coming years.

Beyond these challenges, it is also important to underline the reasons why China's urbanization has progressed at a much faster clip than India's. In China, productivity of urban workers is considerably higher than that of rural workers. This leads to higher wages and a greater incentive to move. The ratio of urban-to-rural wages is also much higher in China than in India. In addition, property prices in urban China, while considered high by global standards, are still less when compared to prices in Indian cities such as Mumbai or Delhi. This is partly due to reservation of vast tracts of land for government use (accommodation for politicians, civil servants and military cantonments) as well as building-code restrictions on concentrated commercial activity.[36]

Some of the policy actions that can help to unlock the benefits of greater urbanization include urban governance reforms, including strengthening the financial position of urban local bodies. Increased revenues from property taxes, as happens elsewhere, will be a key part of financing basic infrastructure services. In addition, monetizing land assets and levying user charges can help shrink the financing gap that currently exists between needs and availability. Forming PPPs as well as creating opportunities for citizen awareness and engagement can facilitate more relevant and progressive urban development policies and programmes. While technology will be a key enabler, we should not misunderstand smart cities to mean just digitally driven cities. Smart cities are about being smart in other ways, such as reducing resource-intensive urban development and seeking sustainable solutions to problems such as heat-island effects that can worsen with climate change.[37]

India's cities need a long-term strategy that involves institutional and policy reforms along with a set of achievable and prioritized programmes. Residents as well as investors should have a clear sense of the direction that city governments and managers are charting. As cities modernize and institutions take hold, the capacity to implement complex reforms and programmes will grow. In all this, we must not forget that urban slums and poverty are a reality and we cannot wish them away. Visions and strategies that do not fully account for the needs of vulnerable sections of society are unlikely to sustain, given the political economy of India's urban areas.

India's rural–urban transition has the potential to not only transform India into an upper-middle-income country but it can change the lives of hundreds of millions of people. It is a key priority that requires long-term strategic thinking and the implementation of changes that will require courageous political leadership. Governments both at the Central and state levels will have their work cut out for them, given that they will have to yield greater power and decision-making to urban local bodies. This calls for leadership that is truly committed to greater decentralization in India. The rewards can be incalculable.[38]

5. UNLEASH THE POTENTIAL OF WOMEN: India still has a long way to go to include women more fully in economic activity. Gender inclusion is not only a social necessity but an economic one too. The WEF tracks gender parity through its *Global Gender Gap*

Report. In 2016, the WEF reported that based on current rates, 'it would take the world another 118 years—or until 2133—to close the economic gap entirely'.[39] Of course, this is for the world as a whole, and some countries such as India might take longer to achieve economic parity between men and women. This would be extremely costly for India and there is plenty of evidence to support a greater role for women in the economy.

In 2013, economists working at the IMF argued that when women participate fully in labour markets, there can be significant gains for an economy.[40] On this finding, there is broad agreement in the economic research community. Research indicates that if women were to work at the same rate as men do in the United States labour market, economic output could grow by 5 per cent, in Japan by 9 per cent and in Egypt by 34 per cent.[41] Christine Lagarde, managing director of the IMF, has suggested that India's GDP would be 27 per cent higher if more women participated in the labour force.[42] Research also indicates that if more women earn and control their incomes, there is greater spending on children's education. This can lead to the development of more productive workers in the future. Basically, greater participation of women in the economy can help power India's future.

Unfortunately, while male LFPRs in India are higher than in China, female rates are extremely low.[43, 44] The LFPR is that section of the working population (fifteen years and older) in the economy currently employed or seeking employment. According to ILO data, India's female LFPR is only 27 per cent compared to China's 61 per cent. For context, the LFPR for Indian men is 79 per cent. In fact, the ILO indicates that in 2013, India's female LFPR was 120th out of 131 countries. Interestingly, female LFPR is lower in urban areas compared to rural areas, indicating that poorer rural women have no choice but to work to make ends meet.

As women become more educated, they are likely to join the labour force in greater numbers and that will increase the competition for non-farm jobs. These shifts can play a big role in India's future. When more women work, our economy will grow more rapidly. This seems to be self-evident, yet the pattern of male–female employment in India suggests that we are not doing enough to support women's economic empowerment. Unless this changes, India cannot grow at its full potential.

Researchers indicate there could be many reasons why female LFPR is so low in India. For example, social norms around marriage, childbearing and women's work outside the home could depress their labour-market participation. It is possible that home-based employment, which women may engage in at a higher rate, is undercounted in labour surveys. It is also possible that there is a mismatch between the skills that employers are looking for versus the skills women may be accumulating. For example, if vocational schools focus on manufacturing skills and women prefer service jobs, there could be a significant negative impact on women's employability. There could also be problems related to women's safety, gender discrimination on account of wages or preference for male workers that could keep women out of jobs. While it is true that some of these factors are also present in other countries, yet it is India that lags far behind the rest of the world when it comes to women participating in labour markets.

There is a wide variety of ideas for increasing greater participation of women in the economy. Improved education quality and length of schooling can have a positive impact. Improving transport connectivity in rural areas can be helpful, and visible improvements in women's security can play a part as well. Encouraging affordable childcare opportunities can encourage women to rejoin work after childbirth. Reducing the gap between maternity and paternity benefits could reduce

Labor force participation rate (females)

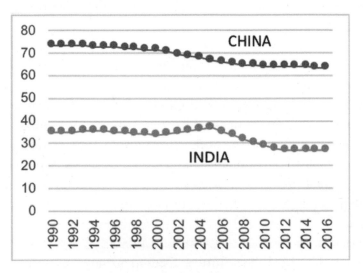

Source: International Labour Organization

Labor force participation rate (males)

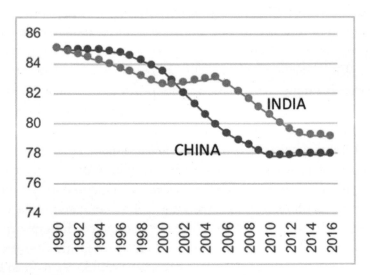

Source: International Labour Organization

chances of gender-based discrimination in hiring. Enforcement mechanisms of anti-discrimination laws require strengthening too.

The idea here is not to lay out in detail all the possible ways in which we can improve female labour-force participation; what is more important is to recognize that there is a serious problem that requires our attention. This is not only about women's economic empowerment. It is also about helping India achieve its full economic potential. Without women, that is just not possible. Governments at all levels must devote ever greater attention to issues of women's economic empowerment. This will go a long way in enabling India's economic transformation.

6. INVEST IN PEOPLE—ACCUMULATE HUMAN CAPITAL: Let's be honest. The Modi government focused far more on improving India's standing in the World Bank's EODB rankings than on other measures of development such as the HDI produced by the United Nations Development Programme (UNDP). As discussed earlier, the EODB rankings show a vast improvement but what about measures such as the HDI and why do they matter? For any economy to do well, it must have a strong foundation.

While economists usually talk in terms of a stable macroeconomic framework as a foundation on which to build sustained growth, development experts have also highlighted the critical role of education and health in sustaining personal well-being as well as broader socio-economic progress. For a variety of reasons, India's health and education sectors have not benefited from the kind of focus and investment that they deserve. With technology evolving rapidly, and amidst fears of job losses to automation, there is renewed interest in improving access to quality education and health. Lack of quality education and health as well as skills are significant hurdles to the kind of job creation that India needs. Before discussing the importance of human capital development (or even its definition), let us quickly review the Modi government's performance in these critical areas since we did not address this in Chapter 4.

If you recall the time of the UPA government, it received much criticism for pushing a welfare agenda that was based on entitlements. Some commentators called the UPA's approach 'dole-nomics', which sought to provide benefits 'without seeking a price for it'.[45] This is not the place to debate such characterizations, but these types of arguments set the stage for the Modi government to push forward a vision of 'empowerment' as opposed to 'entitlement'. As Yamini Aiyar notes, the Modi government never really got down to articulating a road map for empowerment but instead focused on 'announcing schemes without joining the dots'.[46] Aiyar goes on to make a dispiriting observation when she says, 'Crucially, the two key pillars of "empowerment"—quality education and health—remained mostly invisible from the NDA's welfare politics, until the grand announcement of Ayushman Bharat.'[47]

Under the Modi government, there was no significant uptick in investment in health and education—health expenditure remains below 1.5 per cent of the GDP while education expenditure is still around 3 per cent of the GDP.[48] Aiyar argues that the government's 'singular achievement' is the administrative combination of existing schemes including SSA (elementary education), Rashtriya Madhyamik Shiksha Abhiyan or RMSA (secondary education) and Teacher Education (TE). In terms of learning outcomes there really isn't much that is different compared to what was happening earlier.

At this point, a short detour is necessary to explain the challenge India faces. Between 2012 and 2014, I spent a lot of time understanding development challenges in Baramulla in north Kashmir. Given the importance of health and education, what I found was eye-opening. Since that time, I often give the example of a small village called Bandi Payeen in the upper reaches of Baramulla. This village, measuring roughly 1 km by 0.5 km, had eight government schools—a high school, three middle schools and four primary schools. Not one of those eight schools had enough teachers, students, chairs, desks, or anything. On the other hand, I went to a middle school in a village close to Baramulla town. In this school, there were nine students in eight grades and almost a dozen teachers, most of whom were sitting outside chatting.

These are not isolated examples. This was happening across Baramulla and perhaps across India. Government schools did not appear to be serving the interests of students even though teachers in these schools are widely perceived to be more qualified on average than those in private schools. The health sector was not much better. Clearly, we need deep reforms in these sectors but the Modi government has not prioritized them. If the government had done so, perhaps this would show up in some broad measures such as the HDI or in institutional or policy reforms. The Modi government has been working on the NEP for its entire term but a new policy is nowhere on the horizon. The government touted this new policy as transformative in nature. Unfortunately, this has not happened.[49]

Parthasarathi Shome, an economist, explored India's performance on the HDI, which captures progress along ten dimensions, including health, education and basic living standards. Shome finds that India's HDI rose only one spot from 131 in 2015 to 130 in 2017. The actual HDI went up from 0.63 to 0.64 (1 being the maximum). In the same time period, India's gross national product or GNP per capita went up by 12 per cent. Shome notes that this is 'a telltale sign of income growth being concentrated primarily on high deciles'.[50] This disappointing performance on the HDI is not new. This has been going on for years.

A more recent effort to assess cross-country progress on human capital development comes from the World Bank in the form of the Human Capital Index (HCI). The OECD defines human capital as 'the knowledge, skills, competencies and attributes embodied in individuals that facilitate the creation of personal, social and economic well-being'.[51] In explaining the importance of human capital, the OECD notes that in the past, economic growth models used to emphasize the importance of land, labour and capital. Over time, 'there's been increasing agreement on one key part of the growth puzzle, namely, the importance of people—their abilities, their knowledge and their competences—to economic growth. Or, in other words, human capital.'[52] The OECD notes that the American economist Theodore Schultz was among the first to conceptualize human capital in a 1961 paper.[53] However, it is only in recent years that human capital development is shaping up as a powerful advocacy concept in international development.

With this background, let us turn to the World Bank's inaugural HCI rankings. Released in October 2018, the HCI rankings place India in the 115th spot out of 157 countries. Among its neighbours, India trails Sri Lanka (74), Nepal (102), Bangladesh (106) and Myanmar (107), although Pakistan is at a dismal 134.[54] The Modi government was just as quick to reject these rankings as it was in accepting the much-improved EODB rankings. A finance ministry official stated, 'HCI uses metric of industrial era to measure the status of human capital for digital age and its production system.'[55] From Aiyar's perspective, 'The tone and tenor of the government's position and the failure to acknowledge the scale of the challenge India faces offers an important insight into the government's current mindset and policy focus. This doesn't bode well for India's future.'[56]

The point here is that if India does not reform areas that underpin what the government calls 'industrial era' metrics, we

are in deep trouble. It is precisely because we need India to
benefit from and participate in a technology-powered future
that we must initiate major reforms in health, education, skilling,
social protection and related areas. Human capital development
must become the core of the engine of India's transformation.
There simply is no other way around it. Instead of focusing on
China's economic growth and industrial strength, we should first
focus on its HCI ranking. It is 46. No one should underestimate
the role of human capital development in China's progress. For,
there is no such thing as automatic economic development.

7. ENGINEER DIGITAL TRANSFORMATION: Technology is reshaping
economies and creating new challenges as well as opportunities.
For India to make meaningful progress, especially as it relates
to creating opportunities for young people, we must make
technology and innovation an ally in our efforts. Before we can
do that, however, we need to better appreciate the forces that
are impacting our economic trajectory. Sadly, we must begin
with some bad news here.

As established earlier, increasing the share of manufacturing
in economic output has proved challenging. Part of the reason
lies in what experts call 'premature deindustrialization'. As
Harvard economist Dani Rodrik notes, 'This is old news for
most of the advanced economies of the world, which long ago
moved into a new, post-industrial phase of development. These
economies have been deindustrializing for decades, a trend that
is particularly noticeable when one looks at the employment
share of manufacturing.'[57] In his 2015 paper, 'Premature
Deindustrialization', Rodrik brought attention to a decades-
long trend in which he found that developing countries such
as India were undergoing deindustrialization, which he found
to be 'striking, and puzzling'. Rodrik explained that with the
exception of some countries in Asia, low- and middle-income

countries around the world experienced 'falling manufacturing shares in both employment and real value added, especially since the 1980s'. Rodrik went on to argue that these countries were undergoing 'premature deindustrialization', a term first used by Sukti Dasgupta and Ajit Singh in a 2006 paper.[58]

Rodrik found that industrialization peaked in Western European countries at income levels of around US$14,000 (in 1990 dollars). On the other hand, 'India and many sub-Saharan African countries appear to have reached their peak manufacturing employment shares at income levels of $700.'[59] According to Rodrik, 'Premature deindustrialization is not good news for developing nations.' This may seem obvious but the explanation is that industrialization is a key path to rapid growth and of absorbing excess rural workers in urban factories where they may find more productive employment.[60]

Rodrik's findings found resonance in a new report by World Bank economists Mary Hallward-Driemeier and Gaurav Nayyar, which suggests that new technologies are reshaping the manufacturing landscape and that the old model that utilized low-wage labour may no longer be available to developing countries such as India.[61] This report argues that technologies such as 'advanced robotics, industrial automation, and 3-D printing, are changing the landscape of global manufacturing'. The report also notes that traditional definitions of what constitutes an attractive manufacturing location are also changing, with companies focusing on those areas that can leverage modern technologies better.[62]

While this report does not focus on India per se, the authors did pen an op-ed in the *Economic Times*, where they had suggestions for what India could do to adapt to these global trends in technology and manufacturing. Hallward-Driemeier and Nayyar argue that while India should improve its competitiveness in its traditional areas of strength such as textiles, apparel and leather, the country must leverage its higher-education institutions to develop a skilled talent pool to benefit from opportunities provided by the Fourth Industrial Revolution. They also urge greater connectivity with India's technology-savvy diaspora to spur innovation and technology transfer to India's advantage. Finally, the authors point to the opportunity of 'servicification' of manufacturing. This basically means that manufacturing is not just about production but also about services that accompany manufactured products. Servicification includes conceptual design, product strategy, sales and marketing, aftersales and other such services.

The consequences of not addressing this technology-driven challenge could be significant. It is not rocket science—a burgeoning youth population that is turfed out of decent job opportunities by rapidly evolving technologies is going to be hugely problematic. The next government has to rise to the challenge and make digital transformation a pillar of its development strategy. The preceding discussion on human capital is relevant here. These two dimensions need to work in sync with each other. While the Modi government did initiate Digital India and sought to develop a digital-payments infrastructure, these efforts do not seem to be part of a coherent strategy or framework. You can't have a digitally robust economy without substantially higher investments in education, health, as well as protection of those endangered by all this transformation.

New research by Microsoft and International Data Corporation (IDC) shows that India's digital transformation will add over US$150 billion to the Indian economy by 2021.[63] McKinsey and Company believes that India's digital economy could add US$1 trillion in economic value by 2025. All these are encouraging findings but, as with everything in development, such additions will not be automatic. If we remain mired in debates on how the East Asian economies developed through labour-intensive manufacturing and do not focus more on seizing the moment today and build on our advantages like a young population and substantial experience in technology and services, we may at some point in the future be debating the missed opportunities from today.

India is already high on the list of countries as far as digital adoption is concerned. Despite that, there is plenty of hand-wringing about new technologies and what they mean for India. If we look to the future, the only option is to harness technology and not let it immobilize us. The next government has to build an enabling architecture in which research, innovation and adoption of modern technologies are pillars of a concerted push to benefit from the vast opportunities that digital disruption has to offer.

8. REINVENT THE ROLE OF THE STATE: The focus of this book has been on the Modi government's stewardship of the economy. However, as I mentioned in Chapter 1, the Central government by itself is not responsible for all that happens in an economy. State governments, legal and regulatory institutions, local governments, companies and individuals, all play a part in developing an economy. In India's case, though, the Central government does play an outsized role and that is why its policies and programmes receive so much attention. This may not be a good thing, however.

India is a major economy with a very diverse population that has diverse needs. Some states are fairly advanced and may be closer to reaching upper-middle-income status than others that likely fall in the low-income category. Greater autonomy of decision-making could really benefit India. To be fair, a lot has changed in India over the past few decades, and the states have greater say in their affairs than they used to. However, that too is not sufficient because there is a palpable need to decentralize power quickly. This has been part of a long-standing governance reform agenda, and one hopes that the process speeds up because a changing economy needs to change the way the government functions. Governments also need to make an adjustment in their attitude towards governance. Specifically, governments should shift from being 'doers' to becoming 'enablers'. This is not a suggestion for the wholesale privatization of public enterprises, however. When Narendra Modi spoke about 'minimum government, maximum governance', he had a point. We often talk about economic reforms but we rarely talk about reforming the institutions of governance that are supposed to conceive and implement those reforms.

The question that often comes to mind is whether or not the current institutional and regulatory framework is ideal for a new economy powered by knowledge and innovation. Is there a need for a new social contract between citizens and the state? What are the services that citizens should expect the government to provide and where can the private sector take on a greater role? Since we face enormous deficits in financing critical infrastructure, are there opportunities for us to raise resources by embarking on sensible and meaningful privatization of public enterprises? There are many questions that need answers. The overarching point being that if India has to create a new economy underpinned by human capital and digital development, the supporting institutional architecture must change.

Speaking of institutions, a word of caution is necessary. International experience suggests that strong, transparent and accountable institutions are critical for socio-economic progress. Unfortunately, this lesson has been unlearnt to some extent in India. Remember the dismantling of the Planning Commission within months of Modi taking over?[64] While many cheered this development and marked it as an end to socialist-era planning, it was a little disconcerting to observe that the new government had not engaged in any serious exercise in laying out the reasons for its move. In winding down a sixty-four-year-old institution and creating a new one, the NITI Aayog, the government probably did less work than teams of World Bankers do for preparing a small-scale project. I should know because I have led World Bank teams.

Was this a sign of changing with the times or was this a blatant disregard for what institutional development is all about? Over the last few years, we have received an answer to this question. In undertaking demonetization, the Modi government critically damaged the reputation and autonomy of the RBI. Towards the end of Modi's tenure, there have been further attacks on the RBI's independence and all this cannot be good news for the economy.[65] Eswar Prasad of Cornell University wrote in an op-ed that Modi's criticisms of the RBI were 'an alarming development for India, because the RBI's credibility and effectiveness have contributed substantially to macroeconomic and financial stability, thereby helping to sustain rapid GDP growth in recent years'.[66]

Building strong institutions is a painfully long process. Tearing them down doesn't take that much time. However, for those who care about India's progress, especially in these challenging times, strengthening institutions and making their functioning more transparent and accountable is of utmost importance. On this front, unfortunately, the news from India is not that good. A variety of institutions are losing credibility because it appears that the Modi government has done the opposite of what it promised. There is no minimum government. There is no maximum governance.

In a lecture to students at the University of California in Berkeley, Raghuram Rajan summed up the direction of the Indian state: 'India can't work from the centre. India works when you have many people taking up the burden. And today the central government is excessively centralized.'[67] Clearly, he was referring to Modi and the widespread perception that governance was centralized in the PMO. That is not the kind of change India needs now and certainly not in the future either. Institutions matter greatly and we must nurture them and let them grow strong even as we insist that they help India realize her potential.

In the context of policy failures that resulted in the 1997 East Asian Crisis, Joseph Stiglitz, former World Bank chief economist, remarked, 'Smart people are more likely to do stupid things when they close themselves off from outside criticism and advice. If there's one thing I've learned in government, it's that openness is most essential in those realms where expertise seems to matter most.'[68] This is sage advice for India's leaders and policymakers.

9. MAKE CLIMATE CHANGE A TOP PRIORITY: A recent ranking compiled by HSBC Bank ranks India as the most vulnerable country to climate change.[69] The ranking also includes neighbours such as Pakistan and Bangladesh. HSBC compiled its ranking after considering criteria such as vulnerability to the physical impacts of climate change, sensitivity to extreme weather events, exposure to energy-transition risks and the ability to respond to climate change. Agricultural incomes could decline, especially in water-stressed areas that could take a big hit from increased temperatures and a shortfall in rains.[70]

Support for such conclusions comes in the form of a World Bank report that predicts that changing monsoon patterns could cost India 2.8 per cent of the GDP and result in declining living standards for nearly half of the country's population by 2050.[71] A sector that is hugely important for India, and one which already suffers from low productivity, would be subject to further declines in living standards and agricultural yields. Of course, climate change will have broader impacts as well, from more intense weather events leading to bigger natural disasters to damaging changes to ecosystems.

The World Bank report provides a very detailed look at India (and other South Asian countries) and identifies 'hotspots', using very granular geographical and household data. The report shows that 'approximately 600 million people live in locations that could either become moderate or severe hotspots by 2050 under a business-as-usual scenario'. Northern, north-western and central Indian states are particularly vulnerable. The report identifies Chhattisgarh and Madhya Pradesh as the states that will suffer almost double-digit declines in living standards while the Vidarbha region in Maharashtra will account for some of the most vulnerable 'hotspot' districts.

Reports such as the one by the World Bank provide sensible policy recommendations for adapting to India's climate reality. Some of these have to do with making agricultural activity more 'climate smart', changing crop varieties and reducing water stress. To address irreversible economic impacts, the report provides helpful economic prescriptions such as improved education and skills and creation of job opportunities in other sectors to reduce the burden on agriculture.

There is already a lot of work going on in India to combat the impact of climate change. The key is for India to build the institutional capacity that can help integrate growing climate-change concerns with other aspects of economic development. For example, India's energy needs are immense and, for the most part, are met by coal-based plants. While inexpensive energy sources are important right now, they could prove expensive in the long term given their contribution to climate change. Incorporating such calculations into thinking about our future energy mix or advancing technology and innovation to promote climate-sensitive growth will be critical tasks in the coming years.

10. PROMOTE SMART ENERGY SECURITY: India's energy conundrum is devilishly complex. Advanced economies used coal and other fossil fuels to power their economies. They became rich but our environmental commons deteriorated. Just as India and other emerging economies are getting to a stage of ending poverty and ensuring decent living standards for their citizens, climate change is putting the brakes on use of dirty but inexpensive fuels. If we continue on our current path of a high share of fossil fuels, we hurt ourselves later due to climate change. If we shift to a greater share of renewables, presuming we could, it can get very expensive in the short term. Beyond energy generation, India also has to focus a lot more on transmission and distribution challenges.

The energy demand side is just as important. The World Banks's latest SCD notes that India's energy demand is likely to 'grow faster than in any other country in the world over the next 25 years'.[72] While power generation has increased significantly over the last few decades and has also exceeded installed demand, about 23 crore people still lack access to electricity. With almost all rural areas connected to sources of power, it is only a matter of time before power reaches all households. While these new additions to the power demand equation will likely consume less power per capita than established consumers, the additional demand will be considerable. India will also have to make substantial progress in the quality of electricity services. The World Bank points out that 'frequent power outages take a heavy toll on firm performance, household health and overall economic performance'.[73]

India's energy policy choices will matter greatly for the future of the country and the world. Ambitious plans to sharply increase renewable energy and reduce demand for fossil fuels by making only electric vehicles by 2030 are steps in the right direction. An energy policy, as with other critical development areas, requires a comprehensive look. We need to think in terms of a new architecture not for 2030 but for 2050 and beyond. It is helpful to set aspirational targets for India's energy sector, but that in itself doesn't convey to citizens all the ingredients of how that vision is to be realized and how citizens have to contribute.

We need to develop an architecture that works backwards from our goals. A review of legal and institutional frameworks along with an assessment of institutional capacities to implement a strategic plan is necessary. What role the private sector, including consumers, can play is an important ingredient. Showing linkages with other sectors such as education or agriculture is necessary. This gets complex very fast but that is how development works. Setting a target of 1 Terawatt of solar energy by 2025 could be a very interesting target but when citizens are not aware of how India can get there, such targets may become sources of amazement or political grandstanding but not immediately relevant to people's lives. Energy security is a national priority and requires serious consideration that seeps into the country's consciousness.

11. CHANGE THE PUBLIC DISCOURSE: India is going through a difficult phase and I am not talking about the economy. India is in the midst of an upheaval, marked by sharp social divisions and recriminations. Many worry that these divisions could lead to conflict, especially because there is a growing employment challenge in the country. Some of the biggest issues debated in the country are related to disputes over religious activity. Meanwhile, the international development discourse is about the Fourth Industrial Revolution, disruptive technologies, 5G mobile, PayGo models, big data and machine learning, robotics

and countless other concepts that governments, companies and people are experimenting with. These innovations are part of a quest to reshape economies and to make them work to improve the lives of people. India must not only be an active participant in benefiting from these new ideas and innovations but it should aspire to become a central player in shaping the new global economy.

The next government must come in with an attitude to do all it can to foster an environment that promotes dialogue and debate over ideas for India's future. It must help create that bridge between now and tomorrow. However, as a society, we must recognize that we have a choice to make. We either focus our energies on the next generation of ideas and innovations, or we stay mired in the past without learning its many lessons. The Modi government had an opportunity to help the country make that shift. That is what many had expected and what I had hoped for too. What we got instead is not only a return that appears to be below expectation but Modi's tenure has also unleashed forces that are dangerously close to making us lose our focus on what really matters—a better future for Indian citizens.

I discussed the title of this book with many friends. This includes some who supported Modi or were hopeful that he would become a transformative leader. Unfortunately, I have come to an inescapable conclusion. Narendra Modi squandered a unique opportunity to transform the Indian economy. In doing so, he belied the hopes and aspirations of hundreds of millions of people, especially India's youth. For them, and for me, Modi's tenure has been a great disappointment.

Acknowledgements

A lmost two years ago, Swati Chopra at Penguin Random House India asked me if I was interested in writing a book. Until then, I had been writing articles for various newspapers and online sites. However, the idea of writing a book seemed daunting. From writing 800-word columns to writing a book of 80,000 words seemed like a big leap. If you are reading these words today, a lot of credit goes to Swati for her perseverance and patience in making me see that I had to give voice to my ideas. Thank you, Swati!

My thanks also to the team at Penguin that has contributed to the final product. Neeraj Nath deserves special thanks for designing a cover that ingeniously conveys the book's essence.

This book is not mine alone. The ideas and writings of so many have influenced it. Those who wrote about India and its economy around the time of Independence left rich material for us to benefit from. The first chapter on inheritance relies on many such accounts and I am grateful to those writers, many of whom are no longer with us, for sharing their views so that I could draw on them. In a similar vein, the book draws on the work of so many others who have done the hard work of adding to our knowledge of the Indian economy. To all of them, I extend my sincere gratitude.

My work has benefited from conversations (including on social media) over the last few years. Some of these conversations challenged my own world view and others confirmed the logic of my views. At times, some have been kind enough to let me use their material for this book. In this context, I would like to thank Shankkar Aiyar, Sidharth Bhatia, Manas Chakravarty, Ajay Chhibber, Vivek Dehejia, Sadanand Dhume, Amitabh Dubey, Rajeev Gowda, Sanjay Jha, Gaurav Kapoor, Vivek Kaul, Amy Kazmin, Tadit Kundu, Iain Marlow, Puja Mehra, Pratap Bhanu Mehta, Nitin Pai, Mihir Sharma, Joel Selanikio, Rukmini Shrinivasan, Rupa Subramanya, M.K. Venu.

A special thanks to Shashi Tharoor whose prolific writing has inspired so many. In a Washington, DC coffee shop, I had asked him how he managed to write so many books (eighteen at last count) even as he maintained such a hectic schedule. His advice: dedicate time and don't lose momentum. I followed his advice and here we are. Thanks, Shashi!

I do want to express my debt of gratitude to my teachers from schools to universities. Where would I be without their collective effort? There is one teacher in particular who deserves special mention because he has perhaps influenced my writing more than anybody else. Professor David Cromwell at the Yale School of Management taught us a venture capital class when I was doing my MBA (1998–2000). David's class was one that I enjoyed immensely because he kept it simple. I could feel what he taught. His constant appeal was that we write simply and directly. He was the first to bring Microsoft Word's readability statistics to my attention. He wanted us to maintain Flesch Reading Ease above 40 with zero passive sentences. Over time, I tried doing that on a regular basis. I may not have succeeded always, but following that principle has improved my writing. While many of his students learnt to make a lot of money in venture capital and private equity, I learnt to write. Prof. David Cromwell passed away on 26 April 2018. Thank you, David; may you rest in peace.

Writing this book required a lot of research. In this I was very lucky to find Vartika Savarna, a Young India Fellow at Ashoka University. She dug up a vast amount of information, kept track of the latest trends in the economy, and compiled a lot of data that helped me focus on the book's narrative. From pulling together references to reviewing the manuscript multiple times, Vartika accomplished things with quiet efficiency. I am truly grateful for her support and work ethic. She has many accomplishments ahead of her. Thanks, Vartika!

My great thanks to two of my closest friends who reviewed big chunks of the manuscript and helped improve my work. Sajid Malik helped edit the book as I was finishing up the first draft. His insights were invaluable and showed me that Sajid should be writing a book of his own. Any publisher would be lucky to have him!

Julius Gwyer has been a constant intellectual companion for many years. We have brainstormed about development issues since we first became colleagues at the World Bank in 1993. He has been extremely generous with his time and has been very supportive of this book project. Julius was also constantly on my case to not lose focus and to keep writing. The final chapter, which focuses on the future of economic development and technology, is reflective of our many conversations. I am lucky to have him in my corner. Thanks, Jules!

My parents and the rest of my family deserve special mention because more often than not, they help enable my work. My mother, Mumtaz Soz, is the glue that holds our family together. By doing so much by herself, she frees up time for people like me to think and write. My father, Saifuddin Soz, always encouraged me to write a book because he felt I had a contribution to make. His belief in my abilities does cause a bit of embarrassment at times but that's what parents are like. I am truly grateful for his constant encouragement (and pestering) because I needed that to believe in myself. His advice on how to go about writing a book (he has authored quite a few himself) was very helpful too. I know my entire family is as excited about this book as I am.

My lovely little children, Asmara and Zaydan, are big fans of J.K. Rowling. They love books and are voracious readers. When I decided to write a book, perhaps they thought I was going to conjure up a Harry Potter of sorts. Over time, it became clear to them that Narendra Modi was no Harry Potter. However, their enthusiasm for this book has not diminished; it has only grown. They have told everyone at school that their daddy is writing a book and that they will bring it to school. Of course, writing this book (and other work) has meant that I have not been able to spend the kind of quality time with them that they deserve. I hope when they grow up, they understand that this is something that I had to do. Their excitement about this book makes all the effort worth it. In addition to Asmara and Zaydan, we have a third little one at home. Soola, our Havanese dog, has been my constant companion. He is a source of unrestrained love and I will remember how he always sat quietly by my feet while I typed away at the keyboard.

Finally, it is time to acknowledge that this book or my other work would simply not be possible were it not for my wife, Asia Mubashir. She is the rock of our little family. I couldn't have asked for more in a life partner. Asia has constantly pushed me to do better because she believes in me so completely. Asia knew that if I wrote a book, she would have to shoulder significant additional burden. Our kids are young and need the attention of both parents. Yet Asia encouraged me to write because she knows that it is important for me to give voice to my views. She is my biggest supporter (and critic). We are a team and our successes and failures belong to both of us. This book, too, belongs to both of us.

Notes

Introduction

1. 'Minimum Government, Maximum Governance'. www. narendramodi.in. 14 May 2014. Accessed 16 November 2018. https://www.narendramodi.in/minimum-government-maximum-governance-3162.
2. Daniel, Frank Jack and Rajesh Kumar Singh. 'Advisers to Narendra Modi Dream of a Thatcherite Revolution'. Reuters. 6 April 2014. Accessed 16 November 2018. http://in.reuters.com/article/india-election-modi-idINDEEA3500520140406.

Chapter 1: The Inheritance

1. 'Preliminary Transcript of the Q&A Portion of the Prime Minister's Press Conference at the National Media Centre, New Delhi.' Press Information Bureau. 3 January 2014. Accessed 7 January 2019. http://pib.nic.in/newsite/PrintRelease. aspx?relid=102296.
2. ET Online. 'Narendra Modi: You Gave Congress 60 Years, Give BJP 60 Months to Change India's Future'. *Economic Times*. 25 October 2013. Accessed 7 December 2018. https://

economictimes.indiatimes.com/news/politics-and-nation/
narendra-modi-you-gave-congress-60-years-give-bjp-60-
months-to-change-indias-future/articleshow/24702719.cms.

3. Sibal, Rajeev. 'India: The Next Superpower?: The Untold Story
    of India's Economy'. LSE IDEAS, London School of Economics
    and Political Science. May 2012. Accessed 16 October 2018.
    http://eprints.lse.ac.uk/43443/1/India_the   untold   story   of
    India's economy(lsero).pdf.

4. Nehru, Jawaharlal. 'Jawaharlal Nehru: A Tryst with Destiny.'
    Guardian. 30 April 2007. Accessed 7 January 2019. https://www.
    theguardian.com/theguardian/2007/may/01/greatspeeches.

5. An Indian Official. 'India as a World Power.' Foreign Affairs.
    July 1949 issue. Accessed 16 October 2018. https://www.
    foreignaffairs.com/articles/india/1949-07-01/india-world-power.

6. Chetty, Shanmukham. Budget Speech of the Minister of Finance
    for 1947–48. Ministry of Finance, India. Accessed 15 October
    2018. https://www.indiabudget.gov.in/bspeech/bs194748.pdf.

7. Galbraith, John Kenneth. 'Rival Economic Theories in India'.
    Foreign Affairs. July 1958 issue. Accessed 16 November 2018.
    https://www.foreignaffairs.com/articles/india/1958-07-01/
    rival-economic-theories-india.

8. Ministry of Finance. 'Economic Survey 2017–18'. Economic
    Survey 2018. February 2018. Accessed 16 November 2018.
    http://mofapp.nic.in:8080/economicsurvey/.

9. Visaria, Pravin. 'Mortality and Fertility in India, 1951–1961'.
    Milbank Memorial Fund Quarterly Vol. 47, No. 1, Part 1 (January
    1969), pp. 91–116. Accessed 2 November 2018. https://www.
    jstor.org/stable/3349133?read-now=1&refreqid=excelsior%3A
    d866ce90cfad7bb334c2ed45cec6c851&seq=1#page_scan_tab_
    contents.

10. Joe, William, Suresh Sharma, Jyotsna Sharma, Y. Manasa
    Shantana, Mala Ramanathan, Uday Shankar Mishra and B.
    Subha Sri. 'Maternal Mortality in India: A Review of Trends
    and Patterns'. IEG Working Paper No. 353. 2015. Accessed 16
    November 2018. http://www.iegindia.org/upload/publication/
    Workpap/wp353.pdf.

11. Zodpey, Sanjay and Preeti H. Negandhi. 'Tracking India's Progress in Health Sector after 70 Years of Independence'. *Indian Journal of Public Health*. Vol. 62, Issue 1, pp. 1 3. Accessed 2 November 2018. http://www.ijph.in/article.asp?issn=0019-557X;year=2018;volume=62;issue=1;spage=1;epage=3;aulast=Zodpey.

12. Singh, Mahendra. 'Modi Govt Has Just Scrapped Five-Year Plan, New "Three-Year Action Plan" Will Replace It'. Indiatimes. com. 13 April 2017. Accessed 16 November 2018. https://www.indiatimes.com/news/india/modi-govt-has-just-scrapped-five-year-plan-new-three-year-action-plan-will-replace-it-275507.html.

13. Biswas, Kishore Kumar. 'Why Should One Remember Mahalanobis?' *Business Economics*. 1 August 2017. Accessed 16 November 2018. http://businesseconomics.in/why-should-one-remember-mahalanobis.

14. Desai, A.R. *Social Background of Indian Nationalism*. Sixth Edition. New Delhi: Sage Publications, 2016.

15. Bowles, Chester. 'New India'. *Foreign Affairs*. October 1952 issue. Accessed 12 October 2018. https://www.foreignaffairs.com/articles/india/1952-10-01/new-india.

16. Balakrishnan, Pulapre. 'The Recovery of India: Economic Growth in the Nehru Era'. *Economic and Political Weekly* 42, No. 45/46 (23 November 2007): 52–66. Accessed 16 November 2018. https://www.jstor.org/stable/40276833?read-now=1&seq=1#page_scan_tab_contents.

17. Panagariya, Arvind. *India: The Emerging Giant*. Oxford: Oxford University Press, 2010.

18. Nayyar, Deepak. 'Economic Growth in Independent India'. *Economic and Political Weekly* 41, No. 15 (15 April 2006). Accessed 17 September 2018. https://www.epw.in/journal/2006/15/special-articles/economic-growth-independent-india.html.

19. Life expectancy at birth indicates the number of years a newborn infant would live if prevailing patterns of mortality at the time of its birth were to stay the same throughout its life. Source: (1) United Nations Population Division. World Population

Prospects: 2017 Revision, or derived from male and female life expectancy at birth from sources such as: (2) Census reports and other statistical publications from national statistical offices, (3) Eurostat: Demographic Statistics, (4) United Nations Statistical Division. Population and Vital Statistics Report (various years), (5) US Census Bureau: International Database, and (6) Secretariat of the Pacific Community: Statistics and Demography Programme.

20. Dhar, P.N. *Indira Gandhi, the 'Emergency', and Indian Democracy*. New York; New Delhi: Oxford University Press, 2000.

21. Rajadhyaksha, Niranjan. 'The Man Who Could Have Reformed Our Economy'. Livemint.com. 15 March 2013. Accessed 16 November 2018. https://www.livemint.com/Leisure/VBKnp4FAprlOZppLLpvuJP/The-man-who-could-have-reformed-our-economy.html.

22. Panagariya, Arvind. 'Miracles & Debacles: In Defense of Trade Openness.' Department of Economics, University of Columbia. 2004. Accessed 12 January 2019. http://www.columbia.edu/~ap2231/Policy Papers/miracles and debacles-March-04.pdf.

23. Singh, Hemant. 'Census 2011: Literacy Rate and Sex Ratio in India since 1901 to 2011'. Jagranjosh.com. 17 October 2016. Accessed 16 November 2018. https://www.jagranjosh.com/general-knowledge/census-2011-literacy-rate-and-sex-ratio-in-india-since-1901-to-2011-1476359944-1.

24. 'Mortality Rate, Under-5 (per 1,000 Live Births)'. Literacy Rate, Adult Female (% of Females Ages 15 and Above). Data. Accessed 16 November 2018. https://data.worldbank.org/indicator/SH.DYN.MORT.

25. Joshi, Vijay and I.M.D Little. 1994. 'India—Macroeconomics and Political Economy, 1964–1991 (English)'. World Bank Comparative Macroeconomic Studies, World Bank. 31 July 1994. Accessed 16 November 2018. http://documents.worldbank.org/curated/en/259451468772490617/India-Macroeconomics-and-political-economy-1964–1991.

26. Ibid.

27. Ibid.

28. Banerjee, Abhijit V., Esther Duflo and Shawn Cole. 'Banking Reform in India'. Department of Economics, MIT. June 2004. Accessed 16 November 2018. https://economics.mit.edu/files/508.

29. Joshi, Vijay and I.M.D. Little. 'India—Macroeconomics and Political Economy, 1964–1991 (English)'. World Bank comparative macroeconomic studies, World Bank. 31 July 1994. Accessed 16 November 2018. http://documents.worldbank.org/curated/en/259451468772490617/India-Macroeconomics-and-political-economy-1964–1991.

30. Sibal, Rajeev. 'India: The Next Superpower?: The Untold Story of India's Economy'. LSE IDEAS, London School of Economics and Political Science. May 2012. Accessed 16 October 2018. http://eprints.lse.ac.uk/43443/1/India_the untold story of India's economy(lsero).pdf.

31. Bhagwati, Jagdish and Arvind Panagariya. *Why Growth Matters: How Economic Growth in India Reduced Poverty and the Lessons for Other Developing Countries*. New York: PublicAffairs, 2014.

32. Ibid.

33. Life expectancy at birth indicates the number of years a newborn infant would live if prevailing patterns of mortality at the time of its birth were to stay the same throughout its life. Source: (1) United Nations Population Division. World Population Prospects: 2017 Revision, or derived from male and female life expectancy at birth from sources such as: (2) Census reports and other statistical publications from national statistical offices, (3) Eurostat: Demographic Statistics, (4) United Nations Statistical Division. Population and Vital Statistics Report (various years), (5) US Census Bureau: International Database, and (6) Secretariat of the Pacific Community: Statistics and Demography Programme.

34. AICC. 'Let the Comparisons Begin: Let the Comparisons Begin: Full Text of Rajiv Gandhi's Famous 1985 Speech'. *India Today*. 21 January 2013. Accessed 7 January 2019. https://www.indiatoday.in/india/story/full-text-of-rajiv-gandhis-famous-1985-speech-152145-2013-01-21.

35. Nayyar, Deepak. 'Economic Growth in Independent India: Lumbering Elephant or Running Tiger?' *Economic and Political Weekly* 41, no. 15 (15 April 2006). Accessed 7 January 2019. https://www.epw.in/journal/2006/15/special-articles/economic-growth-independent-india.html.

36. Rodrik, Dani and Arvind Subramanian. 'From "Hindu Growth" to Productivity Surge: The Mystery of the Indian Growth Transition'. National Bureau of Economic Research Working Paper 10376. 2004. doi:10.3386/w10376.

37. As per Dani Rodrik and Arvind Subramanian, the four major internal liberalization measures that were implemented in 1985 and 1986 involved: (i) Eliminating the licensing of twenty-five categories of industries subject to certain fairly onerous conditions; (ii) extending delicensing to large companies in twenty-two industries which were previously restricted by the MRTP Act and FERA Act; (iii) allowing companies in twenty-eight industries to expand the scope of their operations into related activities; and (iv) allowing companies that had reached 80 per cent capacity utilization to expand their capacity up to 133 per cent of that reached in any of the previous years. Apart from the first, all the remaining measures essentially allowed incumbents to operate more freely rather than facilitate the entry of new domestic firms and promote competition. Even the limited reduction in the protection of capital-goods industries served to increase the effective protection of incumbents in final-goods industries.

38. Ibid.

39. Balakrishnan, Pulapre. 'Economic Consequences of Rajiv Gandhi'. *Economic and Political Weekly* 25, No. 6 (10 February 1990). Accessed 16 November 2018. https://www.epw.in/journal/1990/6/roots-specials/economic-consequences-rajiv-gandhi.html.

40. George, Natalia. 'Reforms Shape India's Economy (1980–90)'. Yahoo! News. 14 August 2011. Accessed 16 November 2018. https://www.yahoo.com/news/Reforms-shape-India-economy-yahoofinancein-2531391639.html.

41. Vikraman, Shaji. 'The Years of V P Singh, and the Start-Stop Push to Reforms'. *Indian Express*. 5 April 2017. Accessed 16 November 2018. https://indianexpress.com/article/explained/the-years-of-v-p-singh-and-the-start-stop-push-to-reforms/.

42. Life expectancy at birth indicates the number of years a newborn infant would live if prevailing patterns of mortality at the time of its birth were to stay the same throughout its life. Source: (1) United Nations Population Division. World Population Prospects: 2017 Revision, or derived from male and female life expectancy at birth from sources such as: (2) Census reports and other statistical publications from national statistical offices, (3) Eurostat: Demographic Statistics, (4) United Nations Statistical Division. Population and Vital Statistics Report (various years), (5) US Census Bureau: International Database, and (6) Secretariat of the Pacific Community: Statistics and Demography Programme.

43. Singh, Manmohan. 'Union Budget of India 1991–1992—Minister of Finance's Speech'. Teamwork. 12 August 2018. Accessed 7 January 2019. http://www.theteamwork.com/finance/2546-union-budget-india-1991-1992-minister-finance-speech.html.

44. Panagariya, Arvind. 'India's Economic Reforms: What Has Been Accomplished? What Remains to Be Done?' Asian Development Bank, Economics and Research Department. November 2001. Accessed 16 November 2018. https://www.adb.org/sites/default/files/publication/28060/pb002.pdf.

45. Basu, Kaushik and Annemie Maertens. 'The Pattern and Causes of Economic Growth in India'. *Oxford Review of Economic Policy* 23, No. 2 (2007). doi:10.1093/icb/grm012.

46. Ibid.

47. Nayyar, Deepak. 'Then and Now: Economic Liberalisation in India'. *Economic and Political Weekly* 52, no. 2 (14 January 2017). Accessed 7 January 2019. https://www.epw.in/journal/2017/2/25-years-economic-liberalisation/economic-liberalisation-india.html.

48. Nayyar, Deepak. 'Then and Now: Economic Liberalisation in India'. *Economic and Political Weekly* 52, No. 2 (14 January

2017). Accessed 16 November 2018. https://www.epw.in/
journal/2017/2/25-years-economic-liberalisation/economic-
liberalisation-india.html.

49. Ibid.
50. Ibid.
51. Ministry of Finance. 'Economic Survey 1996–97'. Union Budget.
     Accessed 16 November 2018. https://www.indiabudget.gov.in/
     previouses.asp.
52. Ibid.
53. Ministry of Finance. 'Economic Survey 1997–98'. Union Budget.
     Accessed 16 November 2018. https://www.indiabudget.gov.in/
     previouses.asp.
54. FE Online. 'Atal Bihari Vajpayee No More: Look Back at 4 Key
     Reforms under Ex-PM Which Helped India Shine'. *Financial
     Express*. 16 August 2018. Accessed 16 November 2018. https://
     www.financialexpress.com/economy/atal-bihari-vajpayees-
     health-critical-here-are-4-key-reforms-by-ex-pm-which-
     helped-india-shine/1282018/.
55. Ibid.
56. Ibid.
57. Panagariya, Arvind. 'India's Economic Reforms: What Has Been
     Accomplished? What Remains to Be Done?' Asian Development
     Bank, Economics and Research Department. November 2001.
     Accessed 16 November 2018. https://www.adb.org/sites/
     default/files/publication/28060/pb002.pdf.
58. Nayyar, Deepak. 'Then and Now: Economic Liberalisation
     in India'. *Economic and Political Weekly* 52, No. 2 (14 January
     2017). Accessed 16 November 2018. https://www.epw.in/
     journal/2017/2/25-years-economic-liberalisation/economic-
     liberalisation-india.html.
59. Life expectancy at birth indicates the number of years a newborn
     infant would live if prevailing patterns of mortality at the time
     of its birth were to stay the same throughout its life. Source:
     (1) United Nations Population Division. World Population
     Prospects: 2017 Revision, or derived from male and female life
     expectancy at birth from sources such as: (2) Census reports and

other statistical publications from national statistical offices, (3) Eurostat: Demographic Statistics, (4) United Nations Statistical Division. Population and Vital Statistics Report (various years), (5) US Census Bureau: International Database, and (6) Secretariat of the Pacific Community: Statistics and Demography Programme.

60. In the years following the CAG's 'presumptive loss', assessments related to allocation of telecom spectrum have been widely criticized and a Central Bureau of Investigation court could not convict accused persons based on these reports.

61. Rediff.com. 'Indian Economy under Manmohan Singh Is in ICU'. 28 August 2013. Accessed 16 October 2018. https://www.rediff.com/business/report/indian-economy-under-manmohan-singh-is-in-icu/20130828.htm.

62. PTI. 'Rupee Has Lost Its Value, PM Has Lost His Grace: Sushma Swaraj'. 30 August 2013. Accessed 16 October 2018. https://timesofindia.indiatimes.com/india/Rupee-has-lost-its-value-PM-has-lost-his-grace-Sushma-Swaraj/articleshow/22167355.cms.

63. Chatterjee, Urmila, Rinku Murgai, Ambar Narayan and Martin Rama. 'Pathways to Reducing Poverty and Sharing Prosperity in India'. Documents and Reports, World Bank. 1 January 2016. Accessed 16 November 2018. http://documents.worldbank.org/curated/en/559851468910056173/Pathways-to-reducing-poverty-and-sharing-prosperity-in-India-lessons-from-the-last-two-decades.

64. Kotwal, Ashok, Maitreesh Ghatak and Parikshit Ghosh. 'Growth in the Time of UPA: Myths and Reality'. *Economic and Political Weekly* 49, No. 16 (19 April 2014). Accessed 16 November 2018. https://www.epw.in/journal/2014/16/insight/growth-time-upa.html.

65. Ibid.

66. Gupta, Poonam. 'This Is the Story of India's GDP Growth'. World Economic Forum. 13 April 2018. Accessed 16 November 2018. https://www.weforum.org/agenda/2018/04/india-s-remarkably-robust-and-resilient-growth-story.

67. Kotwal, Ashok, Maitreesh Ghatak and Parikshit Ghosh. 'Growth
     in the Time of UPA: Myths and Reality'. *Economic and Political
     Weekly* 49, No. 16 (19 April 2014). Accessed 16 November
     2018. https://www.epw.in/journal/2014/16/insight/growth-
     time-upa.html.
68. Jain, Anurodh Lalit. 'The UPA Regime: A Decade of Massive
     Healthcare Reform'. *Economic Times*. 27 January 2014. https://
     economictimes.indiatimes.com/opinion/et-commentary/
     the-upa-regime-a-decade-of-massive-healthcare-reform/
     articleshow/29430774.cms.
69. Ibid.
70. Life expectancy at birth indicates the number of years a newborn
     infant would live if prevailing patterns of mortality at the time
     of its birth were to stay the same throughout its life. Source:
     (1) United Nations Population Division. World Population
     Prospects: 2017 Revision, or derived from male and female life
     expectancy at birth from sources such as: (2) Census reports and
     other statistical publications from national statistical offices, (3)
     Eurostat: Demographic Statistics, (4) United Nations Statistical
     Division. Population and Vital Statistics Report (various years), (5)
     US Census Bureau: International Database, and (6) Secretariat of
     the Pacific Community: Statistics and Demography Programme.

Chapter 2: The Promise

1. Gowen, Annie. 'India's Likely Next Leader, Narendra Modi,
    Promises Economic Success. Can He Deliver?' *Washington Post*. 15
    May 2014. Accessed 9 April 2017. https://www.washingtonpost.
    com/world/asia_pacific/indias-likely-new-leader-narendra-
    modi-promises-economic-success-can-he-deliver/2014/05/14/
    d27864ac-daca-11e3-8009-71de85b9c527_story.html?utm_
    term=.7ad7c309fcaa.
2. Aiyar, Swaminathan S. Anklesaria. 'Don't Expect Major Reforms
    from Manmohan as FM'. Swaminomics. 1 July 2012. Accessed
    20 May 2017. https://swaminomics.org/dont-expect-major-
    reforms-from-manmohan-as-fm/.

3.   Burke, Jason. 'Bharatiya Janata Party Leader Predicts Landslide
      Win in Indian Elections'. *Guardian*. 26 March 2014. Accessed
      20 May 2017. https://www.theguardian.com/world/2014/
      mar/26/india-opposition-bjp-leader-rajnath-singh-deep-
      economic-reforms.
4.   Bengali, Shashank. 'India's Narendra Modi Leads Conservatives
      to Election Day Victory'. *Los Angeles Times*. 16 May 2014.
      Accessed 20 May 2017. http://www.latimes.com/world/asia/
      la-fg-india-conservatives-elections-modi-20140516-story.html.
5.   Sen, Amartya and Jean Drèze. *An Uncertain Glory: India and Its
      Contradictions*. Princeton: Princeton University Press, 2013.
6.   The Economist Online. 'Indian Development–Beyond
      Bootstraps. Why the World's Biggest Democracy Still Fails
      Too Many of Its People'. *Economist*. 29 June 2013. Accessed
      17 September 2018. https://www.economist.com/books-and-
      arts/2013/06/29/beyond-bootstraps.
7.   Ibid.
8.   The Economist Online. 'Letters—On India, Gay Marriage,
      Protesting, Iran, Marc Rich, Political Pi'. *Economist*. 13 July
      2013. Accessed 27 September 2018. https://www.economist.
      com/letters/2013/07/13/on-india-gay-marriage-protesting-
      iran-marc-rich-political-pi.
9.   The Economist Online. 'Letters—On Amartya Sen, Defence
      Spending, Britain, Egypt, Immigration, France, GDP, Sailing'.
      Economist. 20 July 2013. Accessed 27 September 2018. https://
      www.economist.com/letters/2013/07/20/on-amartya-sen-
      defence-spending-britain-egypt-immigration-france-gdp-sailing.
10.   Bhagwati, Jagdish. 'Why Amartya Sen Is Wrong: Jagdish
      Bhagwati.' https://www.livemint.com/. 23 July 2013.
      Accessed 7 January 2019. https://www.livemint.com/
      Opinion/9Qzg05zypjEUbioqK9N1UM/Why-Amartya-Sen-
      is-wrong.html.
11.   Ibid.
12.   Bunsha, Dionne. 'Modi's Mandate'. *Frontline*. 5 January 2008.
      Accessed 27 September 2018. https://www.frontline.in/static/
      html/fl2501/stories/20080118509812400.htm.

13. Khare, Harish. 'The Humbug Called Gujarat Model Statecraft'. *The Hindu.* 8 October 2016. Accessed 27 September 2018. https://www.thehindu.com/todays-paper/tp-opinion/The-humbug-called-Gujarat-model-statecraft/article15156455.ece#!

14. Asher, Mukul G. 'The Gujarat Model'. *Pragati: Indian National Interest Review,* No. 12 (21 March 2008). Accessed 27 September 2018. http://pragati.nationalinterest.in/wp-content/uploads/2008/03/pragati-issue12-march2008-communityed.pdf.

15. *Pragati: Indian National Interest Review* fashions itself as 'an independent community of individuals committed to increasing public awareness and education on strategic affairs, economic policy and governance'.

16. Asher, Mukul G. 'The Gujarat Model'. *Pragati: Indian National Interest Review,* No. 12 (21 March 2008). Accessed 27 September 2018. http://pragati.nationalinterest.in/wp-content/uploads/2008/03/pragati-issue12-march2008-communityed.pdf.

17. 'Sex Ratio in India'. Religion Data: Population of Hindu/Muslim/Sikh/Christian—Census 2011 India. Accessed 27 September 2018. http://www.census2011.co.in/sexratio.php.

18. The Economist Online. 'A La Modi'. *Economist.* 3 January 2008. Accessed 27 September 2018. https://www.economist.com/asia/2008/01/03/a-la-modi.

19. Ibid.

20. Dhume, Sadanand. 'Prime Minister Modi Won't Fly'. *Wall Street Journal.* 30 March 2010. Accessed 27 September 2018. https://www.wsj.com/articles/SB10001424052702304561304575153154130915506.

21. Dhume, Sadanand. 'The Talented Mr. Modi'. *Foreign Policy.* 20 December 2012. Accessed 27 September 2018. https://foreignpolicy.com/2012/12/19/the-talented-mr-modi/.

22. Dehejia, Vivek. '"Modi Model," Template for India's Development?' Rediff.com India News. 16 January 2013. Accessed 27 September 2018. http://www.rediff.com/business/slide-show/slide-show-1-could-the-modi-model-be-template-for-development/20130116.htm.

23. Dehejia, Vivek. 'The Heart of Modinomics'. https://www.livemint.com/. 14 May 2014. Accessed 27 September 2018. https://www.livemint.com/Opinion/PKSqUTdJRzo8OWCssnuLNI/The-heart-of-Modinomics.html.

24. Debroy, Bibek. 'Gujarat's Data on Social Indicators Shows Positive Impact of Policies'. Economic Times Blog. 6 August 2013. Accessed 27 September 2018. https://blogs.economictimes.indiatimes.com/policypuzzles/gujarat-s-data-on-social-indicators-shows-positive-impact-of-policies/.

25. Inamdar, Nikhil. 'Define "Modinomics", Please!' *Business Standard*. 23 December 2013. Accessed 27 September 2018. https://www.business-standard.com/article/economy-policy/define-modinomics-please-113122300279_1.html.

26. Bhalla, Surjit S. 'Lessons from the Gujarat Model'. Indian Express Archive. 26 October 2013. Accessed 27 September 2018. http://archive.indianexpress.com/news/lessons-from-the-gujarat-model/1187332/0.

27. N.P., Ullekh. 'Gujarat Promises Continued, Accelerated and All-around Progress: Jagdish Bhagwati & Arvind Panagariya.' *Economic Times*. 20 June 2013. Accessed 17 September 2018. https://economictimes.indiatimes.com/opinion/interviews/gujarat-promises-continued-accelerated-and-all-around-progress-jagdish-bhagwati-arvind-panagariya/articleshow/17849401.cms.

28. Jaffrelot, Christophe. 'The Modi-Centric BJP 2014 Election Campaign: New Techniques and Old Tactics'. *Contemporary South Asia* 23, No. 2 (2015): 151–66. doi:10.1080/09584935.2015.1027662.

29. 'Modi Woos India Inc, Says Country in Despair as UPA Takes No Responsibility'. *Indian Express*. 15 January 2014. Accessed 7 January 2019. https://indianexpress.com/article/india/politics/modi-woos-india-inc-says-country-in-despair-as-upa-takes-no-responsibility-2/.

30. Shaikh, Samira. 'Narendra Modi Shares His Vision of "Brand India" in 5 Ts'. NDTV.com. 20 January 2014. Accessed 7 January 2019. https://www.ndtv.com/cheat-sheet/narendra-modi-shares-his-vision-of-brand-india-in-5-ts-548337.

31. Soz, Salman Anees. 'Narendra Modi's Economic "Vision": Is BJP Selling What UPA Made?' *DNA*. 28 January 2014. Accessed 27 September 2018. https://www.dnaindia.com/analysis/standpoint-narendra-modi-s-economic-vision-is-bjp-selling-what-upa-made-1957948.

32. Shrivastava, Rahul and Deepshikha Ghosh. 'BJP's "Modi-festo" Headlines Economy, Downplays Ram Mandir'. NDTV.com. 7 April 2014. Accessed 11 November 2018. https://www.ndtv.com/elections-news/bjps-modi-festo-headlines-economy-downplays-ram-mandir-556500.

33. Chattopadhyay, Suvojit. 'Why the BJP Did Not Need a Manifesto for 2014'. https://www.livemint.com/. 15 April 2014. Accessed 11 November 2018. https://www.livemint.com/Opinion/XMVsWaAq6Vr9OXUgxepjgL/Why-the-BJP-did-not-need-a-manifesto-for-2014.html.

34. Ibid.

35. 'Woolly Promises'. *Frontline*. 2 May 2014. Accessed 11 November 2018. https://www.frontline.in/columns/Jayati_Ghosh/woolly-promises/article5914765.ece.

36. Ibid.

37. Note: As we now know, economic growth in the ten years of UPA rule is the highest ever for such a period. A change in the methodology of calculating economic output led to a revision of GDP growth in 2013–14 from 4.7 per cent to 6.4 per cent.

38. Ghosh, Jayati. 'India's Official Poverty Line Doesn't Measure Up'. *Guardian*. 4 October 2011. Accessed 11 November 2018. https://www.theguardian.com/global-development/poverty-matters/2011/oct/04/india-measuring-poverty-line.

39. Joshi, Poornima. 'Modi Promises a Gujarat for Uttar Pradesh'. *The Hindu BusinessLine*. 23 January 2014. Accessed 11 November 2018. https://www.thehindubusinessline.com/news/modi-promises-a-gujarat-for-uttar-pradesh/article20715478.ece1.

40. Varma, Gyan. 'Narendra Modi Promises Higher Support Price to Farmers.' https://www.livemint.com/. 15 April 2014. Accessed 7 January 2019. https://www.livemint.com/Politics/

bYMbXRsL3eYQw2Bp4iMaXI/Narendra-Modi-promises-higher-support-price-to-farmers.html.

41. 'Modi Promises One Crore Jobs if BJP Comes to Power'. Firstpost. 22 November 2013. Accessed 27 September 2018. https://www.firstpost.com/india/modi-promises-one-crore-jobs-if-bjp-comes-to-power-1243037.html.

42. Kumar, Manoj. 'Business Looks to Modi to Defuse India's Jobs Time Bomb'. Reuters. 4 May 2014. Accessed 11 November 2018. https://www.reuters.com/article/us-india-election-employment/business-looks-to-modi-to-defuse-indias-jobs-time-bomb-idUSBREA4309B20140504.

43. FP Staff. 'Health, Defence, Government: Modi Lists His Plans if He Becomes PM'. Firstpost. 1 April 2014. Accessed 11 November 2018. https://www.firstpost.com/lok sabha-election-2014/news/health-defence-government-modi-lists-his-plans-if-he-becomes-pm-1459553.html.

44. Special Correspondent. 'Economy in a Shambles Because of UPA's Policy Paralysis, Says Modi'. *The Hindu*. 28 May 2016. Accessed 11 November 2018. https://www.thehindu.com/news/national/other-states/economy-in-a-shambles-because-of-upas-policy-paralysis-says-modi/article5391091.ece.

45. BS Reporter. 'FDI Policy Needs to Be Reviewed, Says Modi'. *Business Standard*. 18 April 2014. Accessed 11 November 2018. https://www.business-standard.com/article/elections-2014/fdi-policy-needs-to-be-reviewed-says-modi-114041800482_1.html.

46. IndiaToday.in. 'Won't Do Anything for Myself or out of Ill Intent, Says Narendra Modi'. *India Today*. 7 April 2014. Accessed 11 November 2018. https://www.indiatoday.in/elections/highlights/story/bjp-manifesto-promises-prosperous-and-vibrant-india-187932-2014-04-07.

47. Pant, Anuj and PTI. 'What about 15 Lakh in Accounts Promised by PM Modi, Asked RTI. The Reply'. NDTV.com. 23 April 2018. Accessed 11 November 2018. https://www.ndtv.com/india-news/what-about-15-lakh-in-accounts-promised-by-pm-narendra-modi-asked-rti-the-reply-1841652.

48. TNN. 'We'll Bring Back Black Money in 150 Days: BJP President Rajnath Singh'. *Times of India*. 20 April 2014. Accessed 11 November 2018. https://timesofindia.indiatimes.com/news/Well-bring-back-black-money-in-150-days-BJP-president-Rajnath-Singh/articleshow/34016640.cms.

49. ET Bureau. 'PM Modi's Promise of "Rs 15 Lakh in Each Account" an Idiom: Amit Shah'. *Economic Times*. 6 February 2015. Accessed 11 November 2018. https://economictimes.indiatimes.com/news/politics-and-nation/pm-modis-promise-of-rs-15-lakh-in-each-account-an-idiom-amit-shah/articleshow/46139139.cms.

50. FP Staff. 'Health, Defence, Government: Modi Lists His Plans if He Becomes PM'. Firstpost. 1 April 2014. Accessed 11 November 2018. https://www.firstpost.com/lok-sabha-election-2014/news/health-defence-government-modi-lists-his-plans-if-he-becomes-pm-1459553.html.

51. PTI. 'Fighting Inflation, Developing 100 Smart Cities in Modi's Vision 2014'. *The Hindu BusinessLine*. 19 January 2014. Accessed 11 November 2018. https://www.thehindubusinessline.com/news/national/Fighting-inflation-developing-100-smart-cities-in-Modi's-Vision-2014/article20713491.ece.

52. Varma, Gyan and PTI. 'Narendra Modi Promises Relook at Taxation if Elected PM'. https://www.livemint.com/. 5 January 2014. Accessed 11 November 2018. https://www.livemint.com/Politics/bWxAq03OWAUDTIK9VJt7jI/Narendra-Modi-Born-to-serve-people-not-hold-a-post.html.

53. PTI. 'Raise IT Slab from Rs 2 Lakh to Rs 5 Lakh, Demands Arun Jaitley'. *Economic Times*. 20 April 2014. Accessed 11 November 2018. https://economictimes.indiatimes.com/news/politics-and-nation/raise-it-slab-from-rs-2-lakh-to-rs-5-lakh-demands-arun-jaitley/articleshow/34013531.cms.

54. Varma, Gyan. 'Narendra Modi Promises Higher Support Price to Farmers'. https://www.livemint.com/. 15 April 2014. Accessed 11 November 2018. https://www.livemint.com/Politics/bYMbXRsL3eYQw2Bp4iMaXI/Narendra-Modi-promises-higher-support-price-to-farmers.html.

55. Ibid.

56. Menon, Aditya. 'Modi Charms Students of DU College with Gujarat Story, Says This Century Belongs to India'. *India Today*. 7 February 2013. Accessed 7 January 2019. https://www.indiatoday. in/india/north/story/gujarat-chief-minister-narendra-modi-srcc-college-delhi-university-153399-2013-02-06.

57. BS Reporter. 'FDI Policy Needs to Be Reviewed, Says Modi'. *Business Standard*. 18 April 2014. Accessed 11 November 2018. https://www.business-standard.com/article/elections-2014/fdi-policy-needs-to-be-reviewed-says-modi-114041800482_1.html.

58. Panwar, Preeti. 'Narendra Modi Stresses on Education, Health at Belgaum Rally'. https://www.oneindia.com. 23 January 2014. Accessed 11 November 2018. https://www.oneindia.com/belgaum/in-pics-narendra-modi-stresses-on-education-health-at-belgaum-rally/articlecontent-pf6719-1362620.html.

59. FP Staff. 'Health, Defence, Government: Modi Lists His Plans if He Becomes PM'. Firstpost. 1 April 2014. Accessed 11 November 2018. https://www.firstpost.com/lok-sabha-election-2014/news/health-defence-government-modi-lists-his-plans-if-he-becomes-pm-1459553.html.

60. Ibid.

61. Bhaskar, Utpal. 'Renewable Is the Way Forward for India's Energy Security: Narendra Modi'. https://www.livemint.com/. 26 February 2014. Accessed 11 November 2018. https://www.livemint.com/Politics/7EkcrE6zgNmZJSlta0exlK/Renewable-is-the-way-forward-for-Indias-energy-security-Na.html.

62. Goyal, Piyush. 'Blog: Narendra Modi's Agenda vs Congress' Agenda for India's Economy'. NDTV.com. 24 February 2014. Accessed 11 November 2018. https://www.ndtv.com/blog/blog-narendra-modis-agenda-vs-congress-agenda-for-indias-economy-by-piyush-goyal-551158.

Chapter 3: The Policies and Programmes

1. Hayek, F.A. *Fatal Conceit: The Errors of Socialism*. Chicago: University of Chicago Press, 1991.

2. Mantri, Rajeev and Harsh Gupta. 'Narendra Modi as the Anti-Nehru'. https://www.livemint.com/. 2 September 2013. Accessed 24 October 2018. http://www.livemint.com/Opinion/DCrr6B9v1MvR6QTEMGDcJM/Narendra-Modi-as-the-antiNehru.html.

3. Administrator. 'Ek Bharat Shreshta Bharat, Election Manifesto 2014'. BJP Manifesto 2014. Accessed 24 October 2018. http://www.bjp.org/manifesto2014.

4. Singh, Rajesh Kumar. 'India's Pro-business Modi Storms to Historic Election Win'. Reuters. 16 May 2014. Accessed 24 October 2018. http://www.reuters.com/article/us-india-election-idUSBREA4E0XG20140516.

5. Barry, Ellen. 'Narendra Modi's Ambitious Agenda Will Face Difficult Obstacles'. New York Times. 16 May 2014. Accessed 24 October 2018. https://www.nytimes.com/2014/05/17/world/asia/india-elections.html?mtrref=www.google.com&auth=login-email.

6. Ibid.

7. Panagariya, Arvind. 'Modinomics at Four'. Foreign Affairs. 22 June 2018. Accessed 10 January 2019. https://www.foreignaffairs.com/articles/india/2018-06-22/modinomics-four.

8. Kumar, Rajiv and Pankaj Vashisht. 'The Global Economic Crisis: Impact on India and Policy Responses'. The Global Financial Crisis and Asia–ADB Institute Working Paper Series No. 164. November 2009. doi:10.1093/acprof:oso/9780199660957.003.0008.

9. Ibid.

10. Ibid.

11. Ibid.

12. Ibid.

13. Ibid.

14. Ibid.

15. Izvorski, Ivailo. '10 Years Later: 4 Fiscal Policy Lessons from the Global Financial Crisis'. Brookings. 25 June 2018. Accessed 24 October 2018. https://www.brookings.edu/blog/future-

development/2018/06/25/10-years-later-4-fiscal-policy-lessons-from-the-global-financial-crisis/.

16. IMF. 'World Economic Outlook Database October 2008—IMF'. Accessed on 10 January 2019. https://www.imf.org/external/pubs/ft/weo/2008/02/weodata/index.aspx.

17. Kumar, Rajiv and Pankaj Vashisht. 'The Global Economic Crisis: Impact on India and Policy Responses'. The Global Financial Crisis and Asia–ADB Institute Working Paper Series No. 164. November 2009. doi:10.1093/acprof:oso/9780199660957.003.0008.

18. World Bank Group. 'India Development Update, October 2014'. Open Knowledge Repository. 1 October 2014. Accessed 24 October 2018. https://openknowledge.worldbank.org/handle/10986/20794?show=full.

19. FE Online. 'Land Norms Eased for Infra, Defence Projects'. *Financial Express.* 29 December 2014. Accessed 7 January 2019. https://www.financialexpress.com/economy/land-norms-eased-for-infra-defence-projects/24359/.

20. World Bank Group. 'India Development Update, April 2015'. Open Knowledge Repository. 1 April 2015. Accessed 24 October 2018. https://openknowledge.worldbank.org/handle/10986/21872.

21. 'Dressing Down'. *Business Standard.* 23 July 2014. Accessed 24 October 2018. https://www.business-standard.com/article/opinion/dressing-down-114072301659_1.html.

22. Anuja. 'Congress Releases List of "U-turns" Made by BJP Government'. https://www.livemint.com/. 1 December 2014. Accessed 24 October 2018. https://www.livemint.com/Politics/d3fh99eZOgDLnStZ92pmoI/Congress-releases-list-of-Uturns-made-by-government.html.

23. TNN. 'No Ordinance to Amend Land Acquisition Law, Law Minister Sadananda Gowda Says'. *Times of India.* 20 November 2014. Accessed 24 October 2018. https://timesofindia.indiatimes.com/india/No-ordinance-to-amend-land-acquisition-law-law-minister-Sadananda-Gowda-says/articleshow/45211921.cms.

24. Express News Service. 'PM Narendra Modi Flags "Lies" on Land Bill, Says "Can't Think of Sin of Cutting Relief"'. *Indian Express*. 22 March 2015. Accessed 24 October 2018. https:// indianexpress.com/article/india/india-others/pm-modi-to-farmers-lies-being-spread-on-land-bill/.

25. Jog, Sanjay. 'On Land Ordinance Issue, BJP Allies in Maharashtra Don Opposition Hat'. *Business Standard*. 25 February 2015. Accessed 24 October 2018. https://www.business-standard. com/article/politics/on-land-ordinance-issue-bjp-allies-in-maharashtra-don-opposition-hat-business-standard-news-115022500268_1.html.

26. Bhattacharya, Suryatapa. 'Narendra Modi's Suit and Its Message to Obama.' Wall Street Journal Blog. 26 January 2015. Accessed 7 January 2019. https://blogs.wsj.com/ indiarealtime/2015/01/26/narendra-modis-suit-and-its-message-to-obama/.

27. TNN. 'Rahul Gandhi Tears into Modi's "Suit-Boot ki Sarkar"'. *Times of India*. 21 April 2015. Accessed on 4 January 2019. https://timesofindia.indiatimes.com/india/Rahul-Gandhi-tears-into-Modis-suit-boot-ki-sarkar/articleshow/46993611. cms.

28. Kazmin, Amy. 'India's Narendra Modi Stumbles on Land Reform'. *Financial Times*. 9 August 2015. Accessed 24 October 2018. https://www.ft.com/content/ee2fb6ec-3e55-11e5-9abe-5b335da3a90e.

29. Aiyar, Swaminathan S. Anklesaria. 'Why Land Acquisition Bill Reveals PM Modi as Indecisive, Happier Retreating than an Authoritarian'. Economic Times Blog. 5 August 2015. Accessed 24 October 2018. https://blogs.economictimes.indiatimes.com/ Swaminomics/why-land-acquisition-bill-reveals-pm-modi-as-indecisive-happier-retreating-than-an-authoritarian/.

30. Mehta, Pratap Bhanu. 'Loud but Silent: Modi's Actions Are Opposite to the Mythology Surrounding Him'. *Indian Express*. 7 August 2015. Accessed 24 October 2018. https://indianexpress. com/article/opinion/columns/loud-but-silent/.

31. Ministry of Finance. 'Economic Survey, 2013–14'. Economic Division, Department of Economic Affairs, India. 2014.

32. Lokare, Shashidhai M. 'RBI Working Paper Series No. 03 Re-emerging Stress in the Asset Quality of Indian Banks: Macro-Financial Linkages'. Reserve Bank of India—Publications. 7 February 2014. Accessed 24 October 2018. https://rbi.org.in/Scripts/PublicationsView.aspx?Id=15720.

33. Unnikrishnan, Dinesh. 'Here's the Solution to All Banking Sector Ills. Does Jaitley Have the Guts to Take It Up?' Firstpost. 15 July 2014. Accessed 24 October 2018. https://www.firstpost.com/business/economy/heres-the-solution-to-all-banking-sector-ills-does-jaitley-have-the-guts-to-take-it-up-2010497.html.

34. 'Basel III: International Regulatory Framework for Banks'. Bank for International Settlements. Accessed on 4 January 2019. https://www.bis.org/bcbs/basel3.htm.

35. PIB. 'Union Budget 2018: Full Text of Arun Jaitley's Budget Speech'. https://www.livemint.com/. 1 February 2018. Accessed 7 January 2019. https://www.livemint.com/Politics/6ZTmv653VqU5ghPAcWCfTJ/Union-Budget-2018-Full-text-of-Arun-Jaitley-budget-speech.html.

36. Ibid.

37. ET Bureau. 'Six Ways in Which Black Money Is Created'. *Economic Times*. 17 November 2011. Accessed on 7 January 2019. https://economictimes.indiatimes.com/slideshows/economy/six-ways-in-which-black-money-is-created/slideshow/10763537.cms.

38. IE Bureau. 'Both Sides of the Coin: What Top Economists Think about Demonetisation'. *Indian Express*. 28 November 2016. Accessed on 7 January 2019. https://indianexpress.com/article/india/india-news-india/both-sides-of-the-coin-what-top-economists-think-about-demonetisation/.

39. Annual Report (2015–16). Reserve Bank of India. 29 August 2016. Accessed on 7 January 2019. https://rbidocs.rbi.org.in/rdocs/AnnualReport/PDFs/0RBIAR2016CD93589EC2C4467793892C79FD05555D.PDF.

40. PTI. 'Finance Minister Arun Jaitley Knew about Demonetisation in Advance: Piyush Goyal'. *Indian Express*. 3 December 2016. Accessed 24 October 2018. https://indianexpress.com/article/india/finance-minster-arun-jaitley-knew-about-demonetisation-in-advance-piyush-goyal-4408418/.

41. PTI. 'Can't Disclose if Arun Jaitley Was Consulted on Demonetisation: Finance Ministry'. https://www.livemint.com/. 5 March 2017. Accessed 24 October 2018. https://www.livemint.com/Politics/SNYhOxicsUtjCLttnYT91K/Cant-disclose-if-Arun-Jaitley-was-consulted-on-demonetisati.html.

42. Nair, Vishwanath. 'RBI Gets Its Messages Mixed with 50 Notifications in 30 Days'. https://www.livemint.com/. 7 December 2016. Accessed 24 October 2018. https://www.livemint.com/Industry/8vOWvnEwbV3JcwBPTzSI8I/RBI-gets-its-messages-mixed-with-50-notifications-in-30-days.html.

43. Ibid.

44. Daniyal, Shoaib. 'Why Is There Now a 4-Year Jail Term for Keeping Demonetised Notes (That Are Worthless Anyway)?' Scroll.in. 28 December 2016. Accessed 9 December 2018. https://scroll.in/article/825356/why-is-there-now-a-4-year-jail-term-for-keeping-demonetised-notes-that-are-worthless-anyway.

45. Hebbar, Nistula. 'Modi Urges Country to Become a Cashless Society'. *The Hindu*. 27 November 2016. Accessed 24 October 2018. https://www.thehindu.com/news/national/Modi-urges-country-to-become-a-cashless-society/article16710453.ece.

46. Rashid, Omar. 'Demonetisation Has Equalised the Rich and the Poor, Claims Modi'. *The Hindu*. 14 November 2016. Accessed 24 October 2018. https://www.thehindu.com/news/national/Demonetisation-has-equalised-the-rich-and-the-poor-claims-Modi/article16447877.ece.

47. Ibid.

48. Quartz Staff. '"Organised Loot, Legalised Plunder": The Man Who Opened up India's Economy Trashes Modi's Demonetisation'. Quartz India. 28 November 2016. Accessed 24 October 2018. https://qz.com/india/845609/organised-loot-legalised-plunder-manmohan-singh-the-man-who-opened-

up-indias-economy-trashes-narendra-modis-demonetisation-
move-in-the-rajya-sabha/.

49. Bhagwati, Jagdish, Vivek Dehejia and Pravin Krishna.
'Demonetisation Fallacies and Demonetisation Math'. *Mint*. 27
December 2016. Accessed on 7 November 2018. https://www.
livemint.com/Opinion/niFH9uM377oUSHEQcRuUWP/
Demonetisation-fallacies-and-demonetisation-math.html.

50. Bhalla, Surjit S. 'No Proof Required: Demonetisation
Dispassionately Demystified'. *Indian Express*. 13 December 2016.
Accessed 24 October 2018. https://indianexpress.com/article/
opinion/columns/success-of-demonetisation-economists-
demonetised-india-4425646/.

51. IndiaToday.in. 'Demonetisation Is Modi's Napoleon Moment:
Amartya Sen to India Today'. *India Today*. 11 January 2017.
Accessed 7 December 2018. https://www.indiatoday.in/
india/story/demonetisation-nobel-prize-winning-economist-
amartya-sen-pm-narendra-modi-954297-2017-01-10.

52. Prasad, Gireesh Chandra. 'Demonetisation May Not Deliver Long
Term Benefits to India: Paul Krugman'. https://www.livemint.
com/. 2 December 2016. Accessed 9 December 2018. https://
www.livemint.com/Politics/6WQRkoCktgAJdagFSkcIVN/
Demonetisation-may-not-deliver-long-term-benefits-to-India.
html.

53. 'Modi's Attempt to Crush the Black Economy Is Hurting the
Poor'. *Economist*. 3 December 2016. Accessed 24 October 2018.
https://www.economist.com/asia/2016/12/03/modis-attempt-
to-crush-the-black-economy-is-hurting-the-poor.

54. FE Online. 'Who Is Anil Bokil? The Man Who Suggested Note
Ban to Modi'. *Financial Express*. 8 November 2017. Accessed 24
October 2018. https://www.financialexpress.com/economy/
who-is-anil-bokil-the-man-who-suggested-note-ban-to-
modi/923526/.

55. Rajan, Raghuram. *I Do What I Do*. Uttar Pradesh, India: Harper
Business, 2017.

56. 'National Manufacturing Policy (2011)'. Department of Industrial
Policy and Promotion, Government of India. Accessed 20 May 2017.

http://dipp.nic.in/English/Policies/National_Manufacturing_
Policy_25October2011.pdf.

57. Stratfor. 'The Difficulties of Retooling the Indian Economy'.
     20 July 2016. Accessed 24 October 2018. https://www.stratfor.
     com/analysis/difficulties-retooling-indian-economy.

58. World Bank Group. 'India Development Update, October
     2014'. Open Knowledge Repository. 1 October 2014. Accessed
     24 October 2018. https://openknowledge.worldbank.org/
     handle/10986/20794?show=full.

59. Banyan. 'Time to Make in India?' *Economist*. 25 September
     2014. Accessed 24 October 2018. https://www.economist.
     com/banyan/2014/09/25/time-to-make-in-india.

60. 'How Modi Can Deliver on the Promise of "Make in India"'.
     Knowledge@Wharton. Accessed 24 October 2018. http://
     knowledge.wharton.upenn.edu/article/how-modi-can-deliver-
     on-make-in-india/.

61. Bhuyan, Rituparna. 'Four Years of the Modi Government:
     Make in India, Launched with Much Pomp, Is Now Struggling'.
     CNBCTV18.com. Accessed 24 October 2018. https://www.
     cnbctv18.com/politics/four-years-of-the-modi-government-
     make-in-india-launched-with-much-pomp-is-now-
     struggling-67253.htm.

62. *The Hindu BusinessLine*. 'Old Wine in New Bottle, Says
     Congress'. 25 September 2015. Accessed 24 October 2018.
     https://www.thehindubusinessline.com/economy/Old-wine-
     in-new-bottle-says-Congress/article20873783.ece.

63. Fontanella-Khan, Amana. 'India's Rock-Star PM Wowed
     Madison Square Garden—but Can He Deliver More than a Great
     Show?' Reuters. 29 September 2014. Accessed 24 October 2018.
     http://blogs.reuters.com/great-debate/2014/09/29/indias-
     rock-star-pm-wowed-madison-square-garden-but-can-he-
     deliver-more-than-a-great-show/.

64. ENS Economic Bureau. 'No Space for Another Export-Led
     China: Raghuram Rajan'. *Indian Express*. 12 December 2014.
     Accessed 9 December 2018. https://indianexpress.com/article/

business/economy/make-in-india-should-not-merely-focus-
on-manufacturing-raghuram-rajan/.

65. Mishra, Asit Ranjan, Garima Singh and Sakshi Arora. 'Make for
India Better Approach than Make in India: Raghuram Rajan'.
https://www.livemint.com/. 12 December 2014. Accessed
24 October 2018. https://www.livemint.com/Politics/
nEPZGnUMtLN3o86upKbPsI/Raghuram-Rajan-questions-
Modis-Make-in-India-strategy.html.

66. Ibid.

67. Banyan. 'Time to Make in India?' *Economist*. 25 September
2014. Accessed 24 October 2018. https://www.economist.
com/banyan/2014/09/25/time-to-make-in-india.

68. Ibid.

69. Ibid.

70. 'How Modi Can Deliver on the Promise of "Make in India"'.
Knowledge@Wharton Accessed 24 October 2018. http://
knowledge.wharton.upenn.edu/article/how-modi-can-deliver-
on-make-in-india/.

71. Ibid.

72. Akbar, Prayaag. 'Sardar Patel: An Unexamined Life'. https://www.
livemint.com/. 10 April 2015. Accessed 24 October 2018. https://
www.livemint.com/Leisure/vkB9XJTYAe0EtDZuby3eBK/
Sardar-Patel-An-unexamined-life.html.

73. Gulati, Ashok and Shweta Saini. 'Reading Modi Government's
Agri-performance Right'. *Financial Express*. 29 April 2018.
Accessed 24 October 2018. https://www.financialexpress.
com/opinion/reading-modi-governments-agri-performance-
right/1150192/.

74. Ibid.

75. Swaminathan, M.S. 'The Agriculture Mission: How the Modi
Government Is Shaping the Future of Farming and Farmers'.
Times of India Blogs. 6 August 2018. Accessed 24 October 2018.
https://blogs.timesofindia.indiatimes.com/toi-edit-page/the-
agriculture-mission-how-the-modi-government-is-shaping-
the-future-of-farming-and-farmers/.

76.   Mukherjee, Sanjeeb. 'Centre Laps up Swaminathan Endorsement
      of PM Modi's Farm Policies'. *Business Standard.* 8 August 2018.
      Accessed 24 October 2018. https://www.business-standard.
      com/article/economy-policy/centre-laps-up-swaminathan-
      endorsement-of-pm-modi-s-farm-policies-118080801450_1.html.
77.   PTI. 'Farmers' Agitation Demanding Implementation of NCF Is
      Justified, Says M S Swaminathan'. *Financial Express.* 8 August 2018.
      Accessed 24 October 2018. https://www.financialexpress.com/
      india-news/farmers-agitation-demanding-implementation-of-
      ncf-is-justified-says-m-s-swaminathan/1274166/.
78.   Gulati, Ashok and Siraj Hussain. 'From Plate to Plough: Premium
      Delayed, Farmer Denied'. *Indian Express.* 14 May 2018. Accessed
      24 October 2018. https://indianexpress.com/article/opinion/
      columns/narendra-modi-govt-crop-insurance-scheme-indian-
      farmers-distress-protests-rural-economy-5175487/.
79.   Gulati, Ashok and Siraj Hussain. 'From Plate to Plough:
      Everybody Loves a Good Crop'. *Indian Express.* 30 July 2017.
      Accessed 24 October 2018. https://indianexpress.com/article/
      opinion/columns/from-plate-to-plough-everybody-loves-a-
      good-crop-pradhan-mantri-fasal-bima-yojana-4774696/.
80.   Gulati, Ashok and Shweta Saini. 'Creating a National Agriculture
      Market'. *Financial Express.* 27 May 2018. Accessed 24 October
      2018. https://www.financialexpress.com/opinion/creating-a-
      national-agriculture-market/1183317/.
81.   Ibid.
82.   Express News Service. 'Yashwant Sinha on Moody's Rating:
      "Explain It to a Farmer in Vidarbha"'. *Indian Express.* 23
      November 2017. Accessed 24 October 2018. https://
      indianexpress.com/article/india/yashwant-sinha-on-moodys-
      rating-explain-it-to-a-farmer-in-vidarbha-4951929/.
83.   'I Want to Run the Government Professionally: Narendra
      Modi'. www.narendramodi.in. 17 April 2014. Accessed 7
      January 2019. https://www.narendramodi.in/i-want-to-run-
      the-government-professionally-narendra-modi-3173.
84.   ThePrint Team. 'Manmohan, Sonia, Chidambaram, Sibal,
      All Opposed Retrospective Tax: Pranab Mukherjee'. Print.

27 October 2017. Accessed 12 January 2019. https://
theprint.in/pageturner/excerpt/retrospective-tax-pranab-
mukherjee/13673/.

85. Panagariya, Arvind. 'India: Three and a Half Years of
Modinomics'. Working paper. Columbia University. Columbia
University, SIPA, Deepak and Neera Raj Center on Indian
Economic Policies. 2018.

86. Prasad, Gireesh Chandra and Remya Nair. 'India Set to
Step Up Efforts to Recover Tax Dues from Cairn'. https://
www.livemint.com/. 18 October 2018. Accessed 24
October 2018. https://www.livemint.com/Companies/
GpE4eEO2nhcgaX8byRF3TM/India-set-to-step-up-efforts-
to-recover-tax-dues-from-Cairn.html.

87. Panicker, Raija Susan. '"I Doubted GST as Chief Minister":
PM Modi Answers Critics'. NDTV.com. 9 August 2016.
Accessed 24 October 2018. https://www.ndtv.com/india-
news/i-had-concerns-on-gst-as-gujarat-chief-minister-says-pm-
modi-1441730.

88. IndiaToday.in. 'GST Launched: All You Need to Know about
Parliament's Special Midnight Session'. *India Today*. 30 June
2017. Accessed 24 October 2018. https://www.indiatoday.
in/india/story/live-updates-gst-midnight-parliament-
session-1021729-2017-06-30.

89. Ibid.

90. Gandhi, Rahul. 'A Reform That Holds Great Potential Is
Being Rushed through in a Half-baked Way with a Self-
promotional Spectacle #GSTTamasha.' Twitter. 30 June 2017.
Accessed 7 January 2019. https://twitter.com/RahulGandhi/
status/880718465333690370.

91. Sridhar, V. 'Taxing Times'. *Frontline*. 24 April 2018. Accessed
24 October 2018. https://www.frontline.in/the-nation/taxing-
times/article9749812.ece.

92. Banerjee, Shoumojit. 'GST Rollout Disastrous, Says Sinha'. *The
Hindu*. 23 November 2017. Accessed 24 October 2018. https://
www.thehindu.com/news/national/other-states/gst-rollout-
disastrous-says-sinha/article20734233.ece.

93. FE Bureau. 'Multiple Rates: India's GST Complex, Says World Bank'. *Financial Express*. 16 March 2018. Accessed 24 October 2018. https://www.financialexpress.com/economy/multiple-rates-indias-gst-complex-says-world-bank/1100552/.

94. Einhorn, Bruce. 'In India, Falling Oil Prices Make Modi's Job Much Easier'. Bloomberg.com. 21 October 2014. Accessed 24 October 2018. https://www.bloomberg.com/news/articles/2014-10-21/india-s-modi-ends-fuel-subsidies-showing-he-is-a-reformer.

95. Anand, Rahul, David Coady, Adil Mohommad, Vimal V. Thakoor and James P. Walsh. 'The Fiscal and Welfare Impacts of Reforming Fuel Subsidies in India'. IMF Working Papers 13, No. 128 (2013). doi:10.5089/9781484305164.001.

96. Einhorn, Bruce. 'In India, Falling Oil Prices Make Modi's Job Much Easier'. Bloomberg.com. 21 October 2014. Accessed 24 October 2018. https://www.bloomberg.com/news/articles/2014-10-21/india-s-modi-ends-fuel-subsidies-showing-he-is-a-reformer.

97. Press Information Bureau. 'Subsidy on Petroleum Products'. 25 April 2016. Accessed 24 October 2018. http://pib.nic.in/newsite/PrintRelease.aspx?relid=141145.

98. Sarkar, Soumeet. 'Union Budget 2018: Petroleum Subsidy Allocation May Fall Short. Here's Why'. BloombergQuint. 2 February 2018. Accessed 24 October 2018. https://www.bloombergquint.com/markets/union-budget-2018-petroleum-subsidy-allocation-may-fall-short-heres-why#gs.ckOknfw.

99. Sundria, Saket and Debjit Chakraborty. 'Why India's Fuel Prices Are Sky-High When Oil Isn't'. Bloomberg.com. 30 April 2018. Accessed 24 October 2018. https://www.bloomberg.com/news/articles/2018-04-29/why-india-s-fuel-prices-are-sky-high-when-oil-isn-t-quicktake.

100. Aiyar, S.A. 'Yes, Petrol and Diesel Taxes Are Steep. No, Don't Cut Them'. Times of India Blogs. 16 September 2018. Accessed 24 October 2018. https://blogs.timesofindia.indiatimes.com/Swaminomics/yes-petrol-and-diesel-taxes-are-steep-no-dont-cut-them/.

101. Surabhi. 'Excise Duty on Petrol, Diesel to Give Big Boost to Centre's Revenue Kitty'. *The Hindu BusinessLine*. 11 February 2018. Accessed 24 October 2018. https://www.thehindubusinessline.com/economy/policy/excise-duty-on-petrol-diesel-to-give-big-boost-to-centres-revenue-kitty/article22723716.ece.

102. Panagariya, Arvind. 'India: Three and a Half Years of Modinomics'. Working Paper. Columbia University. Columbia University, SIPA, Deepak and Neera Raj Center on Indian Economic Policies. 2018.

103. Dhume, Sadanand. 'Opinion | Modi Abandons Reform for Populist Nostrums'. *Wall Street Journal*. 23 August 2018. Accessed 7 December 2018. https://www.wsj.com/articles/modi-abandons-reform-for-populist-nostrums-1535063402.

104. Sharma, Mihir. 'India Looks for Money in All the Wrong Places'. Bloomberg.com. 19 October 2018. Accessed 24 October 2018. https://www.bloomberg.com/view/articles/2018-10-18/india-shouldn-t-treat-big-oil-companies-as-piggy-banks.

105. Misra, Prakhar and Kadambari Shah. 'Decoding PMJDY, an Intriguing Work in Progress'. *The Hindu*. 13 September 2017. Accessed 24 October 2018. https://www.thehindu.com/thread/politics-and-policy/decoding-pmjdy-an-intriguing-work-in-progress/article19677006.ece.

106. Dutta, Prabhash K. 'Mudra Yojana Is a Mission or Mess? 5-Point Fact Checker'. *India Today*. 19 September 2018. Accessed 24 October 2018. https://www.indiatoday.in/india/story/mudra-yojana-is-a-mission-or-mess-5-point-fact-checker-1244538-2018-05-29.

107. Misra, Prakhar and Kadambari Shah. 'Decoding PMJDY, an Intriguing Work in Progress'. *The Hindu*. 13 September 2017. Accessed 24 October 2018. https://www.thehindu.com/thread/politics-and-policy/decoding-pmjdy-an-intriguing-work-in-progress/article19677006.ece.

108. Ibid.

109. Ibid.

110. PTI. '30 Crore Families Got Jan Dhan Accounts, Rs 65,000
     Crore Deposited: Narendra Modi'. *Indian Express*. 27 August
     2017. Accessed 24 October 2018. https://indianexpress.
     com/article/india/30-crore-families-got-jan-dhan-accountsrs-65000-
     crore-deposited-narendra-modi-4815995/.

111. Nageswaran, V. Anantha. 'Measuring Mudra's Success'.
     https://www.livemint.com/. 30 May 2016. Accessed 24
     October 2018. https://www.livemint.com/Opinion/
     E79FsbWqrzdkBB8db6q7BJ/Measuring-Mudras-success.
     html.

112. Ibid.

113. Ibid.

114. *Assessing Private Sector Contributions to Job Creation and
     Poverty Reduction*. Publication. IFC Jobs Study, IFC. 2013.
     Accessed 24 October 2018. https://www.ifc.org/wps/wcm/
     connect/0fe6e2804e2c0a8f8d3bad7a9dd66321/IFC_FULL
     JOB STUDY REPORT_JAN2013_FINAL.pdf?MOD=
     AJPERES.

115. 'India - Country Partnership Strategy for the Period FY13–FY17
     (English)'. World Bank. Accessed 24 October 2018. http://
     documents.worldbank.org/curated/en/207621468268202774/
     India-Country-partnership-strategy-for-the-period-FY13–
     FY17.

116. Ibid.

117. Chopra, Ritika. 'Back to PISA after 2009 Poor Show: How
     Does It Assess 15-Year-Olds?' *Indian Express*. 11 September
     2018. Accessed 24 October 2018. https://indianexpress.com/
     article/explained/back-to-pisa-after-2009-poor-show-how-
     does-it-assess-15-year-olds-5349458/.

118. Govindarajan, Padmapriya. 'India's New Education Policy:
     Creeping "Saffronization"?' *Diplomat*. 21 July 2016. Accessed 24
     October 2018. https://thediplomat.com/2016/07/indias-new-
     education-policy-creeping-saffronization/.

119. Sharma, Kritika. '4 Years On, India's Still Waiting for New
     Education Policy - Modi Govt's Big 2014 Promise'. Print. 14
     September 2018. Accessed 24 October 2018. https://theprint.in/

governance/4-years-on-indias-still-waiting-for-new-education-policy-modi-govts-big-2014-promise/117022/.

120. Nanda, Prashant K. 'Education in 4 Years of Modi Government: Implementation Remains a Key Hurdle'. https://www.livemint. com/. 26 May 2018. Accessed 24 October 2018. https://www. livemint.com/Politics/zOwRwPTKYp1SKPflDAY2QI/ Education-in-4-years-of-Modi-government-Implementation-rema.html.

121. Ibid.

122. Pandey, Neelam. 'Four Years of Modi Govt: Autonomy Granted but Education Policy Yet to Take Off'. *Hindustan Times*. 26 May 2018. Accessed 7 December 2018. https:// www.hindustantimes.com/education/four-years-of-modi-govt-autonomy-granted-but-education-policy-yet-to-take-off/story-NcSABKXAPl2Vgy53zwahCN.html.

123. 'National Skill Development Mission'. Ministry of Skill Development and Entrepreneurship, Government of India. Accessed 9 December 2018. https://www.msde.gov.in/ nationalskillmission.html.

124. PTI. 'Serious Conflict of Interest in NSDC's Functioning, Says Govt Panel'. https://www.livemint.com/. 26 April 2017. Accessed 9 December 2018. https://www.livemint.com/ Politics/BDOMzwlJHO4gIDBCD2mXNN/Serious-conflict-of-interest-in-NSDCs-functioning-says-gov.html.

125. Makkar, Sahil. 'Why India's Skill Mission Has Failed'. *Business Standard*. 1 September 2017. Accessed 24 October 2018. https:// www.business-standard.com/article/economy-policy/why-india-s-skill-mission-has-failed-117090200098_1.html.

126. Ibid.

127. 'Industry Must Lead the Way in Skilling India'. https://www. livemint.com/. 24 August 2016. Accessed 9 December 2018. https:// www.livemint.com/Opinion/cgqSiIbBeR56QACiVKGAWJ/ Industry-must-lead-the-way-in-skilling-India.html.

128. Ibid.

129. Zargar, Haris. 'Lack of Quality Trainers Impending India's Skill Mission'. https://www.livemint.com/. 15 February

2018. Accessed 9 December 2018. https://www.livemint.
com/Industry/iLeYEW1rqsxkIS3DA7FIeN/Lack-of-quality-
trainers-impending-Indias-skill-mission.html.

130. Singh, Mausami. 'India Today Expose: Skill India Initiative Weaves More Scams than Success Stories'. *India Today.* 21 September 2018. Accessed 24 October 2018. https://www.indiatoday.in/india/story/india-today-expose-finds-out-skill-india-initiative-weaves-more-scams-than-success-stories-1345024-2018-09-20.

131. 'India Systematic Country Diagnostic'. *World Bank Systematic Country Diagnostic.* 6 June 2018. doi:10.1596/29879.

132. Ibid.

133. Ibid.

134. Das, Jishnu, Alaka Holla, Aakash Mohpal and Karthik Muralidharan. 'Quality and Accountability in Healthcare Delivery: Audit-Study Evidence from Primary Care in India'. *American Economic Review,* 3799th ser., 106 (12), No. 3765 (2015). Accessed 24 October 2018. https://www.povertyactionlab.org/sites/default/files/publications/329_Quality-and-Accountability-in-Health-Care-Delivery-2016.pdf.

135. Coarasa, Jorge and Jishnu Das. 'Primary Care for the Poor: The Potential of Micro-Health Markets to Improve Care'. *WB Open Data* 345 (January 2015). Accessed 24 October 2018. https://openknowledge.worldbank.org/bitstream/handle/10986/23657/944240BRI00PUB0e0for0Poor0FINAL0Web.pdf?sequence=1&isAllowed=y.

136. Teltumbde, Anand. 'Dissecting "Modicare"'. *Economic and Political Weekly* 53, No. 42 (20 October 2018). Accessed 24 October 2018. https://www.epw.in/journal/2018/42/margin-speak/dissecting-'modicare'.html.

137. Ghosh, Abantika. 'Mission Indradhanush: How Govt Vaccinated over 2.55 Crore Children across the Country'. *Indian Express.* 7 January 2018. Accessed 24 October 2018. https://indianexpress.com/article/india/how-mission-indradhanush-vaccinated-over-2-55-crore-children-across-the-country-5014477/.

138. Chandna, Himani. 'This MBA-turned-IRS Officer Is Curing Modi's Ailing Scheme for Affordable Medicines'. Print. 12 October

2018. Accessed 24 October 2018. https://theprint.in/governance/
this-mba-turned-irs-officer-is-curing-modis-ailing-scheme-for-
affordable-medicines/132556/.
139. Ibid.
140. 'India's Government Launches a Vast Health-Insurance
Scheme'. *Economist*. 27 September 2018. Accessed 24 October
2018. https://www.economist.com/asia/2018/09/29/indias-
government-launches-a-vast-health-insurance-scheme.
141. Ibid.
142. Ibid.
143. PTI. 'India Will Need $4.5 Trillion by 2040 for Infrastructure:
Report'. *Economic Times*. 25 July 2017. Accessed 7 December
2018. https://economictimes.indiatimes.com/news/economy/
infrastructure/india-will-need-4-5-trillion-by-2040-for-
infrastructure-report/articleshow/59759648.cms.
144. Vaishnav, Milan. 'Modi's Reform Agenda: Change You Can
Believe In?' Asia Policy Brief 2015/04, November 2015. AEI
Banner. 1 November 2015. Accessed 24 October 2018. http://
aei.pitt.edu/73889/.
145. Damodaran, Harish and Santosh Singh. 'Pradhan Mantri
Gram Sadak Yojana: How the Programme Impacted Indian
Hinterland'. *Indian Express*. 25 February 2016. Accessed 24
October 2018. https://indianexpress.com/article/india/india-
news-india/pradhan-mantri-gram-sadak-yojana-how-the-
programme-impacted-indian-hinterland/.
146. Singh, Rajesh Kumar. 'Every Village Has Electricity, Says
Government. A Reality Check'. NDTV.com. 30 April 2018.
Accessed 7 December 2018. https://www.ndtv.com/india-
news/every-village-has-electricity-says-government-a-reality-
check-1844791.
147. Bhaskar, R.N. 'Opinion | Why Discom Losses Continue to
Hurt despite Modi Govt's UDAY Scheme'. Moneycontrol.
24 September 2018. Accessed 24 October 2018. https://www.
moneycontrol.com/news/business/economy/opinion-why-
discom-losses-are-continuing-to-hurt-despite-modi-govts-
uday-scheme-2974191.html.

148. Bhaskar, R.N. 'UDAY and the Politics of Appeasement and Largesse'. AsiaConverge. 6 April 2017. Accessed 24 October 2018. http://www.asiaconverge.com/2017/04/uday-and-politics-of-appeasement-and-largesse/.

149. PTI. 'UDAY No Panacea, Pushed States' Fiscal Deficit by 0.7%: Survey'. *Times of India*. 15 August 2017. Accessed 7 December 2018. https://timesofindia.indiatimes.com/business/india-business/uday-no-panacea-pushed-states-fiscal-deficit-by-0-7-survey/articleshow/60072929.cms.

150. FE Online. '4 Years of Modi Government: How India Performed in Renewable Energy Sector'. *Financial Express*. 5 June 2018. Accessed 7 December 2018. https://www.financialexpress.com/economy/4-years-of-modi-government-how-india-performed-in-renewable-energy-sector/1194517/.

151. Sudhalkar, Ravindra. 'Three Years of Modi Govt: A Squeaky Clean Housing Policy'. *BW Businessworld*. 29 May 2017. Accessed 7 December 2018. http://www.businessworld. in/article/Three-Years-Of-Modi-Govt-A-Squeaky-Clean-Housing-Policy/29-05-2017-119124/.

152. Nageswaran, V. Anantha and Gulzar Natarajan. 'Can India Grow?' Carnegie Endowment for International Peace. Accessed 24 October 2018. http://carnegieendowment.org/files/CEIP_CanIndiaGrow_Final_.pdf.

153. Bloomberg. 'In Free Trade U-turn, Modi Raises India's Wall of Import Duties'. *Economic Times*. 15 February 2018. Accessed 24 October 2018. https://economictimes.indiatimes.com/news/economy/policy/in-free-trade-u-turn-modi-raises-indias-wall-of-import-duties/articleshow/62925283.cms.

154. Panagariya, Arvind. 'India's Trade Policy Folly: Current Turn to Import Substitution Will Take Economy down from Turnpike to Dirt Road'. Times of India Blogs. 25 July 2018. Accessed 24 October 2018. https://blogs.timesofindia.indiatimes.com/toi-edit-page/indias-trade-policy-folly-current-turn-to-import-substitution-will-take-economy-down-from-turnpike-to-dirt-road/.

155. Ibid.

156. Sharma, Mihir. 'India Can't Turn Its Back on Free Trade' Bloomberg.com. 14 August 2018. Accessed 24 October 2018. https://www.bloomberg.com/view/articles/2018-08-14/india-can-t-afford-to-play-spoiler-in-rcep-talks.
157. Ibid.
158. Dhume, Sadanand. 'Opinion | Modi Abandons Reform for Populist Nostrums'. Wall Street Journal. 23 August 2018. Accessed 24 October 2018. https://www.wsj.com/articles/modi-abandons-reform-for-populist-nostrums-1535063402.
159. Chaudhary, Archana and Bloomberg. 'Modi—the Protectionist: 30-Year High Import Duty to Spur "Make in India"'. Business Standard. 15 February 2018. Accessed 24 October 2018. https://www.business-standard.com/article/economy-policy/modi-the-protectionist-30-year-high-import-duty-to-spur-make-in-india-118021500127_1.html.
160. 'The Modi Government's Reform Program: A Scorecard'. CSIS. Accessed 24 October 2018. http://indiareforms.csis.org/.

Chapter 4: The Results

1. 'Economic Survey of India 2013–2014'. Ministry of Finance, Government of India. Accessed 6 November 2018. http://mof.gov.np/en/archive-documents/economic-survey-21.html.
2. Ibid.
3. Ibid.
4. Vaishnav, Milan. 'Modi's Reform Agenda: Change You Can Believe In?' Bertelsmann Stiftung, Asia Policy Brief. November 2015. Accessed 6 November 2018. http://carnegieendowment.org/files/Modiss_Reform_Agenda.pdf.
5. 'Economic Survey of India 2014–2015'. Ministry of Finance, Government of India. Accessed 6 November 2018. http://mof.gov.np/en/archive-documents/economic-survey-21.html.
6. Ibid.
7. Vaishnav, Milan. 'Modi's Reform Agenda: Change You Can Believe In?' Bertelsmann Stiftung, Asia Policy Brief. November

2015. Accessed 6 November 2018. http://carnegieendowment.
org/files/Modiss_Reform_Agenda.pdf.

8. 'Economic Survey of India 2014–2015'. Ministry of Finance, Government of India. Accessed 6 November 2018. http://mof. gov.np/en/archive-documents/economic-survey-21.html.

9. Ibid.

10. Vaishnav, Milan. 'Modi's Reform Agenda: Change You Can Believe In?' Bertelsmann Stiftung, Asia Policy Brief. November 2015. Accessed 6 November 2018. http://carnegieendowment. org/files/Modiss_Reform_Agenda.pdf.

11. 'Oil Price Steadies after Falling below $28 a Barrel'. BBC News. 18 January 2016. Accessed 6 November 2018. https://www. bbc.com/news/business-35340893.

12. Gupta, Nikhil. 'The Impact of Rising Oil Prices on Indian Economy'. https://www.livemint.com/. 21 May 2018. Accessed 6 November 2018. https://www.livemint.com/Opinion/ PnHcP040QNZYkLT5BWK5rL/The-impact-of-rising-oil-prices-on-Indian-economy.html.

13. ET Online. 'Oil, Modi's Best Friend, Can Now Turn His Enemy as Crude Prices Start Rising'. *Economic Times*. 31 October 2017. Accessed 6 November 2018. https://economictimes. indiatimes.com/industry/energy/oil-gas/oil-modis-best-friend-can-now-turn-his-enemy-as-crude-prices-start-rising/ articleshow/61359971.cms.

14. PTI. 'If My Luck Is Benefitting People, Then Vote for BJP: Modi'. *The Hindu*. 1 April 2016. Accessed 6 November 2018. https://www.thehindu.com/elections/delhi2015/if-my-luck-is-benefitting-people-then-vote-for-bjp-modi/article6845367.ece.

15. Damodaran, Harish. 'Oil, Naseeb and the Economy'. *Indian Express*. 6 February 2015. Accessed 6 November 2018. https:// indianexpress.com/article/business/business-others/oil-naseeb-and-the-economy/.

16. Vaishnav, Milan. 'Modi's Reform Agenda: Change You Can Believe In?' Bertelsmann Stuftung, Asia Policy Brief. November 2015. Accessed 6 November 2018. http://carnegieendowment. org/files/Modiss_Reform_Agenda.pdf.

17. Dhume, Sadanand. 'Modi Abandons Reform for Populist Nostrums'. *Wall Street Journal*. 23 August 2018. Accessed 6 November 2018. http://www.aei.org/publication/modi-abandons-reform-for-populist-nostrums/

18. Debroy, Bibek. 'NDA Government Nothing but Same UPA Regime with Better Implementation'. *India Today*. 1 August 2014. Accessed 6 November 2018. https://www.indiatoday.in/magazine/up-front/story/20140811-bibek-debroy-narendra-modi-nda-government-expectations-804797-2014-07-31.

19. Bhalla, Surjit S. 'In the Name of India, Why?' *Indian Express*. 31 July 2014. Accessed 6 November 2018. https://indianexpress.com/article/opinion/columns/in-the-name-of-india-why/.

20. Panagariya, Arvind. 'India's Best Hope Is That the Budget Due February 2015 Chooses Growth and Jobs'. Times of India Blogs. 26 July 2014. Accessed 6 November 2018. https://blogs.timesofindia.indiatimes.com/toi-edit-page/indias-best-hope-is-that-the-budget-due-february-2015-chooses-growth-and-jobs/?utm_source=TOInewHP_TILwidget&utm_medium=ABtest&utm_campaign=TOInewHP.

21. Crabtree, James, Vivek Dehejia and Mihir Sharma. 'Can Narendra Modi Be India's Thatcher?' American Enterprise Institute. 14 May 2014. Accessed 7 November 2018. http://www.aei.org/events/can-narendra-modi-be-indias-thatcher/.

22. PTI. 'Unreasonable to Expect Big Bang Reforms in India: Arvind Subramanian'. *The Hindu BusinessLine*. 24 January 2018. Accessed 6 November 2018. https://www.thehindubusinessline.com/economy/macro-economy/unreasonable-to-expect-big-bang-reforms-in-india-arvind-subramanian/article6985858.ece.

23. 'Economic Survey of India 2014–2015'. Ministry of Finance, Government of India. Accessed 6 November 2018. http://mof.gov.np/en/archive-documents/economic-survey-21.html.

24. Roy, Rajesh. '5 Quotes from The Wall Street Journal's Interview with Narendra Modi'. *Wall Street Journal*. 26 May 2016. Accessed 6 November 2018. https://blogs.wsj.com/briefly/2016/05/26/5-quotes-from-the-wall-street-journals-interview-with-narendra-modi/.

25. 'Economic Survey of India 2016–2017'. Ministry of Finance,
     Government of India. Accessed 6 November 2018. http://
     mof.gov.np/en/archive-documents/economic-survey-21.
     html.
26. Ibid.
27. 'World Economic Outlook, October 2018: Challenges to Steady
     Growth'. IMF. October 2018. Accessed 6 November 2018.
     https://www.imf.org/en/Publications/WEO/Issues/2018/
     09/24/world-economic-outlook-october-2018.
28. Bakshi, Ishan. 'Elephant Starts Running: Q1 GDP Growth
     Soars to 9-quarter High of 8.2%'. *Business Standard.* 31
     August 2018. Accessed 6 November 2018. https://www.
     business-standard.com/article/economy-policy/elephant-
     starts-running-q1-gdp-growth-soars-to-9-quarter-high-
     of-8-2-118090100065_1.html.
29. 'Economic Survey of India 2017–2018'. Ministry of Finance,
     Government of India. Accessed 6 November 2018. http://mof.
     gov.np/en/archive-documents/economic-survey-21.html.
30. 'PRESS NOTE - Mospi.nic.in'. Ministry of Statistics and
     Programme Implementation, Government of India. 3 January
     2015. Accessed 6 November 2018. http://mospi.nic.in/sites/
     default/files/press_release/nad_pr_31jan18_0.pdf.
31. Ghoshal, Devjyot. 'India's GDP Numbers Are So Dodgy That
     Even the Central Bank Has Doubts about Them'. Quartz.
     5 February 2016. Accessed 6 November 2018. https://
     qz.com/610767/indias-gdp-numbers-are-so-dodgy-that-its-
     central-bank-is-now-doing-its-own-math/.
32. 'The Elephant in the Stats'. *Economist.* 9 April 2016. Accessed
     6 November 2018. https://www.economist.com/finance-and-
     economics/2016/04/09/the-elephant-in-the-stats.
33. Soz, Salman Anees. 'The GDP Obfuscation'. *Business
     Standard.* 16 June 2018. Accessed 7 December 2018. https://
     www.business-standard.com/article/opinion/the-gdp-
     obfuscation-118061600017_1.html.
34. Mishra, Asit Ranjan. 'GDP Grew in Double Digits Twice in
     UPA Era'. https://www.livemint.com/. 17 August 2018.

Accessed 6 November 2018. https://www.livemint.com/
Politics/oDEHrbcSmIpVvQs1uRhfiN/Indian-economy-grew-
twice-in-double-digits-in-Manmohan-Singh.html.

35. Ibid.

36. Chandna, Himani and Amrita Nayak Dutta. 'What's Modi Govt
"Hiding" Is the Question as GDP Growth Data under UPA Is
Delayed Again'. Print. 4 July 2018. Accessed 7 January 2019.
https://theprint.in/economy/whats-modi-govt-hiding-as-gdp-
growth-data-under-upa-gets-delayed-again/78427/.

37. Express News Service. 'Yashwant Sinha Accuses Centre of
Cooking Up Statistics about Economy'. *New Indian Express*.
30 August 2018. Accessed 6 November 2018. http://www.
newindianexpress.com/states/karnataka/2018/aug/30/
yashwant-sinha-accuses-centre-of-cooking-up-statistics-about-
economy-1864902.html.

38. Soz, Salman Anees. 'Beautiful Headline, Ugly Reality: "India
Surpasses France's GDP" Is a Propaganda Dream and a Real
Nightmare'. DailyO. 23 July 2018. Accessed 6 November
2018. https://www.dailyo.in/business/why-india-surpassing-
frances-gdp-is-a-propaganda-dream-and-a-real-nightmare/
story/1/25629.html.

39. Ibid.

40. Ibid.

41. IANS. 'Falsehood Hallmark of Govt, "Top Boss" Narendra
Modi Insecure: Arun Shourie'. *Business Standard*. 27 November
2017. Accessed 7 December 2018. https://www.business-
standard.com/article/politics/falsehood-hallmark-of-govt-top-
boss-narendra-modi-insecure-arun-shourie-117112600733_1.
html.

42. Mehra, Puja. 'Rate of Poverty Reduction Fastest under UPA'.
The Hindu. 27 May 2015. Accessed 6 November 2018. http://
www.thehindu.com/todays-paper/rate-of-poverty-reduction-
fastest-under-upa/article7249241.ece.

43. Jagannathan, R. 'UPA-nomics: High Growth plus High
Inflation Equals Worse Child Malnutrition'. Firstpost. 10 July
2015. Accessed 6 November 2018. http://www.firstpost.com/

business/upa-nomics-high-growth-plus-high-inflation-equals-worse-child-malnutrition-2336296.html.

44. Bahl, Raghav. 'Modi's Fuel Folly Costs Rs 1 Lakh Crore in One Hour; Confirms Statist Mindset'. BloombergQuint. 5 October 2018. Accessed 6 November 2018. https://www.bloombergquint.com/opinion/modis-fuel-folly-costs-rs-1-lakh-crore-in-one-hour-confirms-statist-mindset#gs.bfKEWlA.

45. Surabhi. 'Excise Duty on Petrol, Diesel to Give Big Boost to Centre's Revenue Kitty'. The Hindu BusinessLine. 11 February 2018. Accessed 6 November 2018. https://www.thehindubusinessline.com/economy/policy/excise-duty-on-petrol-diesel-to-give-big-boost-to-centres-revenue-kitty/article22723716.ece.

46. Reuters. 'MSP Hike Impact on Indian Economy: What Analysts Say'. https://www.livemint.com/. 4 July 2018. Accessed 6 November 2018. https://www.livemint.com/Politics/4sdlBmCic0MMVMKrbb4qoM/MSP-hike-impact-on-Indian-economy-What-analysts-say.html.

47. Mishra, Twesh and Surabhi. 'ONGC-HPCL Deal Saves Govt from Breach of Fiscal Deficit Goals'. The Hindu BusinessLine. 26 January 2018. Accessed 7 December 2018. https://www.thehindubusinessline.com/companies/ongchpcl-deal-saves-govt-from-breach-of-fiscal-deficit-goals/article10052016.ece.

48. Madhavan, N. and Paramita Chatterjee. 'Economic Survey: Cautious on Growth and Cautions on Fiscal Consolidation'. Forbes India. 31 January 2017. Accessed 6 November 2018. http://www.forbesindia.com/article/budget-2017/economic-survey-cautious-on-growth-and-cautions-on-fiscal-consolidation/45661/1.

49. Report of the Comptroller and Auditor General of India for the Year End March 2016, Report No. 3 of 2017. Department of Revenue (Indirect Taxes, Central Excise), Union Government. 16 April 2017. Accessed 6 November 2018. http://cag.gov.in/sites/default/files/audit_report_files/Union_Government_Report_3_of_2017_Revenue_Indirect_Taxes_Central_Excise.pdf

50. PTI. 'Government Exceeds 2016–17 Tax Collection Target by 18%'. Times of India. 4 April 2017. Accessed 6 November 2018.

http://timesofindia.indiatimes.com/business/india-business/
government-exceeds 2016-17-tax-collection-target-by-18/
articleshow/58008546.cms.

51. Malviya, Sagar. 'After-Effects of Poor Monsoon: Demand for
    Consumer Goods Halves in December Quarter'. *Economic
    Times*. 24 March 2016. Accessed 6 November 2018. https://
    economictimes.indiatimes.com/industry/cons-products/
    food/after-effects-of-poor-monsoon-demand-for-consumer-
    goods-halves-in-december-quarter/articleshow/51534625.
    cms?utm_source=contentofinterest&utm_medium=text&utm_
    campaign=cppst.

52. World Development Indicators (World Bank). 'Exports of Goods
    and Services (% of GDP) Data'. Accessed 6 November 2018. http://
    data.worldbank.org/indicator/NE.EXP.GNFS.ZS?locations=
    IN-CN.

53. Ghosh, Jayati and C.P. Chandrasekhar. 'Understanding India's
    Export Collapse'. *The Hindu BusinessLine*. 15 January 2018.
    Accessed 6 November 2018. http://www.thehindubusinessline.
    com/opinion/columns/why-indias-exports-are-falling/
    article9370929.ece.

54. 'China's Export Machine Is Grabbing More of the Global
    Market'. Bloomberg.com. 6 September 2016. Accessed
    6 November 2018. https://www.bloomberg.com/news/
    articles/2016-09-06/china-export-machine-defying-gravity-
    grabs-global-market-share.

55. Singh, Manpreet. 'Exports Drop over PM Modi Period, Trade
    Deficit Highest since 2012–13'. *Business Standard*. 30 June 2018.
    Accessed 6 November 2018. https://www.business-standard.
    com/article/economy-policy/exports-drop-over-pm-modi-
    period-trade-deficit-highest-since-2012-13-118063000804_1.
    html.

56. Joshi, Dharmakirti and Pankhuri Tandon. 'Opinion | Caging
    the Current Account Deficit'. https://www.livemint.com/.
    8 October 2018. Accessed 6 November 2018. https://www.
    livemint.com/Opinion/9eM28tOeYSw2GWthTXC7TM/
    Opinion--Caging-the-current-account-deficit.html.

57. Chinoy, Sajjid Z. 'Boom, Bust'. *Indian Express*. 18 April 2017. Accessed 6 November 2018. http://indianexpress.com/article/opinion/columns/boom-surging-global-equities-foreign-portfolio-inflows-inflation-gdp-rate4618641/.

58. Singh, Manpreet. 'Exports Drop over PM Modi Period, Trade Deficit Highest since 2012–13'. *Business Standard*. 30 June 2018. Accessed 6 November 2018. https://www.business-standard.com/article/economy-policy/exports-drop-over-pm-modi-period-trade-deficit-highest-since-2012-13-118063000804_1.html.

59. Panagariya, Arvind. 'Wrong Way to Make in India: Why We Must Resist the Temptation to Return to Import Substitution Mirage'. Times of India Blogs. 13 December 2017. Accessed 6 November 2018. https://blogs.timesofindia.indiatimes.com/toi-edit-page/wrong-way-to-make-in-india-why-we-must-resist-the-temptation-to-return-to-import-substitution-mirage/.

60. Ninan, T.N. 'T.N. Ninan: Flat-Lined Exports Are Impeding India's Economic Momentum'. *Business Standard*. 23 February 2018. Accessed 6 November 2018. https://www.business-standard.com/article/opinion/t-n-ninan-flat-lined-exports-are-impeding-india-s-economic-momentum-118022300549_1.html.

61. Dehejia, Vivek. 'Opinion | Trade Liberalization Folly: From High Road to Low Road'. https://www.livemint.com/. 23 September 2018. Accessed 6 November 2018. https://www.livemint.com/Opinion/LsmVCb9m6adIvafTdQJ4vN/Opinion--Trade-liberalization-folly-From-high-road-to-low.html.

62. Joshi, Dharmakirti and Pankhuri Tandon. 'Opinion | Caging the Current Account Deficit'. https://www.livemint.com/. 8 October 2018. Accessed 6 November 2018. https://www.livemint.com/Opinion/9eM28tOeYSw2GWthTXC7TM/Opinion--Caging-the-current-account deficit.html.

63. Easterly, William and Stanley Fischer. 'Inflation and the Poor'. *Journal of Money, Credit and Banking* 33, No. 2 (2001): 159–78. doi:10.2307/2673879.

64. Kundu, Tadit. 'How Has the Indian Economy Fared under Modi Govt, in 5 Charts'. https://www.livemint.com/. 22 May 2018. Accessed 6 November 2018. https://www.livemint.com/Politics/9tzyzHyTDO8q8Z0ZooCnYP/How-has-the-Indian-economy-fared-under-Modi-govt-in-5-chart.html.

65. Dugal, Ira. 'The MPC . . . Its Mandate and Beyond'. BloombergQuint. 4 October 2018. Accessed 6 November 2018. https://www.bloombergquint.com/rbi-monetary-policy/the-mpcits-mandate-and-beyond#gs.6MerdZc.

66. Reuters. 'Demonetisation Impact: Retail Inflation Hit Two-Year Low in December'. Business Today. 14 February 2017. Accessed 6 November 2018. https://www.businesstoday.in/current/economy-politics/demonetisation-impact-retail-inflation-hit-two-year-low-in-december/story/244138.html.

67. 'The Systematic Country Diagnostic for India: A Narrative for Discussion'. World Bank. Accessed 6 November 2018. http://www.worldbank.org/en/news/feature/2018/01/12/india-systematic-country-diagnostic-draft-for-consultation.

68. Gulati, Ashok and Tirtha Chatterjee. 'From Plate to Plough: The Limits of MSP'. Indian Express. 22 July 2018. Accessed 6 November 2018. https://indianexpress.com/article/opinion/columns/msp-kharif-crops-narendra-modi-minimum-support-price-gst-farmers-5270286/.

69. Kaul, Vivek. 'MSP for Kharif Crops: Narendra Modi Government's Claim of 50% Margin Is an Eyewash; Devil Lies in Details'. Firstpost. 5 July 2018. Accessed 6 November 2018. https://www.firstpost.com/business/msp-for-kharif-crops-narendra-modi-governments-claim-of-50-margin-is-an-eyewash-devil-lies-in-details-4673991.html.

70. Jebaraj, Priscilla. 'Watershed Development Projects Lagging behind Badly'. The Hindu. 23 July 2018. Accessed 6 November 2018. https://www.thehindu.com/sci-tech/energy-and-environment/watershed-development-projects-lagging-behind-badly/article24489296.ece.

71. TimesofIndia.com. 'Why Firms Love Crop Insurance More than Farmers'. Times of India. 19 July 2018. Accessed 6 November

2018. https://timesofindia.indiatimes.com/business/india-business/why-firms-love-crop-insurance-more-than-farmers/articleshow/65051650.cms.

72. FE Online. 'Crop Insurance: Payout Ratio Jumps after Centre's Prodding'. *Financial Express*. 13 October 2018. Accessed 6 November 2018. https://www.financialexpress.com/economy/crop-insurance-payout-ratio-jumps-after-centres-prodding/1348313/.

73. Gulati, Ashok and Shweta Saini. 'Creating a National Agriculture Market'. *Financial Express*. 27 May 2018. Accessed 6 November 2018. https://www.financialexpress.com/opinion/creating-a-national-agriculture-market/1183317/.

74. Gulati, Ashok and Shweta Saini. 'From Plate to Plough: Why Farmers Agitate'. *Indian Express*. 11 June 2018. Accessed 6 November 2018. https://indianexpress.com/article/opinion/columns/india-farmers-portests-agriculture-sector-rural-economy-narendra-modi-govt-bjp-5212139/.

75. Ibid.

76. Ibid.

77. 'Did You Know . . .?' AQUASTAT - FAO's Information System on Water and Agriculture. Accessed 6 November 2018. http://www.fao.org/nr/water/aquastat/didyouknow/index3.stm.

78. Soz, Salman Anees. 'India's Economy in Flux'. Hudson Institute. October 2017. Accessed 6 November 2018. https://static1.squarespace.com/static/552bd209e4b0090163821585/t/59d6e34ee5dd5b440b21df67/1507255127313/India%27s+Economy+In+Flux.pdf

79. 'Index of Industrial Production'. Central Statistical Office, Ministry of Statistics and Programme Implementation, Government of India. Accessed 6 November 2018. http://mospi.nic.in/iip.

80. 'India Nikkei Markit Manufacturing PMI'. Investing.com. 1 November 2018. Accessed 6 November 2018. https://in.investing.com/economic-calendar/indian-nikkei-markit-manufacturing-pmi-754.

81. Soz, Salman Anees. 'Ease of Doing Business in an Uneasy India Hides, Not Reveals'. *Indian Express*. 1 November 2017. Accessed 6 November 2018. https://indianexpress.com/article/

opinion/ease-of-doing-business-in-an-uneasy-india-hides-not-reveals-4916706/,

82. Ibid.

83. Sandefur, Justin and Divyanshi Wadhwa. 'A Change in World Bank Methodology (Not Reform) Explains India's Rise in Doing Business Rankings'. Center for Global Development. 5 February 2018. Accessed 6 November 2018. https://www.cgdev.org/blog/change-world-bank-methodology-not-reform-explains-indias-rise-doing-business.

84. Ibid.

85. Dhume, Sadanand. 'India Jumped 30 Places in the World Bank's "Ease of Doing Business" Rankings. Here's Why It Matters.' 31 October 2017. Accessed on 6 January 2019. http://www.aei.org/publication/india-just-jumped-30-places-in-the-world-banks-ease-of-doing-business-rankings-heres-why-it-matters/.

86. 'How the Big Emerging Economies Climbed the World Bank Business Rankings'. *Economist*. 3 November 2018. h t t p s : / / w w w . e c o n o m i s t . c o m / f i n a n c e - a n d -economics/2018/11/03/how-the-big-emerging-economiesclimbed-the-world-bank-business-ranking.

87. The Heritage Foundation. 'Government Integrity'. 2019 Index of Economic Freedom. Accessed 6 November 2018. https://www.heritage.org/index/freedom-from-corruption.

88. Mishra, Asit Ranjan and Gireesh Chandra Prasad. 'Regulatory Reform Fails to Cut Red Tape: NITI Aayog'. https://www.livemint.com/. 28 August 2017. Accessed 6 November 2018. https://www.livemint.com/Politics/CanjTwmgHX7FE6PgPZ5gXO/Regulatory-reform-fails-to-cut-red-tape-NITI-Aayog.html.

89. PIB. 'Clarification: Ease of Doing Business Report'. NITI Aayog, Government of India. 29 August 2017. Accessed 6 November 2018. http://pib.nic.in/newsite/PrintRelease.aspx?relid=170329.

90. Dash, Dipak K. 'NDA Pips UPA-II in Building Roads, but Most Are 2 Lanes'. *Times of India*. 8 October 2018. Accessed 6 November 2018. https://timesofindia.indiatimes.com/india/nda-pips-upa-ii-in-building-roads-but-most-are-2-lanes/articleshow/66112824.cms.

91. Ibid.

92. Ghani, Ejaz, Arti Grover Goswami and William Kerr. 'Highway to Success: The Impact of the Golden Quadrilateral Project for the Location and Performance of Indian Manufacturing'. Working Paper No. 18524, National Bureau of Economic Research. 2012. doi:10.3386/w18524.

93. Express Web Desk. 'What Is Bharatmala Project?' *Indian Express*. 26 October 2017. Accessed 6 November 2018. https://indianexpress.com/article/what-is/what-is-bharatmala-project-4907128/.

94. Ministry of Rural Development. 'PMGSY Well on Its Way to Achieve March 2019 Target'. Press Information Bureau. 16 April 2018. Accessed 6 November 2018. http://www.pib.nic.in/PressReleseDetail.aspx?PRID=1529270.

95. BJP4India. 'Connecting and Developing Rural India: Construction of Rural Roads Reached an All Time High of 133 Km/day in 2016–17 under Modi Government. Pic.twitter.com/xAnXNHmE19'. Twitter. 22 May 2017. Accessed 7 January 2019. https://twitter.com/BJP4India/status/866690792458403840.

96. Jawed, Sam. 'Did BJP Bluff on Rural Roads Built in 2016–17 Being All-Time High?' *National Herald*. 29 May 2017. Accessed 7 January 2019. https://www.nationalheraldindia.com/fact-check/did-bharatiya-janata-party-bluff-on-rural-roads-built-in-2016-17-being-all-time-high-modi-govt.

97. Raval, Anjli. 'How to Power India: Modi Tweaks the Energy Mix'. *Financial Times*. 4 November 2018. Accessed 6 November 2018. https://www.ft.com/content/9db641ba-d121-11e8-a9f2-7574db66bcd5.

98. Sethi, Nitin. 'After Bold Estimates, Coal Auctions, Allotments Get Rs 56.84 Bn in 3.5 Yrs'. *Business Standard*. 17 September 2018. Accessed 6 November 2018. https://www.business-standard.com/article/economy-policy/after-bold-estimates-coal-auctions-allotments-get-rs-56-84-bn-in-3-5-yrs-118092501278_1.html.

99. Ibid.

100. 'Coal and Lignite Production, Annual Report 2017–18'. Ministry of Coal, Government of India. Accessed 6 November 2018. https://coal.nic.in/content/annual-report-2017-18.

101. 'Policies and Publications'. Ministry of Power, India. Accessed 6 November 2018. https://powermin.nic.in/en/content/power-sector-glance-all-india.

102. Sree Ram, R. 'UDAY No Panacea for Power Sector Woes'. https://www.livemint.com/. 14 March 2018. Accessed 6 November 2018. https://www.livemint.com/Money/vQsqL1lhxUlvxVYVER912I/UDAY-no-panacea-for-power-sector-woes.html.

103. Chatterjee, Anupam. 'UDAY Scheme: Discoms Cut Losses, but Their Dues to Gencos Mount'. *Financial Express*. 10 June 2018. Accessed 6 November 2018. https://www.financialexpress.com/economy/uday-scheme-discoms-cut-losses-but-their-dues-to-gencos-mount/1200937/.

104. D'Cunha, Suparna Dutt. 'Modi Announces "100% Village Electrification", but 31 Million Indian Homes Are Still in the Dark'. *Forbes*. 7 May 2018. Accessed 6 November 2018. https://www.forbes.com/sites/suparnadutt/2018/05/07/modi-announces-100-village-electrification-but-31-million-homes-are-still-in-the-dark/#18815a8863ba.

105. Pellegrini, Lorenzo and Luca Tasciotti. 'Rural Electrification Now and Then: Comparing Contemporary Challenges in Developing Countries to the USA's Experience in Retrospect'. *Forum for Development Studies* 40, No. 1 (2013). doi:10.1080/08039410.2012.732108.

106. Ibid.

107. Special Correspondent. 'India Requires Investment for Two Decades to Meet Its Deficit: Arun Jaitley'. *The Hindu*. 31 March 2017. Accessed 6 November 2018. http://www.thehindu.com/business/Economy/india-requires-investment-for-two-decades-to-meet-its-deficit-arun-jaitley/article17752878.ece.

108. 'The Systematic Country Diagnostic for India: A Narrative for Discussion'. World Bank. Accessed 6 November 2018. http://www.worldbank.org/en/news/feature/2018/01/12/india-systematic-country-diagnostic-draft-for-consultation.

109. 'Boosting Private Sector Investment in India Challenging - Subramanian'. Reuters. 29 March 2017. Accessed 6 November

2018. http://in.reuters.com/article/india-economy-investment-subramanian-idINKBN1700AF.

110. Vyas, Mahesh. 'Investment Cycle Could Be Turning Around'. CMIE. 7 September 2018. Accessed 6 November 2018. https://cmie.com/kommon/bin/sr.php?kall=warticle&dt=2018-09-07 12:12:15&msec=130.

111. 'India's Twin Balance-Sheet Problem'. *Economist*. 2 March 2017. Accessed 6 November 2018. http://www.economist.com/news/finance-and-economics/21717988-fast-growing-economy-india-stuck-alarming-credit-slump-indias-twin.

112. Mundy, Simon. 'India Inc Walks a Banking Tightrope'. *Financial Times*. 4 June 2017. Accessed 6 November 2018. https://www.ft.com/content/b62802e2-4135-11e7-9d56-25f963e998b2.

113. Mampatta, Sachin P. 'Has the Modi Govt Succeeded in Unclogging Stalled Projects?' https://www.livemint.com/. 23 January 2017. Accessed 6 November 2018. https://www.livemint.com/Politics/m4NKrw6ZMYRi4I8vo5aYoM/Has-the-Modi-govt-succeeded-in-unclogging-stalled-projects.html.

114. Mampatta, Sachin P. 'Value of Stalled Projects Rises to a Record Rs 13.22 Trillion in September Quarter'. https://www.livemint.com/. 2 October 2017. Accessed 6 November 2018. https://www.livemint.com/Politics/eJsGqshJCG4VPGvthnDUVN/Value-of-stalled-projects-reaches-yet-another-high.html.

115. Ranjan, Amitav. 'Stalled Projects Is Bad Optics, so Government Moves to Tweak Label'. *Indian Express*. 26 February 2018. Accessed 6 November 2018. https://indianexpress.com/article/india/stalled-projects-is-bad-optics-so-government-moves-to-tweak-label-5078233/.

116. Kwatra, Nikita. 'Decline in New Projects Dashes Hopes of Quick Economic Turnaround'. https://www.livemint.com/. 3 October 2018. Accessed 6 November 2018. https://www.livemint.com/Politics/cUQynkyZ4ska9paJUFpNKI/Declinein-newprojects-dashes-turnaroundhopes.html.

117. Rossow, Richard M. 'India's FDI Reforms under Modi: Once a Fountain, Now a Drip'. CSIS. 15 August 2017. Accessed 6

November 2018. https://www.csis.org/analysis/india's-fdi-reforms-under-modi-once-fountain-now-drip.

118. FE Online. 'Modi's 30-Reform Report Card: Only 9 Done, 6 Not Started, 15 Partially Done; Here's Full list'. *Financial Express*. 30 November 2018. Accessed 6 November 2018. https://www.financialexpress.com/economy/modis-30-reform-report-card-only-9-done-6-not-started-15-partially-done-heres-full-list/1371252/.

119. 'Fact Sheet on Foreign Direct Investment (FDI) from April, 2000 to March, 2018'. Department of Industrial Policy and Promotion, Government of India. March 2018. Accessed 7 November 2018. http://dipp.nic.in/sites/default/files/FDI_FactSheet_29June2018.pdf.

120. 'Foreign Direct Investment, Net Inflows (% of GDP)'. World Development Indicators (World Bank). Accessed 7 January 2019. https://data.worldbank.org/indicator/BX.KLT.DINV.WD.GD.ZS?end=2017&locations=IN&start=1970.

121. PTI. 'FDI Growth Hits 5-Year Low in 2017–18'. *Economic Times*. 1 July 2018. Accessed 7 January 2019. https://economictimes.indiatimes.com/news/economy/indicators/fdi-growth-hits-5-year-low-in-2017-18/articleshow/64813638.cms.

122. 'Economic Survey 2014: Growth of Non-performing Assets a Cause for Concern'. *Economic Times*. 9 July 2014. Accessed 6 November 2018. https://economictimes.indiatimes.com/industry/banking/finance/banking/economic-survey-2014-growth-of-non-performing-assets-a-cause-for-concern/articleshow/38078081.cms.

123. Ibid.

124. 'Banks' Gross NPAs Rise to 9.1% in September from 7.8% in March: RBI'. *Business Today*. 16 February 2017. Accessed 6 November 2018. http://www.businesstoday.in/current/economy-politics/banks-gross-npas-rise-to-9.1-percent-in-september-rbi/story/243240.html.

125. 'RBI Board "Discusses" NPA Crisis, Liquidity Crunch'. *Week*. 23 October 2018. Accessed 6 November 2018. https://www.

theweek.in/news/biz-tech/2018/10/23/RBI-board-discusses-NPA-crisis-liquidity-crunch.html.

126. Ashima Goyal, 'Indian Banking - Perception and Reality'. *Economic and Political Weekly*. 52, No. 12 (25 March 2017).

127. Ibid.

128. Mathew, George. 'In Parliament: Stressed Infrastructure Sector a Major Cause for the Bad Loan Pile-Up'. *Indian Express*. 8 December 2015. Accessed 6 November 2018. http://indianexpress. com/article/business/business-others/in-parliament-stressed-infrastructure-sector-a-major-cause-for-the-bad-loan-pile-up/.

129. Shetty, Mayur. 'At 5.1%, FY17 Bank Credit Grows Lowest in over 60 Years'. *Times of India*. 15 April 2017. Accessed 6 November 2018. http://timesofindia.indiatimes.com/business/india-business/at-5-1-fy17-bank-credit-grows-lowest-in-over-60-yrs/articleshow/58187037.cms.

130. 'Bank Credit Grows at 10.32%, Deposits at 6.66%'. *Economic Times*. 12 April 2018. Accessed 6 November 2018. https://economictimes.indiatimes.com/industry/banking/finance/banking/bank-credit-grows-at-10-32-deposits-at-6-66/articleshow/63736033.cms.

131. Krishnan, Aarati. 'Far Too Mollycoddled, Frankly'. *The Hindu BusinessLine*. 9 March 2018. Accessed 6 November 2018. http://www.thehindubusinessline.com/opinion/columns/aarati-krishnan/indian-banks-and-consequences-of-bad-decisions/article9608472.ece.

132. Sasi, Anil. 'Tackling NPAs: Lots of Bluster, Too Little Action'. *Indian Express*. 22 September 2015. Accessed 6 November 2018. http://indianexpress.com/article/india/india-others/tackling-npas-lots-of-bluster-too-little-action/.

133. Dugal, Ira. 'Banking Scorecard: Who Was Hit the Hardest by the Asset Quality Review?' BloombergQuint. 16 February 2017. Accessed 6 November 2018. https://www.bloombergquint.com/business/2017/02/15/banking-scorecard-who-was-hit-the-hardest-by-the-asset-quality-review.

134. Sengupta, Rajeshwari and Harsh Vardhan. 'Non-performing Assets in Indian Banks: This Time It Is Different'. *Economic and*

Political Weekly, Vol. 52, Issue No. 12. (31 March 2017) Accessed 7 November 2018. https://www.epw.in/journal/2017/12/money-banking-and-finance/non-performing-assets-indian-banks.html.

135. 'We Will Reassess the NPA Situation in 4-6 Months: Arvind Panagariya'. *Economic Times*. 5 May 2017. Accessed 6 November 2018. http://economictimes. indiatimes.com/articleshow/58531592.cms?utm_source=contentofinterest&utm_medium=text&utm_campaign=cppst.

136. 'Raghuram Rajan NPA Note: Congress Legacy or Modi Didn't Check Bad Loan Crisis in Time?' Print. 11 September 2018. Accessed 6 November 2018. https://theprint.in/talk-point/raghuram-rajan-npa-note-congress-legacy-or-modi-didnt-check-bad-loan-crisis-in-time/115826/.

137. Ibid.

138. NH Web Desk. 'RBI Admits Loan Frauds under Modi Govt Three Times Higher than UPA-II'. *National Herald*. 25 May 2018. Accessed 6 November 2018. https://www.nationalheraldindia. com/india/rbi-admits-loan-frauds-under-modi-govt-three-times-higher-than-upa-ii.

139. PTI. 'RBI Submitted a List of High Profile Fraud Cases to PMO: Rajan'. *Times of India*. 11 September 2018. Accessed 6 November 2018. https://timesofindia.indiatimes.com/business/india-business/rbi-submitted-a-list-of-high-profile-fraud-cases-to-pmo-rajan/articleshow/65772120.cms.

140. Vivek, Vipul. 'Modi Has Merely Renamed 19 Out of 23 Congress Schemes'. Quint. 24 June 2017. Accessed 6 November 2018. https://www.thequint.com/news/india/bjp-has-merely-renamed-19-out-of-23-congress-schemes-report.

141. FE Online. 'PM Narendra Modi Attacks Congress; Says MNREGS "Living Monument" of Poverty.' *Financial Express*. 12 March 2015. Accessed 7 January 2019. https://www.financialexpress.com/india-news/pm-narendra-modi-denounces-communalism-attacks-congress-on-poverty/48577/.

142. *World Development Report 2014*. World Bank Group, Open Knowledge Repository, 2013. Accessed 6 November 2018.

https://siteresources.worldbank.org/EXTNWDR2013/
Resources/8258024-1352909193861/8936935-
1356011448215/8986901-1380046989056/WDR-2014_
Complete_Report.pdf.

143. Kulkarni, Ashwini. 'Budget 2018: Highest Funding to
     MGNREGA in 2017, Yet 56% Wages Were Delayed'. *Business
     Standard*. 29 January 2018. Accessed 6 November 2018. https://
     www.business-standard.com/article/current-affairs/budget-
     2018-was-modi-govt-s-funding-boost-to-mgnrega-in-2017-an-
     eyewash-118012900238_1.html.

144. Dubey, Amitabh. 'When the Facts Fail You, Start Tossing Nazi
     References'. *Chunauti*. 1 April 2018. Accessed 6 November
     2018. https://chunauti.org/tag/jan-dhan-yojana/.

145. FE Online. 'Narendra Modi's Grand Schemes Are "Failing"
     on the Ground? Parliamentary Panel Blames Funding Woes,
     Poor Planning'. *Financial Express*. 20 March 2018. Accessed 6
     November 2018. https://www.financialexpress.com/india-
     news/narendra-modis-grand-schemes-are-failing-on-the-
     ground-parliamentary-panel-blames-funding-woes-poor-
     planning/1104819/.

146. Ibid.

147. Mohammad, Noor. 'Four Years in, How Successful Are Modi
     Government's Schemes?' Wire. 28 May 2018. Accessed 6
     November 2018. https://thewire.in/government/narendra-
     modi-government-four-years-schemes.

148. Ibid.

149. Arora, Rajat. 'Modi's Rs 98,000 Crore Bullet Train Project
     Hits a Land Roadblock'. *Economic Times*. 2 June 2018. Accessed
     6 November 2018. https://economictimes.indiatimes.com/
     industry/transportation/railways/bullet-train-project-hits-land-
     roadblock/articleshow/64423217.cms.

150. BJP4India. 'Change in Work Culture under Modi Government:
     21 Crore LED Bulbs Distributed at a Very Low Cost under Ujala
     Scheme. Pic.twitter.com/CbJKzXMJre.' Twitter. 9 February
     2017. Accessed 12 January 2019. https://twitter.com/bjp4india/
     status/829635240540852225?lang=bg.

151. Dubey, Amitabh. 'Why You Shouldn't Be Bedazzled by Modi's LED Bulb Claims'. BloombergQuint. 25 April 2017. Accessed 6 November 2018. https://www.bloombergquint.com/opinion/why-you-shouldnt-be-bedazzled-by-modis-led-bulb-claims#gs.p0k=CYA.

152. Azad, Rohit and Dipa Sinha. 'The Jan-Dhan Yojana, Four Years Later'. *The Hindu*. 29 May 2018. Accessed 6 November 2018. https://www.thehindu.com/opinion/op-ed/the-jan-dhan-yojana-four-years-later/article24017333.ece.

153. Pandey, Radhika and Rajeswari Sengupta. 'Demonetisation Will Likely Lead to a Protracted Economic Slowdown'. Wire. 12 December 2016. Accessed 6 November 2018. https://thewire.in/economy/demonetisation-economic-slowdown.

154. Ibid.

155. 'The High Economic Costs of India's Demonetisation'. *Economist*. 7 January 2017. Accessed 6 November 2018. https://www.economist.com/finance-and-economics/2017/01/07/the-high-economic-costs-of-indias-demonetisation.

156. Ibid.

157. Kumar, Rajiv. 'Bye-Bye Rs 500 & 1,000 Notes: Modi's "Achhe Din" Are Finally Here'. Quint. 9 November 2016. Accessed 6 November 2018. https://www.thequint.com/voices/opinion/bye-bye-to-rs-500-rs-1000-notes-modis-achhe-din-have-arrived-black-money-income-tax-declaration-mamata-banerjee.

158. Beniwal, Vrishti, Jeanette Rodrigues and Hannah Dormido. 'Was Modi's Grand Cash Ban a Big Waste of Time?' Bloomberg.com. 6 November 2017. Accessed 6 November 2018. https://www.bloomberg.com/news/articles/2017-11-05/modi-s-big-economic-gamble-in-tatters-as-cash-remains-king.

159. Ibid.

160. Bose, Prasenjit. 'Demonetisation Post-Truths'. *Economic and Political Weekly* 52, No. 35 (2 September 2017). Accessed 6 November 2018. https://www.epw.in/engage/article/%E2%80%8B-demonetisation-post-truths-0.

161. Ibid.

162. Ibid.
163. D'Cunha, Suparna Dutt. 'One Year Later: India's Demonetization Move Proves Too Costly an Experiment'. *Forbes.* 8 November 2017. Accessed 6 November 2018. https://www.forbes.com/sites/suparnadutt/2017/11/07/one-year-later-indias-demonetization-move-proves-too-costly-an-experiment/#10b46e61378a.
164. Wilson, James. 'Demonetisation: A Circus, Clowns and a Silver Bullet'. *National Herald.* 4 November 2018. Accessed 6 November 2018. https://www.nationalheraldindia.com/opinion/demonetisation-a-circus-clowns-and-a-silver-bullet.
165. Ibid.
166. Dehejia, Vivek and Rupa Subramanya. 'Demonetisation Failed to Make India a "Less Cash" Society'. https://www.livemint.com/. 18 June 2018. Accessed 7 December 2018. https://www.livemint.com/Opinion/PGRi4ySZO2HOWkARKq8GeM/Demonetisation-failed-to-make-India-a-less-cash-society.html.
167. ENS Economic Bureau. 'CMIE's Mahesh Vyas Says 3.5 Million Jobs Lost Due to Demonetisation'. *Indian Express.* 14 September 2018. Accessed 6 November 2018. https://indianexpress.com/article/business/economy/cmies-mahesh-vyas-says-3-5-million-jobs-lost-due-to-demonetisation-5357295/.
168. 'Economic Survey of India 2016–2017'. Ministry of Finance, Government of India. Accessed 6 November 2018. http://mof.gov.np/en/archive-documents/economic-survey-21.html.
169. Mishra, Asit Ranjan. 'India GDP Growth Rate Slumps to 5.7% in Q1 in Challenge for Economy'. https://www.livemint.com/. 31 August 2017. Accessed 6 November 2018. https://www.livemint.com/Industry/acEAx2TJIDMMzZbuhOBpLN/India-GDP-growth-slumps-to-57-in-Q1-hit-by-GST-implementa.html.
170. Basu, Kaushik. 'Opinion | In India, Black Money Makes for Bad Policy'. *New York Times.* 20 January 2018. Accessed 6 November 2018. https://www.nytimes.com/2016/11/27/opinion/in-india-black-money-makes-for-bad-policy.html.
171. Shah, Ajay. 'Note Ban's Impact in 2017'. *Business Standard.* 25 December 2016. Accessed 6 November 2018. https://www.

business-standard.com/article/opinion/ajay shah-note-ban-s-impact-in-2017-116122500642_1.html.

172. Cerra, Valerie and Sweta Chaman Saxena. 'Growth Dynamics: The Myth of Economic Recovery'. *American Economic Review* 98, No. 1 (2008). doi:10.1257/aer.98.1.439.

173. Cerra, V. and Sweta C. Saxena. 'The Economic Scars of Crises and Recessions'. IMF Blog. 21 March 2018. Accessed 28 December 2018. https://blogs.imf.org/2018/03/21/the-economic-scars-of-crises-and-recessions/.

174. Stacey, Kiran. 'India Passes "Revolutionary" Bill for Goods and Services Tax'. *Financial Times*. 29 March 2017. Accessed 6 November 2018. https://www.ft.com/content/8063ced6-1460-11e7-80f4-13e067d5072c.

175. 'GST to Boost Growth Rate by 1.5 Percentage Points: Experts'. *Economic Times*. 7 May 2015. Accessed 6 November 2018. https://economictimes.indiatimes.com/news/economy/policy/gst-to-boost-growth-rate-by-1-5-percentage-points-experts/articleshow/47176910.cms.

176. Van Leemput, Eva and Ellen A. Wiencek. 'The Fed – The Effect of the GST on Indian Growth'. Board of Governors of the Federal Reserve System. 24 March 2017. Accessed 6 November 2018. https://doi.org/10.17016/2573-2129.29.

177. Express Web Desk. 'GST Set for June 30 Midnight Launch at Special Parliament Session'. *Indian Express*. 20 June 2017. Accessed 6 November 2018. https://indianexpress.com/article/business/economy/gst-launch-midnight-parliament-arun-jaitley-pm-modi-president-june-30-4712918/.

178. Kumar, Arun. 'A Broken Tax Chain'. *The Hindu*. 29 June 2018. Accessed 6 November 2018. https://www.thehindu.com/opinion/op-ed/a-broken-tax-chain/article24294420.ece.

179. 'India Development Update'. World Bank. 14 March 2018. Accessed 6 November 2018. https://www.worldbank.org/en/news/feature/2018/03/14/india-development-update.

180. Sanjai, P.R., Archana Chaudhary and Anirban Nag. 'Anger over GST in Gujarat Shows Why Monday's Election Results Is Key'. https://www.livemint.com/. 15 December 2017.

Accessed 6 November 2018. https://www.livemint.com/
Politics/iDZaIHXZ5OYftKXNKhw0gL/Anger-over-GST-in-
Narendra-Modis-Gujarat-shows-why-Monday-i.html.

181. Mishra, Asit Ranjan. 'GST One of the Most Complex, and Second
Highest Tax Rate in World: World Bank'. https://www.livemint.
com/. 15 March 2018. Accessed 6 November 2018. https://
www.livemint.com/Politics/99hZqzvxfdwmZKgkbWORrO/
GST-one-of-the-most-complex-and-second-highest-tax-rate-
in.html.

182. 'India Development Update'. World Bank. 14 March 2018.
Accessed 6 November 2018. https://www.worldbank.org/en/
news/feature/2018/03/14/india-development-update.

183. BS Web Team & Agencies. 'GST Collection Crosses Rs
1-Trillion Mark in October: Arun Jaitley'. *Business Standard*.
1 November 2018. Accessed 6 November 2018. https://
www.business-standard.com/article/economy-policy/
gst-collection-crosses-rs-1-trillion-mark-in-october-arun-
jaitley-118110100499_1.html.

184. Kundu, Tadit. 'How GST and Demonetisation Impacted
Govt Finances'. *Mint*. 5 November 2018. Accessed 6
November 2018. https://www.livemint.com/Industry/
pkS48kM47yZbxS49jL6MSN/How-GST-and-
demonetisation-impacted-government-finances.html.

185. Ibid.

186. 'India Development Update'. World Bank. 14 March 2018.
Accessed 6 November 2018. https://www.worldbank.org/en/
news/feature/2018/03/14/india-development-update.

187. 'A Market, Unified'. *Finance & Development Magazine* 55, No. 2
(June 2018). International Monetary Fund. Accessed 6 November
2018. https://www.imf.org/external/pubs/ft/fandd/2018/06/
impact-of-indias-new-GST-tax-on-the-economy/trenches.
htm.

188. Ibid.

189. Kant, Krishna. 'Indirect Tax Share in GDP at All-Time High
of 10.5%'. *Business Standard*. 26 September 2017. Accessed 6
November 2018. https://www.business-standard.com/article/

economy-policy/indirect-tax-share-in-gdp-at-all-time-high-of-10-5-117092601343_1.html.

190. 'India's Demographic Dividend'. Thomson Reuters. 24 March 2017. Accessed 6 November 2018. https://blogs.thomsonreuters. com/answerson/indias-demographic-dividend/.

191. Maira, Arun. 'Jobs, Growth, and Industrial Policy'. *Economic and Political Weekly*. 21 August 2014. Accessed 6 November 2018. https://www.epw.in/journal/2014/34/perspectives/jobs-growth-and-industrial-policy.html.

192. Abraham, Vinoj. 'Stagnant Employment Growth: Last Three Years May Have Been the Worst'. *Economic and Political Weekly* 52, No. 38 (23 September 2017). 27 September 2017. Accessed 6 November 2018. https://www.epw.in/journal/2017/38/commentary/stagnant-employment-growth.html.

193. Vyas, Mahesh. 'The Rising Jobs Challenge'. CMIE. 13 March 2018. Accessed 6 November 2018. https://www.cmie. com/kommon/bin/sr.php?kall=warticle&dt=2018-03-13 09:33:58&msec=963.

194. Kapoor, Radhicka. 'A Job Crisis, in Figures'. *Indian Express*. 12 December 2017. Accessed 6 November 2018. http://indianexpress.com/article/opinion/columns/a-job-crisis-in-figures-4979982/.

195. Mishra, Asit Ranjan. 'India Needs to Create More Salaried Jobs: World Bank'. https://www.livemint.com/. 14 February 2018. Accessed 6 November 2018. https://www.livemint. com/Politics/8z4W8cGyFp4JTHBiLwqEWN/India-needs-to-create-more-salaried-jobs-World-Bank.html.

196. FE Online. 'PM Modi's Promise to Create 10 Million Jobs: 3 Years into BJP Government, but Unemployment Rate Slightly Up'. *Financial Express*. 23 May 2017. Accessed 6 November 2018. https://www.financialexpress.com/economy/pm-modis-promise-to-create-10-million-jobs-3-years-into-bjp-government-but-unemployment-rate-slightly-up/681301/.

197. Beniwal, Vrishti. 'World's Fastest-Growing Economy Isn't Creating Jobs Like Before'. Bloomberg.com. 10 October 2018. Accessed 6 November 2018. https://www.bloomberg.com/

news/articles/2018-10-09/world-s-fastest-growing-economy-isn-t-creating-jobs-like-before.

198. Ibid.
199. Ibid.
200. FE Bureau. '5.5 Million Jobs Created in FY18? Here is What EPFO Data Says.' *Financial Express*. 17 January 2018. Accessed 8 January 2019. https://www.financialexpress.com/economy/5-5-million-jobs-created-in-fy18-here-is-what-epfo-data-says/1018218/.
201. Mallapur, Chaitanya. 'Narendra Modi's "7 Million Jobs" Speech: Relying on EPF Data Alone Paints Incorrect Picture of Employment in India'. Firstpost. 30 January 2018. Accessed 6 November 2018. https://www.firstpost.com/india/narendra-modis-7-million-jobs-speech-relying-on-epf-data-alone-paints-incorrect-picture-of-employment-in-india-4326779.html.
202. Ibid.
203. Ramesh, Jairam and Praveen Chakravarty. 'A Misleading Story of Job Creation'. *The Hindu*. 22 January 2018. Accessed 7 January 2019. https://www.thehindu.com/opinion/op-ed/a-misleading-story-of-job-creation/article22486279.ece.
204. Dehejia, Vivek. 'The Myth of the Myth of "Jobless Growth"'. https://www.livemint.com/. 28 January 2018. Accessed 6 November 2018. https://www.livemint.com/Opinion/hl5bd7VHY14oFhIOQEMXJK/The-myth-of-the-myth-of-jobless-growth.html.
205. Ibid.
206. Laha, Rozelle. 'Automation Impact: By 2021, One in Four Job Cuts May Be from India'. https://www.livemint.com/. 2 March 2017. Accessed 6 November 2018. http://www.livemint.com/Industry/lElBJJHqEZBBKkQyL6ycyJ/Automation-impact-By-2021-one-in-four-job-cuts-may-be-from.html.

Chapter 5: The Future

1. Bernanke, Ben S. 'Challenges for the Economy and State Governments'. Board of Governors of the Federal Reserve

System. 2 August 2010. Accessed 7 January 2019, https://www.federalreserve.gov/newsevents/speech/bernanke20100802a.htm.

2. Bunting, Madeleine. 'Amartya Sen. India's Dirty Fighter'. *Guardian*. 16 July 2013. Accessed 7 January 2019. https://www.theguardian.com/world/2013/jul/16/amartya-sen-india-dirty-fighter.

3. Garson. 'The Future Has Arrived—It's Just Not Evenly Distributed Yet'. Quote Investigator. Accessed 7 December 2018. https://quoteinvestigator.com/2012/01/24/future-has-arrived/.

4. Kharas, Homi, Kristofer Hamel and Martin Hofer. 'The Start of a New Poverty Narrative'. Brookings.19 June 2018. Accessed 26 November 2018. https://www.brookings.edu/blog/future-development/2018/06/19/the-start-of-a-new-poverty-narrative/.

5. 'India's Demographic Dividend'. Inside Financial & Risk, Thomson Reuters. 7 July 2016. Accessed 26 November 2018. https://blogs.thomsonreuters.com/answerson/indias-demographic-dividend/.

6. Bhattacharya, Suryatapa. 'India's Labor Force – The Numbers'. *Wall Street Journal*. 23 July 2015. Accessed 26 November 2018. https://blogs.wsj.com/briefly/2015/07/22/indias-labor-force/.

7. Das, Goutam. 'Going, Going, Gone: Automation Can Lead to Unprecedented Job Cuts in India'. *Business Today*. 26 December 2017. Accessed 26 November 2018. http://www.businesstoday.in/magazine/cover-story/going-going-gone/story/253260.html.

8. Kapoor, Radhicka. 'Technology, Jobs and Inequality Evidence from India's Manufacturing Sector'. Indian Council for Research on International Economic Relations, Working Paper No. 313 (February 2016). Accessed 26 November 2018. http://icrier.org/pdf/Working_Paper_313.pdf.

9. 'Speech by World Bank President Jim Yong Kim: The World Bank Group's Mission: To End Extreme Poverty'. World Bank. 3 October 2016. Accessed 26 November 2018. http://www.worldbank.org/en/news/speech/2016/10/03/speech-by-

world-bank-president-jim-yong-kim-the-world-bank-groups-mission-to-end-extreme-poverty.

10. World Bank Group. 'Measuring South Asia's Economy from Outer Space'. *The World Bank in India* 16, No. 4 (January 2018). Accessed 26 November 2018. http://documents.worldbank.org/curated/en/537471520488356991/pdf/124003-NEWS-WBNewsletterJanLR-PUBLIC.pdf.

11. Ibid.

12. 'India's Banking System Is Flirting with a Lehman Moment'. *Economist*. 8 November 2018. Accessed 26 November 2018. https://www.economist.com/business/2018/11/08/indias-banking-system-is-flirting-with-a-lehman-moment.

13. 'Full Text of Raghuram Rajan's Note to Parliamentary Estimates Committee on Bank NPAs'. *Indian Express*. 11 September 2018. Accessed 26 November 2018. https://indianexpress.com/article/business/banking-and-finance/full-text-of-raghuram-rajans-note-to-parliamentary-estimates-committee-on-bank-npas-5351153/.

14. 'India's Banking System Is Flirting with a Lehman Moment'. *Economist*. 8 November 2018. Accessed 26 November 2018. https://www.economist.com/business/2018/11/08/indias-banking-system-is-flirting-with-a-lehman-moment.

15. Ibid.

16. Ibid.

17. Ibid.

18. Barnichon, Regis, Christian Matthes and Alexander Ziegenbein. 'The Financial Crisis at 10: Will We Ever Recover?' Federal Reserve Bank of San Francisco. 13 August 2018. Accessed 26 November 2018. https://www.frbsf.org/economic-research/publications/economic-letter/2018/august/financial-crisis-at-10-years-will-we-ever-recover/.

19. Ibid.

20. 'India's Banking System Is Flirting with a Lehman Moment'. *Economist*. 8 November 2018. Accessed 26 November 2018. https://www.economist.com/business/2018/11/08/indias-banking-system-is-flirting-with-a-lehman-moment.

21. Sharma, Mihir. 'India's New Tax Is Too Complicated'. Bloomberg.com. 22 May 2017. Accessed 26 November 2018. https://www.bloomberg.com/opinion/articles/2017-05-22/india-s-big-new-tax-is-far too complicated.

22. Ibid.

23. PTI. 'GST a Monumental Reform, Hit Growth Only for 2 Quarters: Arun Jaitley'. *Economic Times*. 12 November 2018. Accessed 26 November 2018. https://economictimes. indiatimes.com/news/economy/policy/gst-a-monumental-reform-hit-growth-only-for-2-quarters-arun-jaitley/articleshow/66580241.cms.

24. Xirui, Li. 'Why the GST Became Malaysia's Public Enemy Number One'. *Diplomat*. 16 October 2018. Accessed 26 November 2018. https://thediplomat.com/2018/10/why-the-gst-became-malaysias-public-enemy-number one/.

25. Ibid.

26. Kundu, Tadit. 'How GST and Demonetisation Impacted Govt Finances'. https://www.livemint.com/. 5 November 2018. Accessed 26 November 2018. https://www.livemint.com/Industry/pkS48kM47yZbxS49jL6MSN/How-GST-and-demonetisation-impacted-government-finances.html.

27. Ibid.

28. Sharma, Mihir Swarup. 'India's Next Growth Engine'. Observer Research Foundation. 18 June 2018. Accessed 26 November 2018. https://www.orfonline.org/research/41740-indias-next-growth-engine/.

29. Jethmalani, Harsha. 'One Year of GST: India Still Has Miles to Go before It Has a Good and Simple Tax'. https://www.livemint.com/. 26 June 2018. Accessed 26 November 2018. https://www.livemint.com/Money/p9aS9kcWG64Zp50ow1QKOL/One-year-of-GST-India-still-has-miles-to-go-before-it-has-a.html.

30. Nageswaran, V. Anantha and Gulzar Natarajan. 'Can India Grow? Challenges, Opportunities, and the Way Forward'. Carnegie India, Carnegie Endowment for International Peace. 16 November 2016. Accessed 26 November 2018. https://

carnegieindia.org/2016/11/16/can-india-grow-challenges-opportunities-and-way-forward-pub-65088.

31. Goedde, Lutz, Avinash Goyal, Nitika Nathani and Chandrika Rajagopalan. 'Harvesting Golden Opportunities in Indian Agriculture: From Food Security to Farmers' Income Security by 2025'. McKinsey & Company. July 2018. Accessed 26 November 2018. https://www.mckinsey.com/industries/chemicals/our-insights/harvesting-golden-opportunities-in-indian-agriculture.
32. Ibid.
33. Sankhe, Shirish, Ireena Vittal, Richard Dobbs, Ajit Mohan, Ankur Gulati, Jonathan Ablett, Shishir Gupta, Alex Kim, Sudipto Paul, Aditya Sanghvi and Gurpreet Sethy. 'India's Urban Awakening: Building Inclusive Cities, Sustaining Economic Growth'. McKinsey & Company. April 2010. Accessed 26 November 2018. https://www.mckinsey.com/featured-insights/urbanization/urban-awakening-in-india.
34. Ibid.
35. Ibid.
36. Huang, Yukon. 'Urbanization Is Key to Why India Is So Far in China's Wake'. Carnegie Endowment for International Peace. 8 June 2015. Accessed 26 November 2018. https://carnegieendowment.org/2015/06/08/urbanization-is-key-to-why-india-is-so-far-in-china-s-wake-pub-60336.
37. Sinha, Suveer. 'Combating the Challenges of Urbanization in Emerging Markets: Lessons from India'. McKinsey & Company. January 2018. Accessed 26 November 2018. https://www.mckinsey.com/industries/capital-projects-and-infrastructure/our-insights/combating-the-challenges-of-urbanization-in-emerging-markets-lessons-from-india.
38. World Economic Forum. 'Reforms to Accelerate the Development of India's Smart Cities Shaping the Future of Urban Development & Services'. Industry Agenda, WEF. April 2016. Accessed 26 November 2018. http://www3.weforum.org/docs/WEF_Reforms_Accelerate_Development_Indias_Smart_Cities.pdf.

39. Breene, Keith. 'Will the Future Be Gender Equal?' World Economic Forum. 18 January 2016. Accessed 7 December 2018. https://www.weforum.org/agenda/2016/01/will-the-future-be-gender-equal/.

40. Elborgh-Woytek, Katrin, Gerd Schwartz, Benedict Clements, Philippe Wingender, Kangni Kpodar, Stefania Fabrizio, Kalpana Kochhar and Monique Newiak. 'Women, Work, and the Economy'. IMF. September 2013. Accessed 7 December 2018. https://www.imf.org/external/pubs/ft/sdn/2013/sdn1310.pdf.

41. Ibid.

42. Lagarde, Christine. 'Delivering on the Promise of 2025'. Keynote Address, W-20 Summit. 6 September 2015. Ankara, Turkey. Accessed 8 January 2019. https://www.imf.org/en/News/Articles/2015/09/28/04/53/sp090615

43. Klasen, Stephan. 'Low, Stagnating Female Labour-Force Participation in India'. https://www.livemint.com/. 19 March 2017. Accessed 26 November 2018. http://www.livemint.com/Opinion/vgO1ynMV6UMDnF6kW5Z3VJ/Low-stagnating-female-labourforce-participation-in-India.html.

44. 'Labor Force Participation Rate, Male (% of Male Population Ages 15+) (Modeled ILO Estimate)'. World Bank. September 2018. Accessed 26 November 2018. http://data.worldbank.org/indicator/SL.TLF.CACT.MA.ZS?locations=IN-CN.

45. Jagannathan, R. 'Dole-nomics: Why AAP Is Headed Down the Same Hole as Sonia's NAC'. Firstpost. 20 December 2014. Accessed 26 November 2018. https://www.firstpost.com/politics/dole-nomics-why-aap-is-headed-down-the-same-hole-as-sonias-nac-1278659.html.

46. Aiyar, Yamini. 'What Has India Achieved by Rejecting the Human Capital Index?' Hindustan Times. 24 October 2018. Accessed 26 November 2018. https://www.hindustantimes.com/analysis/what-has-india-achieved-by-rejecting-the-human-capital-index/story-zx8SWbCMfgBvh47AYZogjP.html.

47. Ibid.

48. Sengupta, Jayshree. 'India's Poor HCI Ranking: A Warning, Not an Insult'. Observer Research Foundation. 12 November 2018. Accessed 26 November 2018. https://www.orfonline. org/expert-speak/indias-poor-hci-ranking-a-warning-not-an-insult-45493/.

49. Sharma, Kritika. '4 Years On, India's Still Waiting for New Education Policy—Modi Govt's Big 2014 Promise'. Print. 14 September 2018. Accessed 26 November 2018. https://theprint.in/governance/4-years-on-indias-still-waiting-for-new-education-policy-modi-govts-big-2014-promise/117022/.

50. Shome, Parthasarathi. 'Human Development Index: A Snapshot'. *Business Standard*. 13 November 2018. Accessed 26 November 2018. https://www.business-standard.com/article/opinion/human-development-index-a-snapshot-118111301704_1.html.

51. 'Human Capital—The Value of People'. OECD Insights—OECD. Accessed 26 November 2018. https://www.oecd.org/insights/humancapital-thevalueofpeople.htm.

52. Ibid.

53. Ibid.

54. 'Human Capital Project'. World Bank. Accessed 26 November 2018. http://www.worldbank.org/en/publication/human-capital.

55. IANS. 'Rejecting Human Capital Index, India Says Digital Age Demands Better Metric'. *Business Standard*. 13 October 2018. Accessed 26 November 2018. https://www.business-standard.com/article/economy-policy/rejecting-human-capital-index-india-says-digital-age-demands-better-metric-118101300545_1.html.

56. Aiyar, Yamini. 'What Has India Achieved by Rejecting the Human Capital Index?' *Hindustan Times*. 24 October 2018. Accessed 26 November 2018. https://www.hindustantimes.com/analysis/what-has-india-achieved-by-rejecting-the-human-capital-index/story-zx8SWbCMfgBvh47AYZogjP.html.

57. Rodrik, Dani. 'Premature Deindustrialization'. NBER Working Paper No. 20935. National Bureau of Economic Research. February 2015. Accessed 26 November 2018. https://www. nbor.org/papers/w20935.

58. Dasgupta, Sukti and Ajit Singh. 'Manufacturing, Services and Premature Deindustrialization in Developing Countries: A Kaldorian Analysis'. United Nations University UNU-WIDER. 2006. Accessed 26 November 2018. https://www.wider. unu.edu/publication/manufacturing-services-and-premature-deindustrialization-developing-countries.

59. Rodrik, Dani. 'Premature Deindustrialization'. NBER Working Paper No. 20935. National Bureau of Economic Research, February 2015. Accessed 26 November 2018. https://www. nber.org/papers/w20935.

60. Ibid.

61. Hallward-Driemeier, Mary and Gaurav Nayyar. 'Trouble in the Making?: The Future of Manufacturing-Led Development'. World Bank Group, Open Knowledge Repository. 20 September 2017. Accessed 26 November 2018. https://openknowledge.worldbank. org/bitstream/handle/10986/27946/9781464811746.pdf.

62. Ibid.

63. Baxi, Abhishek. 'Digital Transformation Predicted to Add $154B to India's GDP Over Next 3 Years'. *Forbes*. 30 April 2018. Accessed 26 November 2018. https://www.forbes. com/sites/baxiabhishck/2018/04/30/digital-transformation-predicted-to-add-154b-to-indias-gdp-over-next-3-years/#783d211d5b5a.

64. Chikermane, Gautam. '70 Policies - Planning Commission, 1950'. Observer Research Foundation. 2 August 2018. Accessed 26 November 2018. https://www.orfonline.org/expert-speak/42943-70-policies-planning-commission-1950/.

65. Prasad, Eswar. 'India's Central Bank under Attack'. Project Syndicate. 26 November 2018. Accessed 15 November 2018. https://www.project-syndicate.org/commentary/reserve-bank-of-india-government-attack-by-eswar-prasad-2018-11.

66. Ibid.

67. PTI. 'Centralisation of Power One of India's Main Problems:
     Raghuram Rajan'. NDTV.com. 10 November 2018. Accessed
     26 November 2018. https://www.ndtv.com/india-news/
     raghuram-rajan-centralisation-of-power-one-of-indias-main-
     problems-1945426.
68. Stiglitz, Joseph and Brian Snowdon. 'Redefining the Role of
     the State'. *World Economics* 2, No. 3 (September 2001). Accessed
     15 November 2018. https://ideas.repec.org/a/wej/wldecn/65.
     html.
69. Reuters. 'Why India Is Most at Risk from Climate Change'.
     World Economic Forum. 21 March 2018. Accessed 26
     November 2018. https://www.weforum.org/agenda/2018/03/
     india-most-vulnerable-country-to-climate-change.
70. Ibid.
71. 'Climate Change Could Depress Living Standards in India,
     Says New World Bank Report'. World Bank. 28 June 2018.
     Accessed 26 November 2018. https://www.worldbank.org/en/
     news/press-release/2018/06/28/climate-change-depress-living-
     standards-india-says-new-world-bank-report.
72. 'India—Systematic Country Diagnostic: Realizing the
     Promise of Prosperity'. World Bank. 11 June 2018. Accessed
     26 November 2018. http://documents.worldbank.org/
     curated/en/629571528745663168/India-Systematic-country-
     diagnostic-realizing-the-promise-of-prosperity.
73. Ibid.